Be your own car mechanic

Be your own car mechanic

Chris Webb

Illustrated by Michael Clare

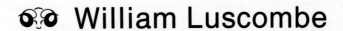 William Luscombe

First published in Great Britain in 1976
by William Luscombe Publisher Limited
Artists House
14 Manette Street
London W1V 5LB

ISBN 0 86002 107 6 (cased)
ISBN 0 86002 150 5 (limp)

Phototypeset by
Tradespools Ltd, Frome Somerset
Printed by Eyre & Spottiswood Ltd,
Grosvenor Press, Portsmouth.

Contents

Acknowledgements

Most of the illustrations in this book come from the picture files of *Practical Motorist* magazine. I would like to thank the Publisher and Editor for kindly allowing me free access to these.

I am also indebted to the major British Motor Manufacturers – British Leyland Motor Corporation, Chrysler UK Ltd., Ford Motor Company Ltd., Vauxhall Motors Ltd., and to scores of other organisations and engineering establishments within the motor trade for their technical assistance and for allowing me to reproduce certain illustrations from their workshop manuals, handbooks and technical leaflets.

The illustrations are as follows:

Automotive Products Co. Ltd., Figs 214, 215, 216, 217, 218, 219, 220, 221, 224a, 224b, 225, 250

British Leyland Motor Co., Figs 13a, 13b, 14, 20, 22, 23c, 24, 25, 26, 107, 251

Ford Motor Company Ltd., Figs 18a, 53

Girling Ltd., Figs 210, 229

Joseph Lucas Ltd., Figs 253, 270a, 270b

The Rawlplug Co. Ltd., Fig 298b

S.U. Carburettor Co. Ltd., Fig 21

Vauxhall Motors Ltd., 13c, 13d, 17a, 23a, 23b, 262, 268, 269, 271

The copyright of these illustrations remains the property of the manufacturers concerned.

My thanks also to Mary and Margaret for typing the manuscript, to Debbie for producing what I thought were long-lost negatives from the filing system and to my wife for not divorcing me for spending countless evenings slaving over a hot typewriter.

Author's note

Whilst all reasonable precautions have been taken to ensure that the information and advice published in *Be Your Own Car Mechanic* is accurate and reliable, it is not possible to guarantee this and no responsibility can be accepted for damage, injury or loss relating from any error or omission.

Introduction

Depending on who you talk to and the sort of axe they have to grind, you'll be told that do-it-yourself car maintenance and repair is either very easy or incredibly hard.

The people who say it is easy usually have some do-it-yourself equipment to sell – such as a paint spray gun or a battery-operated welding kit. They work on the theory that if they can make you think the job is easy, perhaps you will buy one.

The people who say it is difficult (sometimes impossible) are the car manufacturers. Understandably, they feel it is their duty to protect the chain of dealers that they have set up to sell, service and repair their customers' cars.

The truth is somewhere between the two. Working on your own car can be absurdly simple – sometimes twiddling one screw will save you five miles per gallon and smooth out a very lumpy engine. At the other extreme, you may spend two hours trying to undo one rusted nut. Happily, either way it is a lot cheaper than having the work done professionally.

Any competent mechanic will tell you that half the secret of working on cars successfully is knowing what you are doing. In this book I have picked a cross-section of the more common overhaul and repair jobs done on British cars and tried to show exactly what is involved in each one. Where possible, each chapter has been laid out in a logical sequence, with the easier jobs at the front and the more complicated ones towards the end.

You may feel you cannot do some of the jobs. Do not be discouraged – nowadays almost everyone has some mechanical ability, but we all work at different speeds and some are more adventurous than others. If you feel a job is beyond you, my advice is not to do it. At least if you have read about it you will know what the professional is going to do to your car – and this means you will be able to tell whether he has done the work properly.

I should point out that this is not a workshop manual. It would be foolish to suggest that any book dealing with cars in general can give precise details on all maintenance and repair jobs on all cars. On the other hand it has some details – on painting, and body repair for instance – that you won't find in the average manual. I hope you find it helpful.

Chris Webb

Chapter one
Tools and equipment

The most that a car manufacturer reckons the owner should do to his vehicle is change a wheel. To this end, most cars come supplied with a simple jack and wheel brace and precious little else in the toolkit. If you want to take out a spark plug, change a fanbelt, or set the contact breaker points, you nearly always need some extra tools.

The number of extra tools you need depends on what you want to do. For routine maintenance, a few well-chosen spanners, a set of feeler gauges, screwdrivers and pliers will allow you to tackle most jobs. If you want to do your own repairs as well, you'll need more, and I've listed most of the equipment you are likely to need.

The rule when buying tools is that the most expensive ones are the best and will last longer than those costing much less, but don't take this as an encouragement to buy expensive equipment *all* the time. High-priced tools are designed for professional use; unless you are intending to take cars to pieces for 40 hours of every week, you can afford to pay a little less than top price because you won't be working your equipment so hard – something in the middle price range will suit most do-it-yourself motorists.

Before buying any tools it is obviously important to know the sizes of the nuts and bolts that hold your car together. Until about 1970 British and American cars used nuts and bolts having Unified National threads. The sizes of the hexagon heads were quoted in inches, measured across the flats and the spanners and sockets were quoted as, say, $\frac{1}{2}$ in AF, $\frac{5}{8}$ in AF and so on.

At the time of writing, British car manufacturers are in the process of changing over to Metric nuts and bolts. These have a different thread to the Unified ones. Sizes are still quoted across the flats of the hexagon heads, but they are in millimetres and with only the occasional exception, Metric spanners do not fit Unified hexagons properly.

The situation is further confused because some manufacturers are further along the road to metrication than others. A 1974 Ford Escort, for instance, used mostly Metric fixings on its engine and gearbox, but some ancillaries, such as the starter motor, used AF Unified fastenings. British Leyland's 1974 cars, on the other hand, have a higher proportion of Unified nuts and bolts. As a rule of thumb, on cars made before 1973 most of the fastenings will be Unified. But from 1974 onwards, an increasing proportion of Metric fastenings will be used until eventually all British cars will have wholly Metric nuts and bolts. Continental and Japanese cars use Metric fastenings throughout.

Spanners and sockets
The spanner with the greatest grip is the ring spanner. Because it completely encircles the nut or bolt, it won't slip off and is unlikely to cause damage unless the nut or bolt is mis-shapen or the wrong size.

Unfortunately there are many nuts and bolts on the car where the ring spanner cannot be used – for instance on a tube nut securing a brake pipe. In these circumstances an open-ended spanner is used, and to cater for both situations, combination spanners are available with a ring at one end and an open-ended jaw at the other, the ends of each spanner fitting the same size hexagon.

Spanners with open-ended jaws at both ends, will fit two sizes of hexagon. They're useful as a second string to combination spanners and they can be used instead of combination spanners if you are going to invest in a set of sockets. It is not good practice to use only open-ended spanners on a car because they can round off the corners of nuts and bolts which need firm tightening.

Box spanners are used to work on nuts and bolts that are re-cessed. They are turned using a tommy-bar, and the most essential one is the spark plug spanner. Box spanners are also useful in confined spaces where an open-ended or ring spanner is too long to rotate the nut or bolt properly.

Sockets are really sophisticated box spanners. They are sold in sets ranging from around six sockets to about 64 or more. They can also be bought individually. The socket is connected to a ratchet handle, a brace or tommy-bar which turns it by a square drive. There are four sizes of drive in general use $-\frac{1}{4}$ in, $\frac{3}{8}$ in, $\frac{1}{2}$ in, and $\frac{3}{4}$ in. For cars the favourite seems to be a $\frac{1}{2}$ in drive. This can be converted using adaptors to accept sockets with the other drive

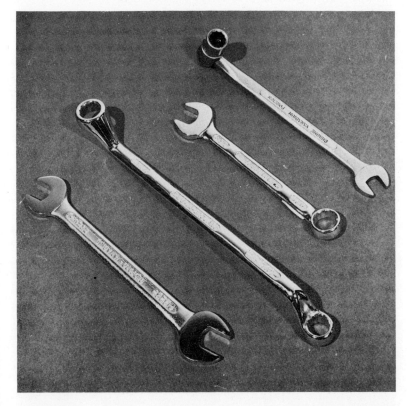

1 The sort of spanners you will need: From left, open-ended, ring, combination and a combined open-ended and socket spanner

11

sizes when necessary, although in practice you will normally only need the $\frac{3}{4}$ in drive adaptor for very large sockets.

The size of your socket set depends on whether the car has a uniform distribution of Unified AF nuts and bolts or Metric fixings, or whether it has a mixture of both. If you are lucky, most serious work should be possible with 10 sockets. If your car has a mixture of Metric and Unified fastenings then purchase a small metric set and add the most popular Unified sockets, buying them individually as necessary.

Some car makers are using bolts that ordinary sockets and spanners will not fit. The best known are Allen bolts which are turned with a hexagon Allen key. Sets of these keys are available reasonably cheaply.

A variation of the Allen bolt is used by Ford on their overhead camshaft engines. The bolt head has a twelve-sided recess in the centre which is engaged by a special splined tool. The tool has a $\frac{1}{2}$ in drive so it fits standard socket attachments.

Screwdrivers

Besides nuts and bolts, the modern car is held together by countless screws. To speed production, most of these have crossed slots in the heads since this discourages a powered screwdriver from wandering. So start your collection with two *good quality*

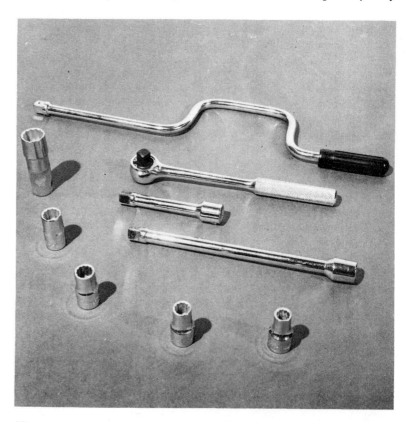

2 The main constituents of a socket set are shown here. From the top they are a speed-brace, ratchet handle, short and long extension and socket-ends. The left-hand socket is for use on spark plugs

cross-head screwdrivers, one with about a 6 in. blade and a short 'chubby' one. In matters of screwdrivers, the most expensive is perhaps worth having since screwdriver points that are a trifle soft will quickly round-off their corners and wreck more screws than they undo. They should have plastic shatterproof handles and the most popular size is called No 1. It has a shaft diameter of $\frac{5}{32}$ in. If you shop around you can pick up chubby screwdrivers with reversible blades with No 1 and No 2 sizes. (No 2 has a $\frac{1}{4}$ in diameter shaft). Even if you can't find an old-fashioned single slot screw on the car, you should have a $\frac{1}{4}$ in slotted screwdriver. It will be worth its weight in gold for opening paint pots and levering, prising, scraping and generally grubbing about. Get one with a blade at least 7 in long. Unless you are unlucky you shouldn't normally need a right-angle screwdriver, but if you come across a screw that's impossible to reach, the better tool shops sell them.

Pliers

Most engineers become quite upset if pliers are used to undo nuts and bolts – they chew up the corners of the hexagon and if they are used often enough the hexagon becomes almost round and unfit to be turned by a spanner. To be correct, pliers should be used for cutting cables, stripping off insulation and for gripping things that you can't hold in your hand – such as pieces of cable that are

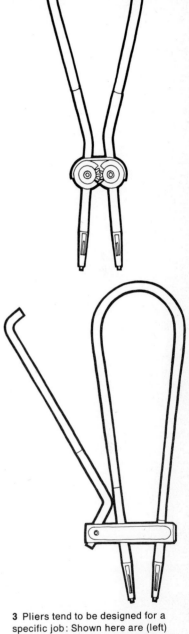

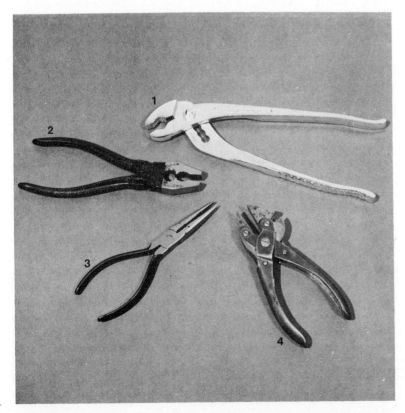

3 Pliers tend to be designed for a specific job: Shown here are (left) pipe grips (1) combination pliers (2) needle-nose pliers (3) parallel jaw pliers (4) and (above) two types of circlip pliers for expanding circlips (top) and for squeezing them up (bottom)

being soldered. If no engineers are looking they are handy for preventing a bolt head turning while you undo the nut with a spanner.

Self-grip pliers, such as a Mole wrench, have the ability to lock their jaws and act as a miniature mobile vice or clamp. They make a useful third hand when two are not enough.

Circuit tester

It looks like a small screwdriver but instead of a blade it should have a point at the end. Dig the point into any live electrical circuit on the car and clip the cable joined to the handle of the tester to chassis earth and a bulb in the handle will light. Circuit testers are invaluable for checking for the existence or otherwise of power in the wiring. They are also useful when setting the ignition timing.

Measuring equipment

Feeler gauges top the list here. If you have a British car, get one calibrated in thousandths of an inch (thous). It's not necessary to have one with a vast number of feeler blades, but before you pick one up, have a look in the car handbook and jot down the valve gaps, spark plug gaps and contact-breaker gap and make sure you get a gauge that can cope with all these. It doesn't matter if two blades have to be laminated to measure some of the bigger gaps. Ideally, Continental and Japanese cars will need gauges marked in millimetres, although most handbooks also quote clearances in inches.

A micrometer, which looks like a highly-sophisticated G-clamp, is essential if you are planning to adjust the valve gaps on some overhead-camshaft engines which have shim adjusters. The micrometer can measure the thickness of the shims to the nearest .001 in — more expensive ones measure to 0.0001 in. The one to have will measure from 0 to about 1 inch. Metric micrometers are readily available. Get one calibrated from 0–25 mm which will work to an accuracy of at least 0.01 mm.

A tyre pressure gauge is obviously useful if you are maintaining your own car. A steel rule is useful — its straight edge is invaluable for checking wear on flat surfaces.

Hammers

For maintenance you don't, in theory, need a hammer at all. But for repairs a 2 lb one is a good all-rounder — light enough to tap out small dents and heavy enough to use behind a cold chisel and chop off a rusted bolt. Get one with a ball on one end of the head — it's known as a ball pein hammer. If you anticipate doing a lot of body repair work, there's a panel beating hammer for just about every purpose, although a medium sized rubber mallet will take care of minor dents. In my view it is better to leave more serious panel beating to the experts.

Cutting and smoothing

Few people imagine they will need to take a hacksaw to their car, yet sooner or later you will need one – even if it is only to trim the end of a mounting bracket so your new car radio doesn't foul the ashtray. For very occasional use, a small junior type hacksaw is cheap and the blades are remarkably sharp. Tin-snips or a sheet metal 'nibbler' are best suited for making long cuts in thin body metal. You will need a flat file after using a hacksaw so you can smooth off the ragged edge. A flat cross-cut file about 1 in wide is a good all-rounder.

Making a hole

Even new cars seem to need holes of various sizes to be bored in them. For instance, fitting a radio, speaker, and aerial may call for the drilling of 10 holes, one of which (for the aerial) may need to be nearly one inch in diameter. Small holes are easy. A power drill is better than a hand-drill simply because it is shorter and can more easily drill holes in cramped places like the rear parcel shelf under a steeply sloping rear window. Use high speed (H.S.) drills and if the power drill offers any choice, select the slow speed. Often even this is not slow enough for double-thickness metal and I find the bits keep cooler, last longer and go through more quickly if the drill is continually switched on and off, slowing it even more.

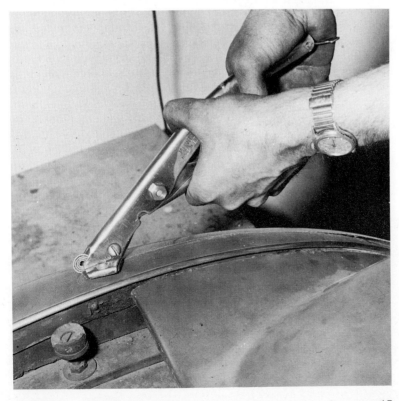

4 This is a Monodex Nibbler – squeeze together the handles and it nibbles a slot in body metal

15

Large holes can be made in a variety of ways. You can mark a circle $\frac{1}{8}$ in smaller than the diameter you want and drill a series of small holes round the edge and join them using a tiny rat-tail file. Alternatively, you can drill a $\frac{3}{8}$ in hole in the centre and open it up to the desired size, using a $\frac{5}{16}$ in round file. There are special hole-boring tools too. The circular hole saw which works well in wood has never worked properly for me on metal, but I have had considerable success using Q-Max cutters and Unicut hole cutters.

The Q-Max is, in effect, a miniature press which punches a hole the required size as the two parts of the cutter are tightened together by a screw. Its disadvantage is that it can only be used on panels where you can reach both sides, so it is no good on double-skinned areas. In addition, each cutter only makes one size of hole. If you want a bigger or smaller hole, you must buy a different sized cutter.

Unicut hole cutters are made by Sykes-Pickavant, are more expensive than Q-Max cutters but more versatile. There are two sizes which cut holes respectively from $\frac{1}{4}$ in to $1\frac{3}{16}$ in and from $\frac{5}{8}$ in to $1\frac{3}{16}$ in. They are used in a power drill and have a conical shape with two cutting grooves, one down each side. In use they are simply drilled into the bodywork until a hole the desired size is obtained – they are very sharp and should be used with caution.

Raising the car

The jack that the manufacturer supplies with the car is intended to get a maximum of two wheels off the ground at any one time. Most of these jacks have a screw thread which raises and lowers a lifting pin or pad and because they are produced down to a price, they are quite likely to be unsafe if required to hold up the car for any length of time.

Nowadays the heaviest cars rarely exceed two tons, so it you reckon to jack up one end at a time, a one ton jack will cope with practically anything. The best jack for home use is a small hydraulic trolley jack. Most have a lift of around 10 in. There are also heavy duty screw type trolley jacks. Providing these can cope with a ton, their only drawback is that they are either hard work to operate or – at the other extreme – a vast number of turns of the handle is required to get them to full lift.

A bottle-type jack is less versatile than a trolley jack (with a trolley the car can be moved while it is still jacked up), but a bottle jack is infinitely preferable to the jack in the toolkit.

In the interest of self preservation you should not get under a car that is supported solely by a jack – it should be blocked up under the chassis either with heavy timber such as old railway sleepers, or with prop-stands. On occasions the jack cannot lift the car high enough from ground level to allow prop-stands to be inserted underneath. You must then fully retract the jack and use a block of heavy timber either to raise the jack off the ground or to pack between the jack pad and the chassis. This allows the car to be lifted higher.

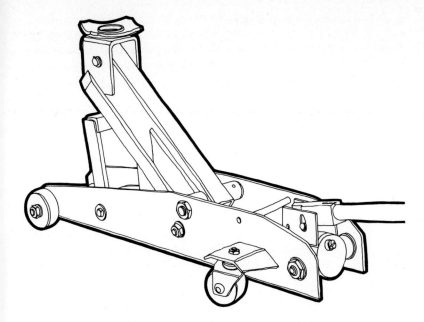

5 The jack which is supplied with the car will usually only lift one side. A trolley jack is more versatile and worth having for serious repairs

Drive-on ramps seem to offer an easier alternative to jacking when it comes to raising a car off the ground. However, they have their drawbacks. One of these is that on some surfaces the ramps tend to run away from the car, skidding across the floor as the wheels try to run up them. The answer is to drill a couple of holes in the floor and insert two long bolts to act as stop-pegs ahead of the ramps.

The other disadvantage is that you cannot take a wheel off with a car on a ramp. This means that ramp work is limited to the areas within the wheels – engine, gearbox, prop-shaft, bodywork, fuel and brake lines and some suspension links. Jobs which require a wheel to be taken off, such as brake adjustment, the majority of work on the steering, suspension and hubs can only be done with the help of a jack.

SPECIALISED EQUIPMENT

The amount of specialised equipment you need depends on the car that you are working on, and the extent of the work you intend to do. If, for instance, you wanted to overhaul the engine cylinder head, in addition to the maintenance tools, you would need a torque wrench, valve spring compressor and a valve grinding tool. If you want to take the engine out, you need some sort of lifting tackle and something to hook it on as well. The specialised tools listed here are arranged where possible in job order – tools needed for the simpler jobs are near the front, and equipment for more complicated jobs is further down.

17

6 Valve spring compressor

Valve spring compressor

This is one of the most widely used specialised tools. The simplest type works like a screw-up G-clamp and is good enough for home decokes. Make sure you get one with enough reach to get to the valve head and spring without fouling the side of the cylinder head.

Valve grinding tool

This is a length of wooden dowelling with a rubber sucker at the end. The suction pad grips the head of the valve which is rotated back and forth against a smear of grinding paste on its seating in the head.

Torque wrench

A torque wrench is used to prevent nuts or bolts being over- or under-tightened. It is essential for instance, when tightening down an engine cylinder head because uneven tightness can cause the head to warp. It is also common for hub nuts, clutch bolts, certain engine and gearbox bolts and suspension fastenings to be tightened to a specified torque.

On British cars torque settings are quoted in pounds-feet, one unit being a force of 1 lb exerted at the end of a wrench 1 ft long. Sometimes torque settings are given in pounds-inches, but bearing in mind that most torque wrenches on general sale are calibrated in lb ft, the lb in figures should be converted by dividing them by 12. Continental torque settings are usually quoted in kilogramme-metres (kg-m).

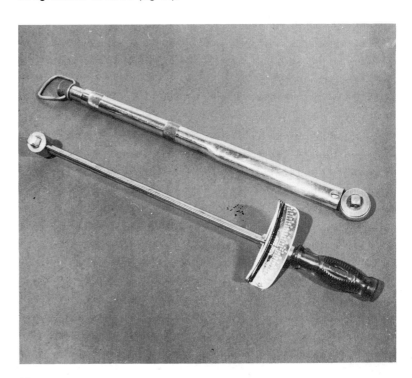

7 Two sorts of torque wrench. The bottom one indicates the torque with a pointer on a scale, the top one is spring-loaded and an internal mechanism 'breaks' when the correct torque is reached.

18

The average torque wrench has a $\frac{1}{2}$ in square drive at the end to mate up with a socket and because it is relatively expensive, most hire shops keep a few in stock.

It is possible to rig up a make-shift torque wrench using a spring balance and the appropriate spanner. Suppose a bolt needs to be tightened to 20 lb ft. Attaching a spanner 1 ft long and applying a 20 lb pull to the end will tighten the bolt correctly. If the spanner is 6 in long, the same result can be obtained by exerting a pull of 40 lb. This method does not work too well if the bolt is buried below surrounding components because an extension is needed to reach it.

Pullers

Some components are an 'interference fit'. This means they will not go together or come apart without a little hammering. Where you cannot get a hammer behind them to tap them out, a puller is used. Most of these work like a bench vice in reverse – as a central thread is tightened, the body of the puller, attached to the thread and the component, draws off the component.

Different pullers are used for different jobs. On some cars, of course, a puller may not be needed at all. Thus, the best course is not to buy one until you need it. If you need a puller only occasionally, try and hire one.

Taper breakers

It is good engineering practice to tighten a component on to a tapered shaft as it is very unlikely to come loose. This poses a problem when the components have to be separated, and to help, there are a number of taper breakers available. Most are designed for use on steering ball-joints which are attached to steering arms or drag links by a tapered pin. These taper breakers fall into two

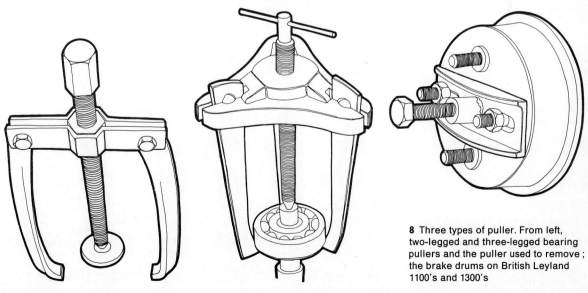

8 Three types of puller. From left, two-legged and three-legged bearing pullers and the puller used to remove; the brake drums on British Leyland 1100's and 1300's

19

categories – there is the sort that push the threaded end of the pin through the arm, and there are wedges which are hammered between the arm and the ball-end of the pin to prise them apart. The wedges are generally a bit cheaper but have the disadvantage that they will damage any rubber seal protecting the ball-joint.

It is possible, using a couple of hammers, to break a taper without a special puller. The secret is to rest a big hammer against the eye through which the pin passes and hit the opposite side of the eye with the other hammer to jar the taper free. This method involves a fair degree of accuracy and the eye must be hit hard. It does work if you hit hard enough and long enough, but it can prove difficult in confined spaces. Other tapered joints – for instance the tapered fit of the Mini flywheel on the end of the crankshaft – are broken using suitable pullers.

Nut splitter

Rusted nuts are sometimes corroded to the point where a spanner no longer fits them. If the nut is too inaccessible to be hacksawn off or chopped off with a sharp cold chisel, a nut splitter will crack it and allow it to be removed. This particular device is most useful when working on the bodywork of older cars.

Impact driver

This is a screwdriver you hit with a hammer. It has a square drive at the end to accept a variety of sockets and an adaptor for special

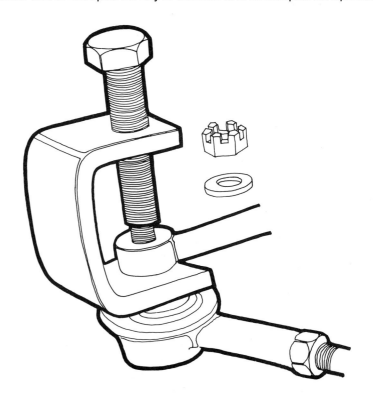

9 A taper breaker is used to separate taper joints. This one is tightened down on the end of the pin, then the screw head is tapped with a hammer to break the joint apart

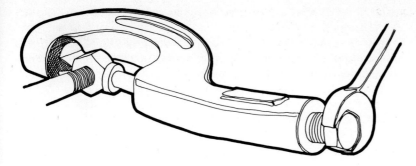

10 A nut-splitter forces a wedge into one flat of the nut until the nut breaks and spreads apart

screwdriver bits. Hitting the end drives the screwdriver bit into the screw head and at the same time imparts a twisting action to the screw. It is only rarely needed on newish cars – to loosen or tighten lock striker plates for instance – but comes in handy sometimes when removing the large cross-head screws that secure the door hinges on some older cars.

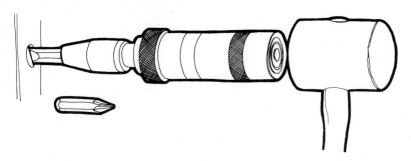

11 The impact driver is in effect a hammer-operated screwdriver. Hitting the end turns the chuck which is attached to a screwdriver bit. Different bits are available to suit cross-head and slotted screws

Screw extractor

If a screw breaks off below the surface, a left-hand thread screw extractor might get it out. The method is to drill a small hole down the centre of the screw, insert the extractor and wind it gently anti-clockwise. If you are lucky, it will grip the remnant of the screw and undo it. If you are unlucky, it either won't grip or the top of the screw will spread and jam in the hole. Then the only remedy is carefully to drill it out and cut a new thread in the hole with an engineer's tap.

Lifting gear

Depending on the car, the weight of the engine and gearbox can be anything from around 300 lbs up to more than 700 lbs. Accessory shops sell hoists that will lift these weights, but it is not always certain whether a beam across the garage will stand the strain. The tables at the end of this chapter give some indication of the maximum loads that various beams will stand. While I have included timber beams, it must be borne in mind that much depends on the individual quality of the timber used – timber that is knotty or has a split in it won't be so strong under load as an unsplit or knot-free beam. As a rough guide, beams of up to 6 ft span should have a 4 in bearing at each end, and those up to 9 ft not less than 6 in.

You can get over the beam problem if you hire lifting tackle from a hire shop. They usually supply a couple of ceiling props which are stood on each side of the engine bay. A hoist is then suspended from a steel tube which is supported each end by the props. If you reckon on doing a lot of engine-out jobs, it is possible to buy a small lifting crane – although it is more expensive than a hoist.

DEALING WITH HEAVY WEIGHTS

The following tables give the dimensions of timber beams and steel joists and indicate the safe loads they can carry.

Timber beams – maximum centrally placed load on a 2 in wide beam in lbs.

Depth (in)	Span (ft)								
	4	5	6	7	8	9	10	11	12
3	150	120	100	90	70				
$3\frac{1}{2}$	205	165	136	115	100	90			
4	270	215	180	150	135	120	100		
$4\frac{1}{2}$	350	275	230	165	170	150	135	120	
5	220	335	280	240	210	170	165	150	140
6	600	485	400	350	300	270	240	220	200
7	825	540	470	470	410	365	330	300	275

Steel joists – maximum centrally placed load in cwt.

Section (in) D B	Span (ft)							
	5	6	7	8	9	10	11	12
$6 \times 3\frac{1}{2}$	90	80	70	60	50	40	30	20
5×3	60	50	40	35	30	25	20	
$4 \times 2\frac{1}{2}$	35	30	25	20	15	10		
3×2	14	12	11	10	7			

Typical weights: small four-cylinder engine and gearbox (Escort, Imp, Herald and the like) 225–300 lbs; small transverse engine and gearbox (Mini-1100) 330–350 lbs; medium four-cylinder engine and gearbox (Hunter, Victor FD) 350–450 lbs; medium four-cylinder transverse engine and gearbox (BL 1800) 550 lbs; medium six-cylinder engine/gearbox (Triumph Vitesse/2000) 460–500 lbs; large six-cylinder engine and gearbox (Ford V6, Vauxhall Ventora) 500–700 lbs.

Car manufacturers encourage buyers of their products to have them serviced by an authorised dealer, and about 50% of the cars in Britain *are* professionally serviced. Of the remaining 50%, a few are not serviced at all, but most are maintained during the weekends by owner-drivers. There are two principal arguments for maintaining your car at home.

*It's cheaper than sending it to a garage.

*You don't lose use of the car during the week while a garage has it for service.

There is also a proportion of car maintenance addicts who derive a certain enjoyment from keeping their car in peak condition.

For the most part, servicing is easy and only calls for a small toolkit. With a bit of planning, it is possible to carry out a major service – the sort most manufacturers reckon their car needs once a year or at 10,000 or 12,000-mile intervals – in a weekend morning, although if you are tackling a job like this for the first time, also allow a fair bit of time in the afternoon.

Before you start, you must know what the service interval is on your car. Most modern vehicles require weekly or monthly checks on simple items such as the levels of the oil, water and hydraulic fluid, the condition and pressure of the tyres and tightness of the wheel nuts. Apart from these, servicing will follow a definite pattern and is required at 3,000, 5,000 or 6,000-mile intervals, depending on the car.

The jobs you have to do at each service will either be detailed in the handbook as a maintenance summary or written on the pages in the manufacturer's service voucher book.

To do the jobs you need to know a number of measurements such as the gap required at the spark plug electrodes, the distributor contact-breaker points gap, the valve gaps and the

Chapter two
Servicing at home

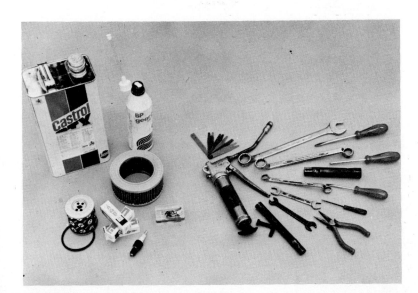

12 This is what you need for a typical 12,000 mile service – engine oil, back axle oil, new oil and air filters, spark plugs and contact-breaker points. Besides appropriate spanners the toolkit includes feeler gauges, a grease gun, fine-nosed pliers, box spanners and – in this instance – a bolt that's bent to act as a key for undoing a drain plug

23

static ignition timing. This information will be in the handbook, usually under the heading 'general data'.

To give an idea of what is involved, the information here is based on a typical 'big' service – the sort you would reckon to carry out annually or at 10,000 or 12,000 miles. A big service usually means at least fitting a new set of sparking plugs, new contact-breaker points, a new paper element in the carburettor air cleaner, changing the engine oil and fitting a new filter – make sure you have these before you start.

Assuming the engine is in fair mechanical condition there are four adjustments which must be correctly made to keep it running sweetly. These are:

*Spark plug gaps.
*Contact-breaker points gap.
*Ignition timing.
*Valve clearances.

They should be tackled in the above order.

Spark plugs

The plugs have to be taken out whether you are merely setting the gaps or changing them, and it saves time on re-assembly if the high-tension cables which connect them to the distributor are labelled with sticky tape.

Undo the plugs with a plug spanner and if they are not due for change, clean the electrodes with a thin file, then check the gaps using a feeler gauge. The gaps can be re-set using a flat-bladed screwdriver – tap the side electrode with the screwdriver handle to close them up, lever the side electrode gently upwards to open them. Avoid putting any leverage on the centre electrode otherwise the ceramic insulation surrounding it may crack.

If you are making further engine adjustments, leave the plugs out at this stage, but remember when they are being fitted that it should be possible to tighten them almost fully by hand. If a plug refuses to screw in, do not force it as it is most likely cross-threaded – take it out and try again. If the plug repeatedly jams up, clean the threads with a wire brush. On engines with aluminium heads, smear a little graphite grease on the threads.

Plugs with electrodes that are excessively carboned-up can be cleaned by soaking them overnight in household vinegar. Next morning the softened-up carbon can be scraped out using a matchstick. Do not use a knife blade or wire brush to clean the electrode areas as both leave metal traces on the insulator round the centre electrode and the current may run down this metal to earth instead of jumping the spark gap.

Contact-breaker points

On cars with coil ignition the points are under the distributor cap. They are operated by a cam on the distributor shaft and generally the cam has as many lobes as the engine has cylinders.

In use, there is a tendency for the points gap to gradually close up as the plastic or fibre rubbing block which bears on the rotating cam gradually wears away. There is also some unavoidable sparking across the contacts and over a period this causes a small peak to form on one contact and a corresponding crater to form in the other. If this has happened, it is best to fit a new set of points – they are reasonably cheap. In practice most cars seem to need new points after about 12,000–18,000 miles.

To set the gap the engine must be rotated so the rubbing block comes to the tip of one of the cam lobes. Rotating the engine was easy when all cars had starting handles, but it's not always so easy now. Most car-makers suggest turning the engine over using a spanner on the crankshaft pulley bolt-head. Unfortunately the bolt is often recessed so it is difficult to reach, and sometimes the head is so big that only a large, rare and comparatively expensive socket will fit. In addition, if the bolt is locked by a tab washer it may be impossible to use a socket.

If the car has manual transmission, the alternative is easy – put the car on a level surface, take out the spark plugs, engage top gear, release the handbrake, and roll the car forward to turn the engine.

On cars with automatic transmission the top-gear trick will not work so you have no choice but to use a spanner on the crankshaft pulley bolt. On automatic Minis, where the bolt is particularly inaccessible, British Leyland suggest the engine is turned using a screwdriver on the ring-gear teeth of the torque converter after removing a rubber plug in the converter housing. Quite often, if the plugs are removed, these engines can be turned using a spanner on the generator or alternator pulley bolt while pressing on the fan belt.

There are two principal distributor layouts. The most widespread has the contact-breaker assembly directly under the rotor arm and the method of adjusting the points on one of these – a Lucas unit – is shown in the drawings. The other type has the advance–retard weights beneath the rotor and the contact-breakers below the weights. On these the rotor arm is removed to give access to the points.

Static ignition timing

Because the petrol and air mixture that the engine draws in takes a little time to burn, the ignition is timed so each spark plug ignites the mixture fractionally before maximum thrust is required above the piston. Usually ignition occurs as the piston reaches the top of its stroke – appropriately called Top Dead Centre – or a few degrees before TDC.

Unlike spark plugs and contact-breaker points which wear out, the ignition timing does not alter much over short mileages, although in the long term, wear in the camshaft drive and distributor drive will cause the setting to alter. As this is a reasonably slow process, from the servicing aspect, it is enough to check the ignition timing and rarely necessary to adjust it. But because the

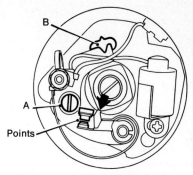

13a On Lucas distributors, set the points with the rubbing block resting on one lobe of the distributor cam (arrowed). Loosen the screw A and use a screwdriver in the slots B to adjust the position of the fixed contact. The correct gap will be given in the handbook

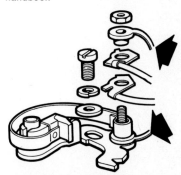

13b When fitting new Lucas points make sure the terminals on the condenser and LT wires are in contact with the spring blade. The spring eye is insulated from the threaded post by nylon insulating bushes (arrowed)

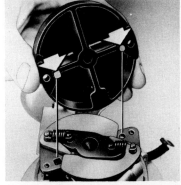

13c On AC distributors with high-mounted centrifugal advance weights, remove the rotor arm before adjusting the points

13d If the points need renewal, they are detached from the base-plate after removing a plastic clip

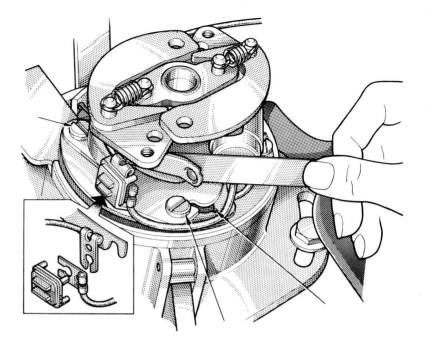

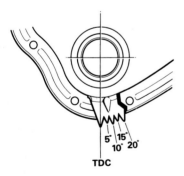

14 Timing marks on the Morris Marina 1.3 are on the timing chain cover immediately behind the radiator. A notch in the edge of the crankshaft pulley is aligned with these pointers. On transverse British Leyland cars the marks are on the flywheel or torque converter.

contact-breaker points gap affects the ignition timing, it is essential the points are adjusted *before* checking the timing.

To enable the timing to be checked, every engine has a set of timing marks. One mark will be on something that is attached to the crankshaft – usually the crankshaft pulley wheel which turns the fanbelt, or on the rim of the flywheel. In its travels this moving mark will go past a nearby fixed mark – usually a pointer behind the pulley or at the edge of the flywheel. On an engine that is timed correctly, the contact-breaker points will *just* be opening as the moving mark and the fixed point align.

On most engines you would need two heads to watch the distributor contact breaker and the timing marks simultaneously, so most mechanics use a timing light or test lamp connected between the side terminal on the distributor and earth. The lamp will light when the contact-breaker points open.

My own favourite timing procedure is as follows:

Put the car on a flat surface, remove the spark plugs, adjust the contact-breaker points gap, leave the distributor cap off.
Select top gear and pull the car forward (on an automatic turn the engine) until the timing marks coincide and the distributor rotor arm is aimed towards the HT cable feeding No. 1 spark plug. If necessary turn the crankshaft one revolution to obtain this condition. Now push the car backwards or turn the engine back to turn the timing wheel about 45 degrees.
Switch on the ignition and connect the test lamp.
Pull the car forwards so the engine turns very slowly and stop immediately the lamp lights. The timing marks should be aligned.

26

If the lamp comes on before the moving mark has reached the fixed pointer, the ignition is too far advanced. If it has gone past the fixed mark, it is too far retarded.

The setting can be altered in two ways. Small adjustments are sometimes possible by turning a knurled adjuster on the distributor body – turn it towards A to advance the ignition, towards R to retard it – it is as easy as that.

Some distributors do not have adjusters. With these, the clamp holding the distributor body to the engine is loosened and the distributor body rotated slightly to alter the setting. Turning the body against the direction of rotor arm rotation advances the ignition; rotating the body in the same direction as the rotor retards it. Always re-check the timing after any adjustments.

The only snag you may encounter when setting ignition timing is that the car manufacturer may not have given sufficient information in the handbook. Quite often the static setting is given, but there is no explanation as to what the timing marks mean. If the handbook is vague, the local dealer will have the data in his workshop manual; alternatively, all British car manufacturers and the principal foreign car importers have a technical service department which is there to help dealers when they hit a service snag. The Service Department will know what the timing marks mean, but before telephoning them, make sure you can give the make, model, year, engine and chassis number of your car if they should ask for it.

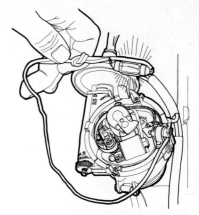

15 Timing light in action. One wire from the light is connected into the terminal on the side of the distributor, the other is clipped to chassis earth. With the ignition on, the bulb will light the instant the points open. Also shown is the knurled adjuster for making small alterations to ignition timing

Valve adjustment

A few manufacturers insist that the valve clearances are set with the engine hot and when this is specified it is important that the engine has fully reached operating temperature; this means at least 5–6 miles running on the road or a long period at a fast idle. If the valves on such an engine are adjusted before it has fully reached operating temperature, performance and economy will suffer. Where the manufacturer recommends setting the clearances with the engine cold, leave the car overnight before adjustment.

Virtually all engines have overhead valves, but the method of actuating the valves can be either through a low-mounted camshaft, pushrods and rockers, or by an overhead camshaft which in some instances bears on inverted bucket tappets mounted directly on the ends of the valve stems. Of the two the overhead camshaft set-up is more efficient and is growing in popularity because it is cheaper to produce.

Because of the greater number of moving parts, a pushrod and rocker layout needs more regular adjustment. Fortunately this is simple. Overhead camshaft layouts tend to need less adjustment, but when it is required, sometimes the camshaft must be taken out and this can be a lengthy business. The differences can best be appreciated by looking at each type separately.

Pushrod overhead valves

The adjustments are made at the rockers above the cylinder head. First remove the rocker cover and any closed-circuit breather pipes. As the engine needs to be rotated, it helps if the spark plugs are removed. When inlet and exhaust valves need different clearances, identify them by the position of the intake and exhaust manifolds.

The clearances are adjusted when each valve is fully closed and the cam-follower is resting on the heel of the camlobe. Since you will not be able to see the camshaft to check this, its position must be calculated.

The most foolproof way is to rotate the engine until the valve you want to adjust is fully open (valve spring compressed) and then turn the engine one full revolution from this point. The gap can then be checked with a feeler gauge – the blade should be what can best be described as a 'firm sliding fit' between the end of the rocker and the top of the valve stem – if the feeler gauge tries to buckle as you press it in, the gap is too tight.

The method of adjustment is either by a screw and locknut at the pushrod end of the rocker, or by turning the nut that the rocker pivots on.

Overhead camshaft systems

The simplest layout from the engineering point of view – and the most difficult to adjust in service – is where each camshaft lobe bears directly on an inverted-bucket-type tappet which sits over the end of each valve stem. Between each valve stem and the tappet is a shim which can be replaced by a thicker or thinner one to set the clearances. If the gaps need altering the camshaft must come out, the bucket tappets are taken off the valve stems, and the appropriate shims fitted. The most popular British cars using this system are the overhead camshaft Austin Allegros and Maxis. A similar system is used on the Hillman Imp.

One consolation is that the gaps do not alter much in service simply because there are so few moving parts. In addition, the valve gaps are very flexible. On the Austin engines, for instance, the rebuild gaps are quoted as .016–.018 in (inlet) and .020–.022 in (exhaust) but as a service check, British Leyland reckon they will operate satisfactorily at .012 in. In other words, the inlet gap can close up as much as .006 in and the exhaust by .010 in before adjustment is deemed necessary.

Since adjustment is comparatively rare, it will not be dealt with in detail here, although the information is given in the overhead camshaft decoke section in Chapter 4.

To check the valve gaps, simply remove the cam cover and rotate the engine. Measure each gap with a feeler gauge when the cam lobe is pointing vertically away from the tappet.

Some manufacturers build in a simpler adjusting system on their overhead camshaft engines. The Vauxhall Victor and Viva ohc units have a system where a screw with a tapered flat on one

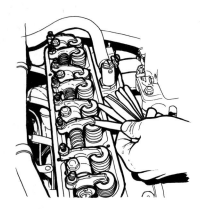

16a Check ohv valve gaps using a feeler gauge between the end of the valve stem and the rocker pad

16b On shaft-mounted rockers, loosen the adjusting screw locknut at the pushrod end of the rocker, and turn the screw until the correct gap is obtained. Re-tighten the locknut. Some rockers use self-locking screws without a locknut

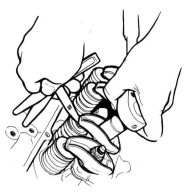

16c On stud-mounted rockers adjustment is achieved by turning a locknut at the rocker pivot point using a socket or box-spanner

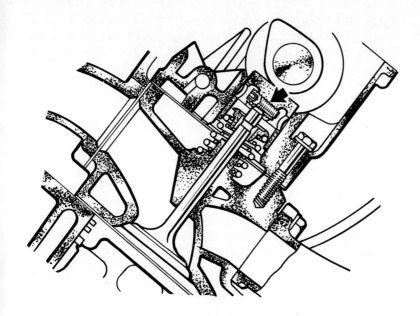

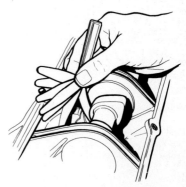

17a Vauxhall use a screw with a ramp on one side instead of a shim to adjust the clearances on their overhead camshaft engines

17b First the gap is checked while the cam lobe points directly away from the tappet

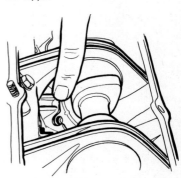

17c Then the tappet is rotated until this cut-out uncovers the head of the adjusting screw

side is interposed between the underside of the bucket tappet and the valve stem and is turned with an allen key to set the gaps.

Ford, on the single overhead camshaft Cortinas and Capris interpose a series of 'fingers' or cam followers between the camshaft and the valves. These would be comparatively easy to adjust if one could reach the locknuts for the adjusting screws. One of these is particularly difficult to reach and Ford recommend using a special tool – a crowsfoot spanner – to tighten these nuts. If you cannot get one, you can either remove the carburettor to reach the nut or get a cheap 19 mm open-ended spanner and bend the jaw at 90 degrees to the handle and use this, turning it with a self-grip wrench.

Carburettor adjustment

Some engines are fitted with emission control equipment and have carburettors sealed so that virtually no adjustment is possible. On these there is little to be gained from tampering unless you have expensive equipment to analyse the exhaust gases. The following information, therefore, is aimed at the carburettors fitted to engines which are not heavily laden with emission control equipment. If applicable, adjustments should be carried out after fitting a new air cleaner element.

From the service point of view, carburettors can be divided into two groups. The most widespread have fixed chokes and mix petrol with air after passing the petrol through a number of fixed jets. They normally have two adjusting screws which are used to alter the mixture at tick-over speed. No further running adjustments are needed. Autolite (Ford), Solex, Weber and Zenith carburettors have fixed chokes and jets.

The other group is the variable-choke carburettor where a

17d The screw is then turned using an Allen key anti-clockwise to increase the gap or clockwise to narrow it. Each complete revolution of the screw alters the gap by .003 in

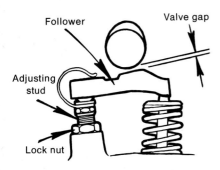

18a Ford use a follower between the camshaft and the valve on their single overhead camshaft engines. On these the gap is altered by loosening the locknut and altering the height of the stud that the follower sits on

18b As before, check the gap with the cam lobe pointing away from the top of the follower

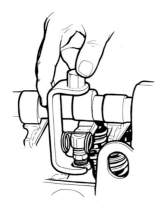

18c Because one of the locknuts is inaccessible, Ford use this special crowsfoot spanner to turn it. If the carburettor is removed, it can be reached with an ordinary spanner

piston or air valve practically blocks off the air-flow down the choke tube at small throttle openings, but lifts to provide less obstruction as the throttle is opened. Attached to the underside of the valve or piston is a tapered needle working in a fixed jet which meters the fuel flow. Mixture settings on these are adjusted by raising or lowering the jet in relation to the needle and by altering the throttle opening at idling speed.

Fixed choke adjustment

Warm up the engine, and locate the two adjusting screws. One – the throttle stop screw – controls the throttle opening at idling speed and normally bears on part of the throttle linkage. The other – the volume control screw – meters the fuel fed into the engine at idling speed. Unscrew the stop screw until the lowest idling speed is obtained without the engine stalling.

Now turn the volume control screw, clockwise, then anti-clockwise and note the effect on engine speed. Stop turning when the engine tick-over reaches its highest speed. If necessary re-set the throttle stop screw to an even tick-over.

Some twin-choke carburettors have two volume control screws and on these the principle is the same as for carburettors with just one, except you have to be more methodical.

Warm up the engine, then screw home each screw, counting the number of turns. In theory they should be open the same amount, give-or-take a quarter-turn. If they are more-or-less the same, reset them to their original position. But if you find one screw is open, say two turns, and the other is open six turns, strike a happy medium and begin with both screws open say, four turns.

Start the engine and set the idle speed with the throttle adjusting screw to approximately 850 rpm. Now open both volume screws by the same amount, a little at a time, until the engine begins to run unevenly. This means it is running too rich.

Reverse the process and screw in both screws by the same amount until the highest engine speed is reached. If you screw them in too far engine speed will drop as the mixture goes too weak. Set the screws to give the highest speed, then if necessary, re-adjust the throttle stop screw to give a smooth tick-over.

Variable-choke carburettors

The principle is the same as fixed-choke units, except the mixture adjuster is beneath the carburettor.

Begin by removing the damper cap at the top of the carburettor and top up the hollow piston rod with engine oil.

Warm-up the engine to operating temperature then run it at around 2,500 rpm (equivalent to a road speed of about 40–45 mph in top gear) for a few moments to clear the inlet and exhaust systems. Allow the engine to idle. If it ticks-over smoothly, and the fuel consumption has not been heavy, the carburettor is correctly adjusted and you might as well leave it alone.

If the car has a heavy fuel consumption, idles erratically or tends to stall, proceed as follows:

Switch off the engine. Under the bottom edge of the suction chamber is a lifting pin. If you cannot find it, take off the air cleaner so you can see the piston or air valve. Using the pin or a small screwdriver, lift the piston or valve about $\frac{1}{4}$ in and allow it to fall. You should hear a metallic click as it drops on the jet bridge. If there is no click the needle is binding in the jet and the jet must be centred – details are given in Chapter 6.

Restart the engine and turn the jet adjusting nut or screw about $\frac{1}{6}$th of a turn at a time and note the effect on engine speed. As the mixture comes right, the tick-over will speed up and become smoother. When the fastest speed has been reached, turn the adjuster up (clockwise looking from underneath) until the idling speed *just* begins to fall. This is the correct setting.

The above adjustment should be carried out within three minutes. If it takes longer, speed up the engine to 2,500 rpm for a brief period to clear inlet and exhaust passages before continuing.

If the mixture adjustment speeds up the idling speed this should be slowed down by backing off the throttle stop screw.

On SU and Stromberg carburettors, when the choke is pulled out, the linkage also opens the throttle slightly and provides a fast idle and both carburettors have a fast idle adjustment screw which ensures this action happens at the right moment.

On Stromberg carburettors, the handbook will indicate the clearance between the adjusting screw head and the choke spindle cam and this should be checked after adjusting the throttle stop screw.

On SU carburettors the choke is pulled out approximately $\frac{1}{2}$ in to the point where the linkage is *just* beginning to move the jet downwards. Start the engine and set the fast idle screw until the engine speed is approximately 1000 rpm.

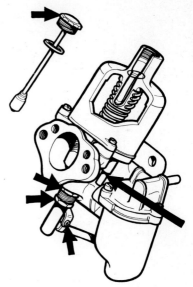

19 The principal components of an SU carburettor. Arrowed (clockwise) from the top are the damper, piston lifting pin, jet link, jet adjusting nut and jet locking nut

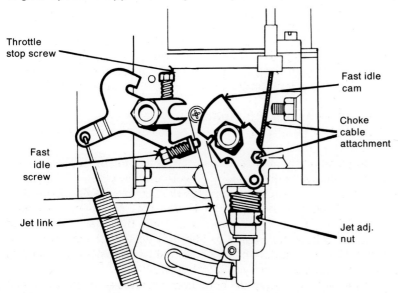

Throttle stop screw

Fast idle cam

Choke cable attachment

Fast idle screw

Jet link

Jet adj. nut

20 On SU's the fast idle cam rubs against the end of the fast-idle screw. This should be set to provide an idling speed of 1000 rpm at the point when the jet link is just about to move the jet – normally with the choke knob pulled out about $\frac{1}{2}$ in from the dashboard

Idling speed

Car manufacturers generally quote the idling speed of their engines to the nearest 50 rpm and recommend using an electronic tachometer for checking them.

If your car has a tachometer (or rev-counter) fitted, by all means use it to set the idling speed and, more important, the fast-idle speed on SU and Stromberg CD carburettors. If you haven't got a tachometer, do not despair, for an intimate knowledge of your particular car is just as effective.

As a rule of thumb, slow down the engine by using the throttle stop screw until it begins to idle lumpily, at which point it will rock on its mountings. Turn the screw about a quarter of a revolution in the other direction until the engine smooths out.

HD-type SU carburettors

As the drawing shows these use an adjusting screw on the side to raise and lower the jet when adjusting the mixture strength, and to confuse matters further, they may not have a throttle stop screw – instead there will be a screw-adjusted slow-running valve.

If the engine is idling roughly, check that the needle is correctly centred using the lifting pin, then warm up the engine and adjust the slow running valve to give the slowest tick-over without the engine actually stalling. Now screw the jet adjusting screw up to

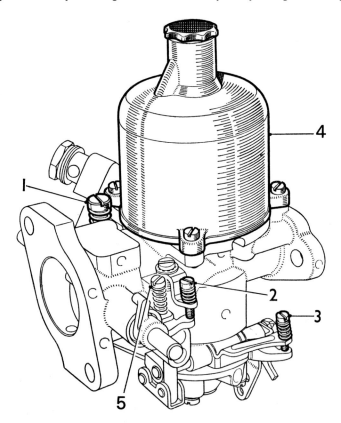

21 The main controls on the HD-type SU carburettor: 1, slow-running valve; 2, fast-idle adjusting screw; 3, jet adjusting screw; 4, piston suction chamber; 5, throttle adjusting screw (when fitted)

weaken or down to richen the mixture until the highest engine speed is obtained. If necessary re-set the slow running valve to give the correct idling speed.

The choke is adjusted similarly to other SU's in that the fast idle screw is set to give an idling speed of 1000 rpm at the point when the choke linkage is just about to lower the jet operating arm.

Some HD's *do* have a throttle adjusting screw. On these the slow running valve is not used for idling adjustment. If one is fitted it should be permanently closed.

Twin carburettors

If a smooth idle cannot be obtained, the first step is to check for needle sticking using the lifting pins. If all is well here, remove the air cleaners and check the airflow through each carburettor with the engine running. To do this you need about 2 ft of flexible hose with an internal diameter of $\frac{1}{4} - \frac{1}{2}$ in. Put one end to your ear and insert the other end into the carburettor air intake. With the engine idling you will hear a hiss or roar of air as it enters the carburettor. Now transfer the pipe to the same position on the other carburettor. The hiss or roar should sound the same.

If the airflow noise is different on each carburettor, the coupling between them must be slackened. Then the throttle stop screws are adjusted until the same sound is made by each carburettor. If adjustment has speeded-up the idling too much, unscrew each throttle stop screw an equal amount to obtain the correct idling speed – check the airflow again after doing this.

If the idling is still poor, stop the engine and fully screw up the jet adjusting nut or screw (turning it clockwise looking from

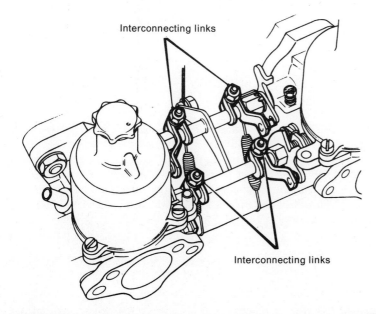

Interconnecting links

Interconnecting links

22 Twin SU carburettors have two sets of connecting links joining the throttle plates and choke mechanisms of the two carburettors. The clamps on these linkages must be slackened before adjusting the carburettors

below) and count the number of turns. From this point, on SU's, undo each jet adjusting nut 2 turns, on Strombergs, slacken each adjusting screw 3–4 turns. Re-start the engine.

Turn both adjusters an equal amount and note the effect on idling speed. If the engine runs roughly, turn in the opposite direction until the highest idling speed is obtained. From this point, turn up each adjuster an equal amount until the speed just begins to drop. This is the correct mixture adjustment.

The above method will work satisfactorily on carburettors that are relatively new, but when they wear, sometimes one carburettor wears a little more than the other and this means that an identical mixture setting for each unit isn't necessarily correct.

So on more senior carburettors, if the above method does not work, remove the dampers and drop a small screwdriver into the oil-filled damper rod. With the engine running, use the lifting pin to raise the air valve or piston $\frac{1}{32}$ in – about the thickness of the wire on a paper clip – and note the effect on engine speed. The screwdriver will help you judge $\frac{1}{32}$ in.

One of three things will happen:

If the engine speeds up, the mixture on that carburettor is too rich. Weaken it by screwing up the adjuster (clockwise looking from below)

If the engine stops or falters badly, the mixture is too weak. Richen it by turning down the adjuster (anti-clockwise looking from below)

If the engine speed remains the same, or only drops slightly, the mixture setting is correct.

Once the mixture setting and balance of the carburettors is correct, re-tighten the linkage. It is common practice to provide a small amount of lost motion where the linkage joins each carburettor. Make sure the amount of lost motion is the same for each carburettor before tightening the clamps – the handbook will give details. The same applies to the choke fast-idle linkage. The fast idle cam mechanism is the same as on single carburettors – adjust it to give a tick-over of 1000 rpm on SU's as already shown, set the appropriate gap between the screw head and choke cam on Stromberg CD's.

On manual cars, get in and press the clutch. If the engine slows to the point of roughness, speed the idle up a fraction more until the engine remains smooth with the clutch depressed. Rev-up the engine and lift off the throttle. It should return to a smooth idle. If it stops, the idling speed is too low or the mixture is wrongly set.

On cars with automatic transmission, put on the handbrake and have a helper hold on the footbrake and select 'D'. The idle should be adjusted to the slowest, smoothest, speed. A small amount of 'creep' is regarded as inevitable on automatic cars with D selected and the brakes off.

Oil changing

Once the carburettor adjustments have been set, and the engine is warmed up, you can drain the oil.

You will need a shallow container to catch the old oil – a low-built plastic bowl will do or you can make one by cutting a square hole with tin-snips or household scissors, in the side of a one-gallon oil can – bend the edges of the hole over to get rid of the sharp edges. To help the oil drain quickly, remove the oil filler cap then take out the sump plug.

Once you have drained the oil, you have a small problem of disposing of it. Some garages will allow you to tip the stuff in their waste oil tanks; or you can take it to the nearest Council rubbish dump. It is illegal to pour it down the drain.

While the oil is draining, the filter can come off. The latest filters are in the form of a canister which is screwed on to the engine block. To replace these, simply unscrew the old one by hand and screw on a new one. If the old canister is very tight it can be loosened with a strap wrench or by spearing the side of the canister with a large screwdriver and using this as a tommy-bar to unscrew it – messy but effective. Once the old canister is off, the surface of the block that it seals on is wiped clean, a smear of oil put on the sealing ring of the new canister which is then screwed on hand-tight.

The other sort of oil filter has a replaceable element which is generally contained in a metal bowl. The bowl is bolted to a casting which houses a rubber sealing ring on which the edge of the bowl makes a seal. Replacement elements come with a new sealing ring.

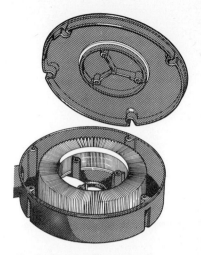

23a Carburettor filters nowadays mostly contain pleated paper elements. Usually these need changing at around 12,000 mile intervals. In the interim service, tap the element against a wall to shake out the dust

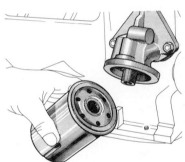

23b Canister type oil filters – providing you can get the old one off – are easy to change. Simply coat the rubber sealing ring with a smear of oil and screw it up hand-tight

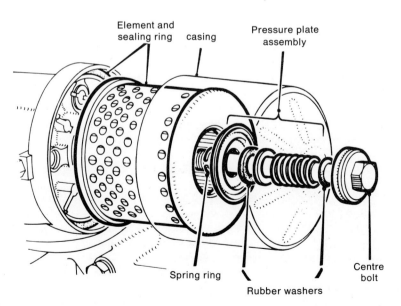

Element and sealing ring casing Pressure plate assembly

Spring ring Rubber washers Centre bolt

23c Cartridge-type filters are more messy because the old cartridge must be taken out, and the filter bowl washed out in paraffin before fitting a new element. Make sure the rubber sealing ring is seated properly

35

Any problems here are confined to the sealing ring. My own experience is that sealing rings which have held up satisfactorily for one oil change period will most likely last for another. Therefore I tend to only change the ring if it leaks oil when the engine is re-started.

If you want to change the sealing ring for a new one the old ring will be at the bottom of a groove which is approximately $\frac{1}{8}$ in wide. It can sometimes be winkled out using a small screwdriver, although you are less likely to damage the casting if you use a compass point or an old darning needle pressed into a block of wood to spear the ring and pull it out. Coat the new one with oil and press it in gently – making sure it is not twisted, for any un-evenness will allow an oil leak. Perhaps you can see now why I leave well alone.

With the old oil out, the sump plug replaced (wipe the plug and its seating before re-tightening it) you can top up with fresh oil. Allow a little time for the oil to pass through the drain holes in the head before checking the level with the dipstick – there is nothing to be gained from over-filling. The last job is to start the engine and make sure from inside the car that the oil light goes out (remember it may stay alight for a few seconds longer than usual as the new oil filter fills up) and then to check that there are no leaks at the oil filter or the sump plug. Recheck the level and top-up if necessary.

Some years ago the oil in the gearbox and back axle was changed as well, but most manufacturers now merely suggest the level is checked and topped-up when necessary. All back axles use an extreme pressure hypoid oil, whereas the recommendations for gearbox vary – some use an EP oil, others run happily in engine oil – the handbook will specify the correct oil for each unit.

The correct oil level is generally in line with the bottom of the filler plug-hole. The only difficulty you are likely to encounter when topping-up gearboxes and back axles is that this work must be carried out with the car level. On most, with the car on its wheels if you lie on your back you can wriggle one arm underneath far enough to undo the filler plug and top-up the level using a squeeze-bottle with a pipe on the end. If you cannot operate the squeeze bottle, raise the car by driving it up on ramps at one end. Over-fill the gearbox and back axle, then insert the filler/level plugs finger tight. Drive the car off the ramps and on to level ground, remove the filler/level plugs and allow the surplus oil to drain out. Refit the plugs.

The other oiling points can be reached with an oil-can full of engine oil. If you have not done so already, top up the damper on variable-choke carburettors and inject a little oil in the rear bearings of Lucas dynamos (do not squirt in too much or you will coat the commutator and partially insulate it). On distributors with their advance weights below the contact-breaker plate, inject a few drops through a gap in the plate, and also take off the rotor and inject a drop or two into the recess at the top of the cam – there is a clearance round the cam securing screw to allow the oil past to lubricate the cam bearing. On distributors with high-mounted advance weights, take off the rotor arm and lightly grease the pivots.

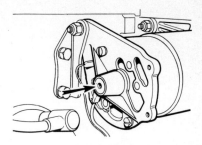

24 On cars still using DC dynamos, inject a few drops of engine oil into the rear bearing housing

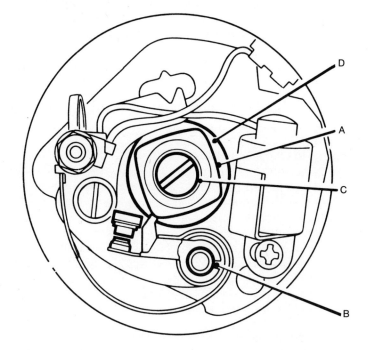

25 The lubrication points on a Lucas distributor. Put a smear of grease on the cam (A) and contact pivot (B), inject a few drops of oil round the screw in the centre of the cam spindle (C), lubricate centrifugal advance weights through the hole in the baseplate (D)

Greasing

Chassis greasing is not entirely dead – a few cars require grease to be injected into their suspension, steering and transmission joints at regular intervals, and providing greasing *is* carried out regularly, there should be no difficulties – after four or five strokes of the grease gun, you should see grease emerging from the edge of the joint.

If you buy a second-hand car with joints stiff with hard-packed and ageing grease and dirt, you *may* be able to persuade some new grease in if you heat the joint with a blow-lamp, although this will destroy any rubber seals in the area. It is also worth trying to pump penetrating oil through a new grease nipple, but if neither of these work, the joint has most likely reached the stage where it needs overhaul to take up the wear. It's worth remembering that some suspension joints should be greased with the vehicle weight off them, whereas others are lubricated with the weight on them. If one method doesn't work, try the other. A piece of rag over the head of the grease nipple before you apply the gun, will sometimes prevent grease from escaping down the sides.

37

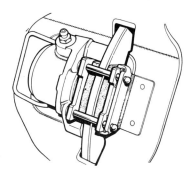

26 Checking disc pad thickness on an Austin Allegro. On some calipers a spring plate must be removed to see the pads

Brakes

There are three main checks – brake fluid level, the condition of brake pipes and hoses and inspection of the friction material for wear. Brake pipes and hoses are best examined with the car up on ramps or axle-stands, while checking the friction material involves removing the road wheel and where applicable, the brake drum. If you are using the car jack, one wheel at a time can be dealt with before moving on to the next. More detailed information on the braking system is given in Chapter 9. The disc brakes used on the front wheels of the majority of British cars are self-adjusting, but in adjusting themselves they draw extra brake fluid from the reservoir. It is therefore important that brake fluid level is checked at service intervals and topped up as required using the manufacturer's recommended fluid.

Checking disc pads

Normally this is merely a matter of observation because on most calipers the pads can be viewed edge-on once the wheel is removed. On a few, an anti-rattle plate, secured by split-pins must be removed to check pad thickness.

On calipers where the pad backing plates are parallel to the disc, fit new pads when the friction material is $\frac{1}{8}$th in thick or less. Lockheed make a swinging caliper where the lining material is intentionally wedge-shaped to allow for the swing of the caliper. Renew these pads when the friction material has worn until it is parallel with the backing plate.

Checking drum brake linings

To check drum brake linings the drum has to come off and here you might meet a snag, for some brake-drums require a special puller to remove them – a ridiculous state of affairs when it is considered that brake linings need examining at least every 6,000 miles or so. Removing these drums is dealt with in Chapter 9.

If you are lucky, the drum will be located on the hub by one or two small screws or the hub nut, and after these are removed and the manual adjusters (where fitted) slackened off, the drum can be pulled off the hub.

If the linings are bonded to the brake shoe, they should be renewed when the minimum thickness is $\frac{1}{16}$ in. If the linings are riveted on, they need renewing when the lining material has worn to within $\frac{1}{32}$ in of any one rivet.

While the drum is off, look for signs of fluid leakage from the wheel cylinders and if no attention is required, wipe the dust from the drum and the backplate with a dry cloth. Refit the drum and adjust the brakes – various adjustment systems are detailed in Chapter 9.

While the front wheels are off, the front flexible hoses can be checked. Look for signs of chafing or cracking and for indications of fluid leakage at the unions. Chafed hoses must be renewed.

Underneath the car, check the metal pipes for rusting. British

27 Remove the brake drums to check lining thickness. Use a dry cloth to remove accumulated dust – don't blow it out as the dust is bad for your lungs

cars have steel brake pipes which are plated to resist corrosion although they don't all resist it very well. Wipe the pipes clean with a paraffin-soaked cloth; rusty ones should be renewed.

Check the handbrake action after adjusting the brakes. Adjustment will be provided to allow for any stretch in the cables, but do not fall into the trap of adjusting the handbrake too tightly. On some cars an over-adjusted linkage can apply the back brakes each time the rear suspension is loaded – such as when the car goes over a bump – and on cars with self-adjusting rear brakes, the handbrake must return to the fully 'off' position or the adjustment will not work.

Clutch adjustment will vary depending on the car and the linkage used. Some hydraulic clutch systems have no provision for adjustment, others have. Cable clutches have an adjustment to compensate for cable stretching.

The adjustment clearance will be detailed in the handbook. As a guide to whether you have done the job correctly or not, the clutch pedal should be about $\frac{2}{3}$ through its travel from the toe-board as the clutch engages.

There is one last adjustment that you can't make. Most service sheets say – 'check front wheel alignment and balance wheels if necessary'. You cannot do this at home, but most tyre fitting centres operate a scheme where they will check the wheel alignment for nothing, although they do obviously charge a fee if it needs re-setting. They can also balance the wheels if the car is suffering from a steering shake.

Chapter three
Engine adjustments

Sometimes an engine does not respond to careful adjustment. Regardless of how carefully you set the valve gaps, adjust the contact-breaker points or twiddle with the carburettor it still runs roughly, mis-fires or consumes inordinate quantities of fuel.

Fortunately, if you know where to look, it is quite often easy to find the cause of the trouble. Most experienced mechanics, faced with an engine that does not perform properly, make a number of basic checks. They will not necessarily be in the order I have given them here because the order changes depending on the symptoms the engine displays, but most would check the adjustments first then test the compression.

Compression

The cheapest sort of compression tester – it is quite effective – looks like a tyre pressure gauge with a spark plug thread on the end. To use it, take out a spark plug, and screw in the tester. With the ignition off, turn the engine on the starter while you hold the accelerator pedal hard down. The tester will indicate the pressure within the cylinder.

Not all compression testers screw in to a plug hole, some have to be pressed against the plug orifice while the engine is rotated. With this sort of tester you obviously cannot operate the starter from inside the car (unless you have a helper to do it) and if you are on your own you will have to operate the starter solenoid by hand.

The solenoid will be in the main feed between the battery and the starter motor and until car manufacturers began costing cars in fractions of a penny most solenoids had a button you could press to work the starter and turn over the engine from under the bonnet. Nowadays not all solenoids have a separate button and with these the only way to turn over the engine while you test compressions is to bridge the main solenoid contacts with a screwdriver blade or a spanner. There will be some sparking, but the starter will operate. On cars with automatic transmission 'P' or 'N' must be selected before the engine can be turned on the starter. On cars with pre-engaged starters, where the solenoid is mounted on top, bridging the solenoid terminals can cause damage – so on these you must have a helper.

For diagnosis purposes, we are looking for uneven cylinder pressures which indicate loss of compression past worn or broken piston rings or a leaking valve. The actual compression pressure is of secondary importance.

Ideally the variation in pressure between cylinders should not be more than 15 lb/sq in. Suppose the compression readings on a four cylinder engine were 160, 160, 80 and 155. Number 3 cylinder is obviously losing compression and it would save a lot of unnecessary work if we could determine whether the leak was past the piston or past a defective valve. Fortunately there is a way.

The spark plugs are out, so, with an oil can inject through the plug holes two or three squirts of engine oil. You want enough

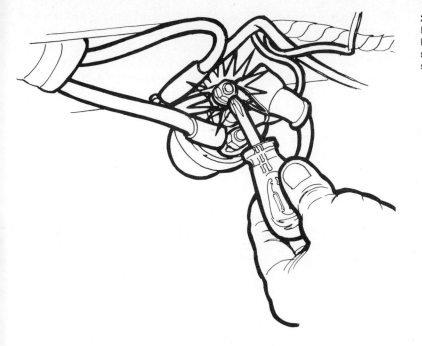

28 On remote solenoids which do not have a manual button, the starter can be operated from under the bonnet by shorting across the terminals with a screwdriver blade

oil to improve the seal at the edges of the pistons, but not enough to spray everywhere when you operate the starter. To avoid everything being soaked with oil, drape a cloth over the plug holes and spin the engine on the starter from inside the car first.

Fit the compression tester to each plug hole in turn and test again. Compared with our previous figures, the readings are now 170, 170, 80 and 165. All have shown an improvement except on No 3, so the compression loss is past a badly-seating valve.

The theory behind this test is that the extra oil in the bores will improve the seal of the pistons. If the trouble is damaged piston rings or a worn bore, the sealing properties of the oil would still give a considerable improvement to the low figure, but a leaking valve will be unaffected by the oil and will continue leaking at the same rate.

Spark plugs

The spark plug makers and the car manufacturers tell us plugs should be renewed at 12,000 miles at the latest. This sometimes seems hard to swallow if the engine appears to be running perfectly smoothly on the old ones.

The problem with spark plugs is that they deteriorate so slowly that any loss of performance is hardly noticed. In fact on the average European car, the spark plug gap increases at the rate of .001 in every 1,000 miles because each time they spark, tiny particles of the electrodes are eroded away. Eventually the action of the spark rounds off the flat end of the centre electrode and nibbles the corners off the other electrode immediately above it.

You can correct the ever-widening gap by bending the side electrode closer, but it is an electrical fact of life that for the spark to jump from a rounded centre electrode requires a higher voltage than if the centre electrode was flat and had sharp edges for the spark to jump from. So with old, rounded-off plugs, you need a higher voltage for a clean spark and this means that at high engine speeds, you might get mis-firing because the ignition system is finding it difficult to cope.

You can get over the rounded electrode problem by opening out the side electrode and filing the end of the centre one flat, and flattening out the corresponding opposite surface in the other electrode. In theory you now have 'as new' electrodes.

Unfortunately there is another snag. Most petrol contains lead to improve its anti-knock properties. Lead salts formed during combustion are strongly attracted to any hot surface and therefore tend to coat and impregnate the spark plug insulator tip which surrounds the centre electrode. When hot these salts conduct electricity and a spark plug which has been in use for 9,000 – 12,000 miles can absorb enough lead salts to provide an alternative electrical leak path for the spark. If this happens, you will get no spark – and a mis-fire.

If you do not change your plugs bang on 12,000 miles, and drive gently the chances are that your car will soldier on for perhaps another 6,000 miles, although its fuel consumption and performance will not be so good compared with a similar engine using new plugs. If you are in the habit of working your engine hard, it is not wise to put off plug changes as a high-speed mis-fire can encourage pre-ignition which causes expensive things like holes in pistons.

If a mis-fire persists after fitting new plugs, the condition of the spark plug electrodes which protrude into the combustion chamber can give an accurate guide to what is going on inside. One of the easiest and quickest checks is to drive the car until mis-firing occurs, then *while the mis-firing is still going on*, switch off the ignition, select neutral and coast to a stop. On cars with steering locks you must be careful not to pull the key out when switching off, otherwise the steering will lock-up. If you are unsure of the locking-up capabilities of your ignition key, have a dry run with the car stationary to make sure you don't make a mistake.

If you have switched off during the mis-firing, the spark plugs, taken fresh from the engine, should indicate the trouble as follows:

Normal: Insulator nose lightly coated with grey-brown deposits. Spark plug gap increases approximately .001 in every 1,000 miles.

Heavy Deposits: Electrodes and insulator tip caked with grey-brown deposits. This indicates oil is being burned in the combustion chambers, possibly due to worn valve guides – cross-check by noting the oil consumption. The plugs should be satisfactory after cleaning.

Carbon fouling: Electrodes and insulator coated in soot. This indicates a rich mixture – check for clogged carburettor air filter, sticking choke, over-rich mixture setting.

Oil fouling: Black, wet deposits on firing end. Most likely causes are worn valve guides, bores or piston rings.

Overheating: The insulator will have a bleached white appearance. Check for over-advanced ignition timing, weak mixture, use of fuel of too low an octane.

Damaged electrodes: Serious overheating will burn away the ends of the electrodes. Check as for overheating.

Split insulator nose: Small cracks in the insulator nose are usually caused by detonation waves in the combustion chamber which indicate over-advanced ignition timing, use of fuel of too low an octane, weak mixture.

Ignition defects

Most ignition trouble can be traced to three sources:

*Incorrect spark plug gaps or worn-out plugs.

*Incorrect contact-breaker points gap.

*Dampness on the high-tension circuit.

In order to save unnecessary words, I have assumed in this section that the battery is in a satisfactory state of charge, and that the car is fitted with new or nearly-new sparking plugs of the correct grade, new correctly-gapped contact points and that the coil top, HT leads, distributor cap (including the inside) and spark plug insulators are clean and dry.

If, despite all this, the engine is mis-firing and the plugs indicate ignition trouble, check further as follows.

HT leads

The current fashion is to fit HT cables which have a centre core of string impregnated with carbon. These prevent radio interference, but if a mechanic in a hurry yanks the leads off the plugs by pulling on the cable, the string sometimes pulls apart.

Without a voltmeter they are difficult to check for continuity but careful examination of a defective cable will show up damaged insulation and burn-marks if the string has parted at a joint and the spark has been jumping the gap. Do not forget to remove each cable individually from the distributor cap as many a broken cable has been masked by the rubber waterproof covers used on distributor cap 'chimneys'. If you have a radio, the onset of unaccountable interference also indicates the break-down of carbon HT cables.

If all spark plugs show evidence of mis-firing, the HT cable from the coil to the distributor centre terminal is most likely faulty. If an individual plug seems to be the cause, then look for trouble at the single HT lead connecting it to the distributor.

Distributor cap

If the HT leads are in good condition, check the cap next. The

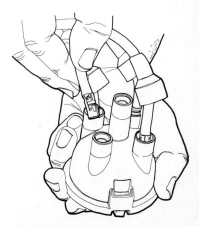

29 When checking ignition HT leads, detach each one from its distributor cap chimney and check for damage at the terminal. Modern terminals are a push-fit and an incorrectly fitted lead will cause arcing and burning at the cap

43

30 It's normal for the electrodes within the cap to look a little rough; if they are practically eaten away, fit a new cap. Where the centre contact is a spring-loaded one, make sure it has plenty of bounce and moves freely. Check the inside of the cap for tracking (see text) and cracks

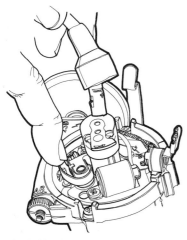

31 Checking rotor arm insulation. With the ignition on, detach the coil lead from the centre of the distributor cap and hold it above the rotor arm while the points are opened. A spark indicates a defective rotor

presence of dust or moisture inside can cause a spark to track from the electrode down the inside of the cap until it earths itself on the distributor body. A tracking mark will be etched on the surface of the cap and will be shaped like forked lightning. As a temporary cure the mark can be scraped away with a pen-knife, but the cap should be renewed as soon as possible. A cracked cap will almost certainly allow HT leakage and should be renewed. If you do renew the cap, and have not changed a distributor cap before, transfer one HT lead at a time and use the old one as a pattern for fixing the cables to the new one – it is possible to get awfully confused if you rip all the wires out of the old cap before noting into which hole they fit.

Under the cap is a contact which bears on the centre of the rotor. Some caps have a fixed carbon contact which sits over a sprung contact on the rotor; other caps have a spring-loaded carbon brush which has been known to drop out when the cap is removed. If the engine mysteriously refuses to start after you have removed the distributor cap, check that this brush is in place.

The electrodes on the inside of the distributor cap collect crusty deposits which are caused by the small spark jumping from the end of the rotor to each electrode. Do not scrape off these deposits because you will increase the gap that the spark has to jump and this can cause a mis-fire. If the electrodes inside the cap appear to be practically eaten away, fit a new cap.

The rotor is checked next. Detach the HT cable from the centre terminal on the distributor and hold it, by its insulation, about $\frac{1}{4}$ in above the centre of the rotor. With the ignition on, flick open the points with your finger or a pencil. You will hear a small crackle as the points separate, but there should be no spark from the end of the HT cable. If there is a spark, the rotor insulation has broken down and it is leaking HT current to earth. If you examine it, you will most likely find it is cracked. Fit a new one.

Coil

Unless you have electronic test equipment it is impossible to check a coil with any accuracy. All you can do is check that it is producing a fat spark and if it is, the chances are that it is all right. But this is not infallible – some coils break down at high engine speeds because they cannot keep up a supply of sparks, but when tested at a slow sparking rate they seem to react normally.

The rough-and-ready coil check is to remove the HT cable from the centre terminal of the distributor cap and hold it, by the insulation, about $\frac{1}{4}$ in from a good earth point – the engine block will do. With the ignition on, flick the points open with a pencil. A bright blue-tinged spark should hop from the end of the HT cable to earth. The spark should jump a gap of around $\frac{3}{8}$ in to $\frac{1}{2}$ in. If the spark seems weak, try the same test on an earth point on the chassis such as a brake pipe. If you get a good spark here and a poor spark from the engine, the engine earth strap has probably broken and the engine is earthing rather inefficiently through the choke cable or throttle linkage.

Wrong polarity

Modern coil ignition systems are intended to produce a negative spark at the plug terminals. If high tension current is positive at the sparking plugs, a higher voltage is required to produce a healthy spark. This incorrect polarity can cause misfiring when the engine is under load and rough idling.

The polarity is reversed if the two low tension wires on the coil are inadvertently interchanged. Some years ago most manufacturers marked their coil LT terminals 'CB' and 'SW' from which one deduced that one wire went to the contact breaker terminal on the side of the distributor and the other accepted the cable which came from the ignition switch. Nowadays coil LT terminals tend to be marked simply with a plus or minus sign. On negative earth car (where the battery minus terminal is connected to the bodyshell) the minus terminal on the coil is connected to the terminal or cable on the side of the distributor. Some coils are now appearing with un-alike LT terminals so the wires can't be interchanged. If your car has a non-standard coil and you think wrong polarity might be responsible for mis-firing, the pencil test will confirm or deny it.

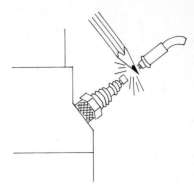

32 With the engine idling, pull off one plug lead and hold it about $\frac{1}{2}$ in from the plug terminal. Now insert a pencil point between the end of the lead and the plug terminal. Correct polarity is indicated by a flash on the plug side of the pencil. If polarity is wrong, interchange the coil LT connections

Low-tension problems

If we rule out complete engine failure such as would be caused by a broken cable, and assume that the contact-breaker points are new and correctly gapped we are left with the possibility of a faulty condenser, a high resistance in the low tension circuit or a worn distributor shaft bearing as the most likely causes of mis-firing.

Condensers are not easily tested, but a faulty one gives itself away by allowing the contact-breaker points to arc heavily and wear out in a remarkably low mileage. Renew the condenser (replacements are cheap) if you need new contact-breaker points every 2,000 miles or if the points appear sooty – a sure sign of excessive arcing.

The distributor shaft normally runs in a sintered bearing pressed into the distributor body. Sintered bearings have the ability to soak up oil and retain it rather like a sponge and since most distributor bearings are splashed with engine oil, they do not normally wear very quickly. You can check the shaft by attempting to move the rotor arm sideways. If there is more than just perceptible movement, either the shaft or the distributor cam bearing is wobbling and the contact-breaker gap will alter as it rotates. Distributor overhaul is covered in chapter 10.

High resistance in the remainder of the LT circuit is most likely due to corroded or loose connections. Look first at the connections on the coil top and the side of the distributor. On Lucas distributors, lift the cap and check the 'pigtail' wire between the side

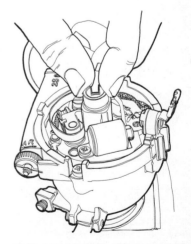

33 Excess play in the distributor shaft or cam assembly will give a variable points gap and cause misfiring. There should be just perceptible play when the shaft is moved sideways. If the shaft is very sloppy, fit a new distributor

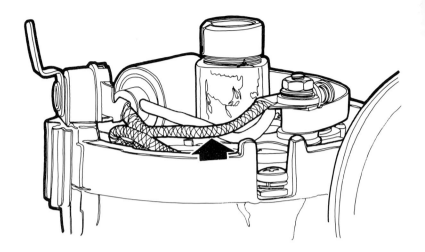

34a Many Lucas distributors use a highly flexible 'pigtail' wire between the LT terminal on the side and the contact-breaker spring post. If this is broken inside the insulation, you'll get a mis-fire as it makes intermittent contact

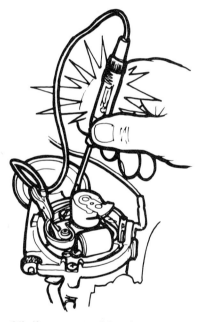

34b If you are suspicious but cannot confirm a broken pigtail wire, turn the engine until the distributor points open, put the ignition on and connect a test-lamp between the contact-breaker spring and chassis earth. The lamp should light, but will flicker as you move the pigtail wire if the wire is broken inside

terminal and the contact-breaker spring. An internal break here will give intermittent mis-firing. Check also that the contact-breaker spring securing nut hasn't loosened.

Ignition advance

As engine speed rises the ignition timing is automatically advanced. The most popular way of doing this is to arrange for centrifugal weights in the distributor to twist the distributor cam and rotor arm in the same direction as the rotation of the disbributor shaft.

In addition, a large number of distributors have a vacuum advance system linked to the engine inlet manifold. This moves the contact-breaker assembly against the direction of rotation of the cam and thus advances the ignition at light throttle openings.

If the centrifugal advance is not working properly, the most obvious symptoms are pinking on acceleration, overheating, lack of acceleration and a lower top speed. Most distributor cams turn anti-clockwise and if you twist the rotor in an anti-clockwise direction, the advance weight springs should pull it back a few degrees when you let go. The spring action on some distributors is weak, so do not worry if the reaction is feeble – the main purpose of this check is to make sure the cam bearing hasn't seized-up.

To test further you need a stroboscopic timing light. These are available from accessory shops and are wired up in series with the HT supply to No 1 spark plug. Some rely on the HT pulse to produce their light while others are powered by the car battery. Both types do the same job – they flash every time No 1 spark plug fires.

In theory if you point the strobe at the timing marks while the engine is running, the flashing light will appear to make the marks stand still and you can check the adjustment. In practice most inexpensive stroboscopes sold for do-it-yourself engine tuning emit such a poor light that it is necessary to help them as much as possible by painting timing marks white or bright yellow, and by using the strobe in a darkened garage. Under these conditions you should just see the marks. Take care you do not get too near the fan – it is easily done in the dark.

To check the centrifugal advance, start the engine and disconnect the vacuum advance pipe (if there is one) between the carburettor and distributor. Now rotate the throttle linkage to speed up the linkage while you watch the timing marks – they should move away from each other smoothly as the speed rises. If the movement is jerky, the weights are sticking and need lubrication. If there is no movement something is wrong – most likely the cam has seized on the shaft.

The vacuum advance system depends on the air-tightness of the pipe between the carburettor and the distributor and the assumption that the diaphragm which does all the work at the distributor end is free from punctures. The professionals attach a tee-piece to the pipe and use a vacuum gauge to check the system, but if you have a healthy set of cheek muscles there is a more basic test – remove the distributor cap and the vacuum pipe at the carburettor end, suck the pipe hard and you should see the contact-breaker plate move slightly. Now pop your tongue over the end of the pipe. If the suction does not vanish within 10 seconds, the diaphragm is sound.

To check whether the vacuum advance is having the desired effect at the distributor, start the engine and screw in the throttle stop screw a known amount (usually about three complete turns) to speed the engine up to around 1500 rpm. With the vacuum pipe disconnected, shine the stroboscope on the timing marks. Still watching the marks, reconnect the vacuum pipe (it is a bit of a fumble, but it can be done) – the timing marks should separate a little more as the pipe is connected. Reset the idling speed by unscrewing the throttle adjusting screw by the same amount that it was screwed up.

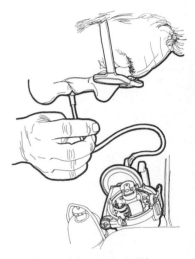

35a The suck-it-and-see test for distributor vacuum diaphragms

Vacuum gauge

Sometimes called an economy gauge, a vacuum gauge measures the depression in the engine inlet manifold. During normal driving, if a vacuum gauge is mounted on the facia, keeping the vacuum as high as possible will result in the most economical fuel consumption.

The gauge can also be used to indicate when the correct mixture strength has been obtained when adjusting variable-choke carburettors.

The gauge is tapped into what is laughingly called a convenient point on the intake manifold. If you have ever bought the average vacuum gauge kit, you will know that the gauge usually comes with about five feet of small-bore flexible pipe and a small screwed adaptor for fitting it to the intake manifold. You are very unlikely to find a hole already in the manifold that the adaptor will

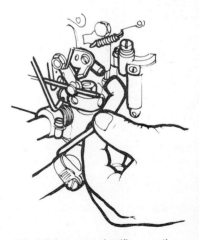

35b A little more scientific – run the engine at 1500 rpm with a stroboscope picking out the timing marks. Remove and reconnect the vacuum pipe at the carburettor and note the effect on the ignition timing

screw into, so you have either got to make one, or find another way of siting the gauge. If you are lucky, the manifold will contain a screwed plug. If you unscrew it, you can take it to the workbench, drill and tap a hole in it, fit the vacuum gauge adaptor and refit the plug and adaptor to the manifold. The whole process takes about 20 minutes.

If there is no plug you may have to drill a hole in the manifold itself. If you do this, it is important that the metal chippings made by the drill do not drop inside where they will get sucked into the engine where they can become trapped under a valve seat and cause the valve to burn out.

Some vacuum gauge fitting instructions suggest that if the drill is coated with grease all the chippings will stick to it when it is withdrawn. A thread is then cut in the hole with a suitable engineer's tap – again suitably greased so it catches all the metal pieces.

The only snag with this method is that it does not work. To drill a hole in a manifold and be sure that no metal particles are fed to the engine, you have to take the manifold off and swill it thoroughly in paraffin after the hole has been drilled and tapped before refitting it to the engine.

A few inlet manifolds have a water jacket in them. The jackets are pretty straight-forward affairs and once you have the manifold off, you will most likely be able to see straight through the water gallery. Obviously any drilling for a vacuum gauge must miss this channel. If you do drill into the water jacket by mistake, do not despair, tap a thread into the hole and seal it with a short screw coated in jointing compound. If you don't like the idea of drilling holes in your engine, there are alternative ways for fitting a vacuum gauge.

One is to fit a carburettor flange adaptor. A firm called Speedo-graph make a composition packing piece about $\frac{1}{4}$ in thick which fits between the carburettor flange and the flange on the intake manifold. From the edge of the adaptor sprouts a small pipe which is connected to the gauge. To fit the adaptor, simply unbolt the carburettor, add the sandwich plate and refit. On paper it couldn't be simpler. Unfortunately even these have their difficulties. On some cars, with the adaptor in place, the studs which hold on the carburettor are no longer long enough. Sometimes this can be overcome by unscrewing the studs a few turns from the manifold flange, but you must be careful not to unscrew them too much, otherwise the stud may spear the float chamber or something similar when the nut is tightened.

On carburettors with rod-type throttle linkages, lifting the carburettor another $\frac{1}{4}$ in might put the rod system under strain – on these check that the accelerator works smoothly and opens and *shuts* the throttle butterfly fully with the spacer in position (the throttle is shut if the stop screw returns fully to its abutment).

If your car has servo brakes, it may be possible to fit a T-piece for the vacuum gauge in the hose between the inlet manifold and the servo unit. Speedwell of Chesham make one, but it should be pointed out that a few servos have their non-return valve at the manifold end of this pipe, so fitting a T-piece on this set-up will only show the vacuum within the servo – not the manifold. The only way for amateurs to check whether a servo union has a non-return valve inside is to take off the hose, unscrew the union and peer through it. If you can see straight through, it is not a non-return valve. Just to complicate things, some servos have a non-return valve actually inserted in the servo pipe. With these the vacuum gauge T-piece should be inserted in the hose between the valve and the manifold.

Using the gauge is much easier than fitting it. On SU and Stromberg carburettors, turning the nut or screw at the base of the carburettor will richen or weaken the mixture strength. Using the vacuum gauge, the best mixture strength has been reached when the highest vacuum reading is obtained. On twin-choke carburettors with two volume control screws, the gauge helps in balancing the slow running mixture. Set the engine to a low tick-over speed. Adjust one volume control screw to obtain the highest reading, then do the same with the other volume screw – the reading will most likely climb a little higher as this one is adjusted.

Fuel consumption

We have already seen how the colour and condition of the spark plug electrodes can indicate when something is wrong. If all the plugs have a sooty appearance, the chances are that the fuel consumption is heavy. The best way to check is by doing a full-to-full test over a distance of at least 200 miles.

Fill the tank to the brim (rocking the car to make sure all the air is out) and note the mileage on the odometer. From this point on,

36a The easy way with vacuum gauges – first separate the carburettor from the intake manifold . . .

36b . . . then insert a spacer with a vacuum pipe tapped into the side

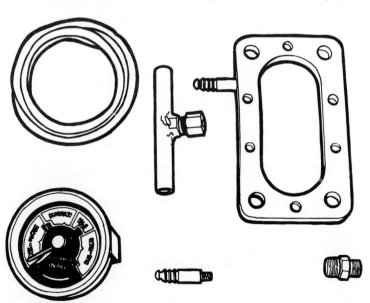

37 A vacuum gauge and some alternative connections. From the gauge, clockwise, the flexible hose which runs between gauge and intake manifold, a brake servo T-piece, carburettor spacer plate (for a twin-choke unit) and two adaptors for screwing into a drilled and tapped hole in the intake manifold

49

make a note of all the petrol that goes into the tank. To make the arithmetic easier, try to avoid adding fractions of a gallon. At the end of the test period, fill the tank to the brim (rock the car) and make a note of the mileage again. Say you have covered 360 miles and used 12 gallons. The car is doing $360 \div 12 = 30$ mpg.

Once you have the overall fuel consumption you can use it as a yardstick for any improvements or otherwise you may make by adjustment of the engine.

Electronic engine tuning

Large garages sometimes use expensive electronic equipment to find engine faults and correct them. The big advantage of the professional electronic equipment is that it can check out the engine while it is running. So for instance, while the ignition system is in operation, a trace of the electrical pulse being served up to each spark plug can be thrown up on an oscilloscope where it can be stretched and expanded to pin-point any defects. Even better than an electronic tuner and tester is the same equipment linked to a rolling road dynamometer. The car is put with its driving wheels on rollers. These are used to measure the power output at the wheels and can be loaded to simulate a steep hill or a stiff headwind so that the electronic gear clipped to the engine can measure what's happening while the engine is under load. A lot of competition engine tuners use a rolling road for fine tuning of cars, because the reading from the rollers will tell them instantly whether the adjustments and modifications they are making are having any effect.

Although the electronic tune-up equipment and rolling road are the ultimate in tuning equipment and are most likely to find an obscure fault when all else has failed, they can only be as good as the operator. Happily the work of ham-fisted tune-up men generates adverse comment, so before booking your car in it is wise to ask around a bit at places like the local motor accessory shop to weed out the doubtful ones.

A top overhaul is the modern equivalent of what our motoring ancestors called a decoke. You did a decoke then because you had to. If you did not then the build-up of carbon within the combustion chambers, around the valves and in the ports severely restricted the gas-flow and seriously reduced the power output. In addition, red-hot layers of surplus carbon would ignite the mixture before the spark plug, causing pre-ignition; when this happened the engine would make loud knocking noises and eventually was likely to burn a hole in a piston.

Nowadays, petrol has improved and the build-up of carbon is a much more gentle process, so a decoke is no longer essential at regular intervals. In fact, because it is a fairly major job, a top overhaul should only be carried out when it is necessary and not before.

The cylinder head contains valves, valve springs, valve guides, combustion chambers, inlet and exhaust ports and sits on a gasket which seals the joint between the head and the block. Trouble in any of these departments indicates that a top overhaul is needed. The signs are as follows.

Valves

Leakage when the valve is shut will allow the combustion gases to escape. The hot gas acts like a blow-torch, burning the edge of the valve as it passes through. The symptoms are loss of power, sometimes popping-back in the exhaust. Confirm the trouble with a compression test.

Valve springs

These can lose their strength over a long mileage or if the engine is overheated – the sort of thing which easily happens if a fan-belt breaks or a water hose bursts. Weak springs have difficulty shutting the valves completely at higher engine speeds so the valves bounce on their seats, allowing combustion gases to escape. The trouble is more prevalent on push-rod engines where the spring has to push back the rocker, a pushrod and a cam-follower as well as the valve. Confirmation is largely subjective: the engine 'runs out of wind' as the revs build up in the lower gears and there is a mechanical rattle as the valves clatter on their seats. If you avoid using high engine speeds you can motor for years with 'tired' valve springs without any ill effects to the engine but it will have little power at high speeds.

Valve guides

These are the holes in the cylinder head through which the valve stems pass. Serious wear here will allow oil to be sucked down past the inlet valve stem and into the combustion chamber. Confirm by running the car downhill with the accelerator pedal released, then accelerate hard at the bottom. If you notice a cloud of blue smoke in the mirror, the guides are most likely worn.

Chapter four
Top overhaul

Combustion chambers and ports

Some cars do not have a combustion chamber formed in the cylinder head, instead it is formed by leaving a bowl in the piston or by leaving a space above the piston at TDC. Regardless of its shape, in time it accumulates combustion deposits and when these reach a certain level they can mask the edges of the valves, interrupting the gas-flow and reducing power output. Up to a point a similar thing can happen within the ports although here the main carbon build-up is on the back of the valve heads where, on the inlet valves, it has an even more damaging effect on the gas-flow. Confirmation of a coked-up cylinder head is not easy for the symptoms – sluggish acceleration and lack of top speed – come about so gradually that if you drive the car regularly you may not notice the fall-off in performance. The only yardstick that can be applied is a personal one: Most drivers using the same route over a period get to know the speed at which the car climbs a certain gradient. When the speed begins to fall off, you know the engine is losing efficiency. If all the adjustments are in order, it could be caused by carbon build-up in the ports and combustion chambers.

Gasket

On a water-cooled engine the gasket provides the seal between the cylinders, the water passages and any oil drillings. If it breaks, any of these can intermingle, sometimes with disastrous results.

If the gasket breaks between two combustion chambers, the cylinder that is firing spills some of its burning gas into the next cylinder. Besides a loss of power, in time this will burn a gutter across the wall between the cylinders. When this happens, the block and head will need resurfacing by an engineering specialist, or might have to be scrapped. Confirmation of the trouble can be obtained using a compression tester.

If the gasket breaks between a water-passage and a combustion chamber, water seeps into the cylinder, the level in the radiator will drop and the engine will overheat. Moisture inside the cylinder alongside the broken area will make the engine more difficult to start from cold, and it will tend to run on three cylinders until it has pumped some of the water out. If this happens, stop the engine and take the plugs out. If one has water droplets on it, the gasket has blown. Another indication is the presence of bubbles in the radiator header tank when the engine is running.

Taking the head off

Unfortunately for me, car manufacturers disagree on the cheapest and most suitable way of making and mounting the cylinder head. Because there are differences, there is no overall recipe which applies to all cars when carrying out a top overhaul. All one can do is take a typical pushrod overhead valve sequence as a basis and say that the same procedure with slight modifications, applies to similar layouts on other cars.

52

I have included information on overhead camshaft engines as well, to point up the differences.

Pushrod overhead valve engines

On water-cooled engines, the first task is to drain the water. If you do not, when you come to lift the head, water will drain into the cylinders and down the pushrod holes into the sump.

Most cars have a drain tap in the bottom of the radiator and a small tap or plug in the side of the cylinder block. On these open both and allow the water to drain out. If you want to save the anti-freeze, use a large clean bowl to collect everything and pour it back into the radiator when you have finished.

Some cars do not have radiator drain taps. On these, undo the bottom radiator hose at the radiator end. The water from the radiator will drain out of the bottom stub, and much of the water in the block will drain out through the disconnected hose. On British Leyland Minis without drain taps, pull off the bottom hose at the water pump end (the bottom connection is particularly difficult to reach). While the water is draining, you can clear the decks. At the carburettor, disconnect the throttle linkage or cable, disconnect the choke, vacuum advance pipe and fuel line. If the air cleaner has a connection to the rocker cover, undo this too. On most cars it helps to take the air-cleaner right off.

38 The first steps: Disconnect the throttle linkage, then the vacuum pipe (A), choke control (B), fuel pipe (C), air cleaner (D) and fume pipe (E)

53

From the cooling system at least one heater hose will be attached to the head – disconnect this, and also detach the top radiator hose and loosen any short by-pass hoses between the head and block.

On the electrical side, disconnect the battery and the HT leads from the spark plugs, marking them for re-assembly, and disconnect the wire from the temperature gauge sender unit.

You can now begin uncovering the cylinder head. Depending on the design it will either have its inlet and exhaust manifolds on the same side, or the inlet manifold on one side and the exhaust manifold on the other. Regardless of the layout, they have to come off. To discourage exhaust manifold nuts from sticking on their threads most manufacturers make them of brass, although a few use a steel bolt. Disconnect the bottom of the exhaust manifold from the down-pipe, then at the upper end, undo all the fixings holding it to the head. On most engines it isn't necessary to detach the carburettor from the intake manifold – the whole lot comes off in one piece.

Undo the bolts holding the rocker cover and lift it off. At its bottom edge will be a gasket – prise it out because there will be a new one in the decoke gasket set.

There are two principal ways of securing valve rockers. You can either pivot them on a common shaft in which case the shaft will be fastened to the top deck of the head by bolts or studs passing through supporting pillars. On these undo the pillar nuts/bolts and lift the shaft and rockers out as a single assembly.

Some Ford and Vauxhall engines pivot each rocker about an individual stud. The stud has a self-locking nut run down its thread and the rocker bears on the underside of this. To take out these, simply undo the nut. To assist re-assembly I make a note of the number of turns each nut has to be undone before it is free. The rockers should be re-fitted on the same studs, so keep them in order.

You can now take out the push-rods. At the bottom end each pushrod sits in a tappet block which rides on the camshaft. Some tappet-blocks are like small upturned buckets and if you tug the pushrods straight out, the blocks can be pulled off their seatings on the camshaft lobes and tip over at the bottom of the pushrod aperture. This is not a major disaster, but on some engines it can involve extra dismantling to put them straight. The problem can be avoided if each pushrod is rotated sharply between finger and thumb to break the grip of the oil before lifting the rod out. Keep the pushrods in order so they can be returned to their original positions – the best way to do this is to poke them through a line of holes in a length of card. Put a figure 1 at one end of the card to indicate which rod belongs to No 1 valve.

Using a socket and long handle, loosen the cylinder head nuts or bolts and take them out. This sounds straightforward, but on a few engines you sometimes meet a long stud which protrudes perhaps an inch or more through a head nut. To undo the nut you

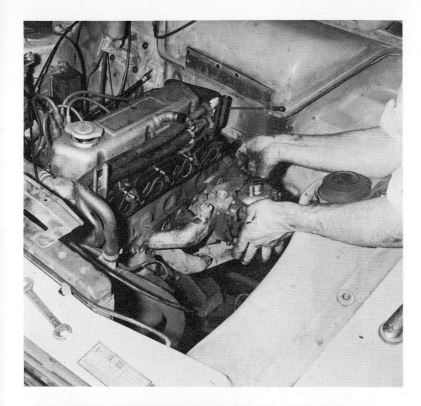

39 Disconnect the exhaust manifold from the down-pipe and if you can, remove the exhaust manifold, inlet manifold and carburettor in one piece

40 The rocker cover has been taken off, exposing the valve gear

41 On this car the rockers are on a shaft. Releasing the supporting pillars from the head allows it to be lifted off in one piece. Remove the pushrods next, keeping them in their correct order

need a long socket. If you have not got one, get a double-ended box spanner that fits the nut, and put a suitable socket over the upper end of the box spanner so it grips it like a nut. This allows the box spanner to be turned by the long socket handle and – more important on re-assembly – the torque wrench.

If you are lucky, the head should now lift off. If it is stuck, reconnect the battery and turn the engine over on the starter – the compression should break the seal of the gasket. If there is still no joy, a sharp sideways tap with a nylon-faced hammer usually gets things moving.

Once the head is off, you can begin to check whether your diagnosis is right. A gasket burned between cylinders is obvious as part of it will be missing. Water seepage into a cylinder also gives itself away because the gasket will be blackened and discoloured where the combustion gases have blown into a water channel.

A burned valve can usually be seen before the valves are taken out as the valve head will not be truly circular – the burning first forms a flat on the edge and in the later stages nibbles out a vee.

Removing carbon

On the engine the piston tops will be coated with carbon. On engines where a substantial combustion chamber is formed in the head, turning it on the fanbelt will bring two pistons up until

42 On the Hillman Avenger 1500 the head is held by 8 bolts and 2 studs. The studs (arrowed) secure heater pipe supports. Once the top nut is off, a deep socket or box spanner is needed to loosen another nut mounted below the support (see fig 52)

43 With the nuts and bolts undone the head is lifted off. The pistons on this engine are well coated with combustion deposits

they are flush with the block face. Stuff a few old rags in the oil holes and scrape the carbon from the piston tops with an old kitchen knife. It is not necessary to bull up the piston crowns until they shine – just scrape off all the carbon. A lot of decoke experts reckon to leave a ring of carbon round the edge of each piston crown because they argue that to remove it will put up the oil consumption. In my view, an engine that relies on a ring of carbon on the piston crown to keep down its oil consumption probably needs a lot more than a decoke to put it right – I always remove all the carbon.

If the engine does not have much of a combustion chamber in the head, the piston will have a bowl in it or the piston may not rise completely to the gasket line. These are a bit more difficult to clean because the carbon must be wiped out of the recess with an oily rag. Do not worry about getting every single speck of carbon out of these – the small stuff will be blown out the exhaust valve as soon as the engine starts.

We can now turn our attention to the head. First remove any odds and ends such as the thermostat housing and heater tap. Now prop it up on the bench and scrape all the carbon from the combustion areas. I prefer to get rid of this surface carbon with the valves in position because the scraper cannot slip and damage the valve seats. If you have one, a small rotary wire brush on a power drill will clean carbon from the combustion chambers quite quickly.

Before you go any further the valves must come out. You need a valve spring compressor, but before using it, give each of the valve caps (not the stem) a light tap with a nylon hammer to break the seal between the collets and the cap. Now hook up the compressor, squeeze up the spring and finger out the split collets. Each valve, its collets, spring and cap should be kept together and stored in line so they can be refitted into the same guides.

Valve guides

If the existing valve guides are badly worn they will need replacing or boring oversize. The way to check is a bit rough-and-ready but it works. Insert the valve into its guide, lift it about $\frac{1}{4}$ in from its seat and try to waggle it sideways. If you can *just* feel fractional sideways play the guides are all right. If there is a lot of slop and the back of the inlet valve heads are covered in thick slightly soft carbon, oil is leaking down the guides on to the back of the valves.

There are two types of valve guide. The simplest is where the car maker drills a hole in the head casting and inserts the valve into it. If these holes are worn, they must be accurately reamed oversize and the appropriate new valves with oversize stems fitted. The Hillman Avenger, for instance, uses this method. Valves are sold in three sizes – standard, the first oversize which is +.015 in or the second oversize, +.030 in. The reaming out of valve guide holes must be carried out with the appropriate

44 The same block after the deposits have been scraped off with a kitchen knife. The crankshaft should be turned to bring two pistons to top dead centre for easier cleaning

45 Off comes the surface carbon from the cylinder head (this car has a flat head without any combustion chamber recesses)

46 Squeezing up a valve cap with the valve spring compressor allows the split collets to be fingered out. As with the pushrods, keep the valves in order

equipment, which for most of us means taking the head to an engineering shop or a garage.

The other sort of valve guides look like small thick-walled steel tubes and are pressed into the cylinder head. These can be renewed at home but first you must measure the height of the top of the guides above the top deck of the head. Once you have noted this, the old guides can be driven out from the top using a punch with a step in it. If you have not got one, get a short bolt that just fits inside the guide and trim the bolt head with a file until it is smaller in diameter than the outside of the guide. Pop it into a guide and hammer the head of the bolt to drive the guide down to the surface of the head. Use another bolt like a punch to hammer it through. Do not hammer directly on the end of the guide otherwise you will spread it and it will not come out.

As you will not have a hydraulic press, the best way of fitting new guides is to draw them in with a length of studding and a bit of tube. You can buy studding from most good ironmongers while a couple of inches of conduit, old heater pipe or domestic central heating pipe will do for the tube. The studding must be small enough to pass through the hole in the guide, while the tube must be big enough to allow the guide to pass through it.

Cut the tube to the length that the guides protrude above the top deck of the head. Now put a nut on the end of the studding, pass the studding through the guide and – from the combustion chamber side – through the hole in the head. From above thread on the tube, add a large washer and screw on another nut. Tightening the top nut will draw in the guide and the guide will be inserted the correct distance when it meets the washer under the top nut. If you are stuck for big washers, there are usually a few from the exhaust manifold that can be used. With the new guides you should fit new valves.

If the head does not need new guides, the old valves should be cleaned of carbon. The quickest way to do this is to mount a power drill in a vice (do not squeeze it too hard) and *lightly* grip the valve stem in the chuck – it is not necessary to tighten the chuck jaws hard and if you do you will burr the stems which will in turn wear out the valve guides. Start the drill and use the edge of a broken piece of hacksaw blade to chisel off the carbon from the rotating valve.

At the cylinder head, an old flat-bladed screwdriver will dislodge any carbon from the area above the valve heads. The inlet and exhaust ports are cleaned with a rotary wire brush or a long-bladed knife. Once all carbon has been removed the head can be washed by brushing it with plenty of paraffin.

Grinding-in valves

For this you need grinding paste and a valve grinding tool.

Most grinding paste comes in a double-ended tin with coarse paste one end, and fine the other. Normally you should not need the coarse paste (some people say *never* use it) but it can be helpful where fine paste won't remove black spots of carbon which are sometimes embedded in the exhaust valve seats. Here a short grind-in with coarse paste will get rid of the black bits and the job can be finished with fine paste. What you should not do is use coarse paste to grind-in a mis-shapen valve, such as a burned one. The only answer here is to fit a new valve.

The valve grinding procedure is easy: The valve head is gripped with the suction cup, a thin layer of fine paste applied to the seat and the valve is inserted into its guide and pressed down on to the seat in the head. The valve is rotated back-and-forth through about half a turn by turning the stick in the palm of your hands and the abrasive grinds a matching surface on the valve seat and the seat in the head. To prevent the paste forming concentric lines on the seats, the valve is lifted and turned through 90 degrees at regular intervals and the process repeated. You have finished when both seats have an even grey matt surface all round.

It is obviously important to remove all abrasive from the valve and combustion chamber after grinding-in and there is a temptation to re-assemble each valve into the head immediately after it is ground in. I do not believe you can wipe away all traces of abrasive paste with a piece of oily rag and prefer to grind in all the valves, then wash the surplus abrasive away with lots of paraffin before re-fitting.

When re-assembling the valves, the stems should be oiled before fitting them to the valve guides. If oil seals are used, these

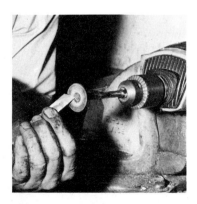

47 Exhaust valve (left) and inlet valve from a 50,000 mile engine. The build-up of carbon on the back of the inlet valve interrupts gas flow and reduces efficiency

48 Spinning a carboned-up valve in a power drill allows the deposits to be turned off using a broken hacksaw blade. Don't grip the valve stem too tightly in the chuck

are fitted next. Most manufacturers use umbrella-shaped oil seals or O-rings threaded on to the stems to discourage oil running down the guides, and supply these in the gasket set. But there are exceptions. Chrysler UK do not supply oil seals in the Avenger gasket set because different sized seals are used depending on whether the valve guides have been enlarged or not. These must be ordered separately. Avenger engines with enlarged guides are stamped with the appropriate oversize on the head adjacent to No 1 inlet port.

After the oil seal, on goes the spring. New valve springs are always worth fitting because they are fairly cheap. The spring is followed by the valve cap and the spring and cap is squeezed up by the compressor while you fit the split collets. Let off the compressor a little and make sure the collets are correctly seated (you will see if one is out of line) before releasing the compressor entirely.

The next step is to refit the head to the block. Clean any dirt off the block face and fit the head gasket. Most gaskets are marked 'top' or 'front' and those that are not marked will only fit one way anyway. Before fitting the head, I usually put a couple of squirts of engine oil on the top of each piston because some old mechanic once told me it tends to carry out any small particles of carbon with it once the engine fires.

49a Adding grinding paste to the seat of a valve (left)

49b The valve is rotated on its seating in the head using a grinding tool (centre)

49c The desired result is an even matt grey surface around the circumference of both seats (right)

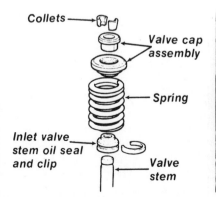

50 Valve spring assembly on the Avenger 1500. The valve stem oil seal is clipped to a protrusion on the head top deck (left)

51 On goes the head gasket. Make sure the block face is completely clean (right)

52 Head nuts and bolts must be tightened in the correct sequence using a torque wrench. On this engine they are tightened to 60 lb ft. The picture shows one way to cope with the recessed nuts – a box spanner is used on the nut and is mated at its other end to a socket which fits the torque wrench

Head tightening

Depending on the design of the engine you will now either fit the rocker assembly then tighten the head or vice-versa. We'll deal with head-tightening first.

It is essential that modern cylinder head nuts or bolts are tightened with a torque wrench and in the correct order. The normal starting point is in the centre of the head, working outwards. If this sequence is not followed, particularly on aluminium heads, the head may warp. The tightening sequences and torques are given in the workshop manual and can be verified from a dealer.

If the rockers are mounted on a shaft, all this entails is fitting the pedestal nuts and bolts and tightening them. A few rocker systems have an external oil pipe which must be connected – make sure this is a secure fit.

If the rockers pivot on studs, tighten the locking nuts the same amount as when they were removed. The reason for this is to assist setting the valve clearances – if the nuts are under-tightened, turning the engine will not operate the rockers so you will not know which one to adjust. Set the valve clearances as detailed in chapter 2 and oil the rocker assembly.

The rest is simply a straight-forward re-assembly job. Fit the intake and exhaust manifolds using a new gasket, reconnect the carburettor controls, refit the thermostat, heater take-off, hoses, spark plugs and leads and top up with water. Leave off the rocker cover for a moment.

Reconnect the battery and start the engine – it may need several attempts if the carburettor float chamber has emptied. As soon as the engine starts, watch for a flow of oil to the rocker gear before stopping the engine and re-fitting the rocker cover using a new gasket.

OVERHEAD CAMSHAFT ENGINES

There are two principal types – what I call direct-acting ohc engines where the camshaft bears directly on an inverted bucket tappet on top of the valve stem, and indirect ohc engines where the camshaft in the head operates the valves by a series of 'fingers' or short rocker arms. The most difficult is the direct-acting type as

53 Fitting the carburettors and manifolds is relatively easy. But you may have trouble fitting the downpipe. The secret is to clean off all carbon, grease the mating parts lightly, and hold the down-pipe in position with *gentle* pressure from a jack underneath while you tighten the clamp nuts

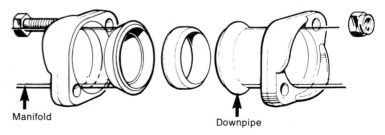

Manifold

Downpipe

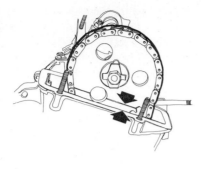
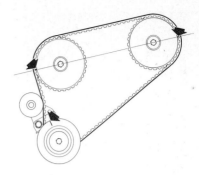

54 On overhead camshaft engines the correct camshaft position will be marked when the engine is at TDC with No 1 cylinder firing. Markings vary. These are on the 1750 Maxi (left), Hillman Imp (centre) and Vauxhall 2300

fitted to the Hillman Imp and ohc Allegros and Maxis, and I will deal with these first.

In a nutshell, the main difference between top overhauling one of these engines and a pushrod ohv unit is that the camshaft has to come out. When the camshaft is taken out of any engine it is essential that it is replaced in exactly the same position in relation to the crankshaft and distributor. Providing this is done, there should be no problems.

The clearing the decks operation is the same as on a pushrod engine. After this the top cover is taken off to reveal the camshaft.

Before removing the camshaft, turn the engine until No 1 piston is at Top Dead Centre and on its firing stroke – this can be checked by aligning the timing marks, then lifting the distributor cap and making sure the rotor is pointing towards the HT feed to No 1 spark plug – if the rotor is 180 degrees out, rotate the engine one more revolution. Incidentally, the engine must always be rotated in its normal direction – turning it backwards can damage a timing chain tensioner.

In this position, a mark on the camshaft sprocket or pulley will align with another adjacent mark. Unfortunately it is not possible to be more explicit because the markings vary depending on the engine – some examples are given in the illustrations.

On chain-driven camshafts the usual procedure is first to back off the chain tensioner – this may involve simply pressing back a spring blade with a screwdriver or, as on the Maxi, de-adjustment of the tensioner by turning a bolt. With the chain loose the drive sprocket can be removed, disengaged from the chain and if necessary the chain hooked up on a piece of bent wire to prevent it dropping into the timing case.

It is usual to mount the camshaft in a carrier which is bolted to the cylinder head. On the Hillman Imp, the camshaft is mounted to the carrier by three bearing caps. If you do the job according to the workshop manual, removal of the caps allows the camshaft to be lifted out. The tappets can then be drawn from the carrier using the suction cup of a valve grinding tool. The tappets should be kept in order with the shims which go between them and the valve stems.

55 The timing chain tensioner on the Maxi must be slackened off by turning an adjusting bolt 90 degrees clockwise using a $\frac{1}{8}$ in Allen key. With this adjuster it's not necessary to tie up the timing chain – it will rest on top of the adjuster

56a To remove a Hillman Imp camshaft, release and remove the cam cover

56b Align the timing marks on the sprocket, then remove the sprocket and tie up the timing chain. Remove the camshaft bearing caps (mark them for re-assembly) to take the camshaft out

56c Carefully lifting the camshaft will uncover the carrier and bucket tappets which can be removed using a valve grinding sucker

There is another way on this engine: unless the small shell bearings in the caps require renewing there is no real need to disturb them. Instead undo the nuts securing the carrier to the head progressively so that the valve spring tension lifts the carrier evenly. When the nuts have been removed, slide the carrier, with the camshaft still in position, up the studs, taking care not to let any of the tappet blocks slide out of the guides in the carrier (usually only two are likely to drop).

As soon as it is free, the carrier and camshaft can be turned upside down so the tappets cannot fall out. The valve adjustment shims will normally stay inside the tappet blocks sticking to the film of oil, but any which remain in the recesses in the valve spring caps should be picked off and placed inside their own tappet. In this way all items remain correctly related within the carrier to await re-assembly. During refitting, place each shim in the recess provided in its appropriate valve spring cap, but keep the tappets in the carrier and fit this as an assembly. Valve clearances can be checked in the way detailed for the Maxi engine further on.

On the Maxi the camshaft cannot be lifted on its own because the camshaft bearings are in one piece. And the carrier and cam-shaft cannot be lifted straight off because the inlet and exhaust valves are fitted at different angles. The trick is to remove the carrier bolts evenly then use the two longest bolts (from the front of the carrier) to prop up the carrier front and rear. This makes the

57 On the Maxi, inlet and exhaust
valves are inclined at different angles.
Prop up the carrier front and rear to
remove the camshaft

tappets drop down and allows the camshaft to be drawn out towards the clutch end of the engine. You can now remove the head.

The Maxi timing chain cannot drop out and at the bottom will
hang clear of the crankshaft sprocket and this means that the
engine can be turned to bring each piston to TDC when scraping
the carbon off. On engines where the timing chain must be held up
against the crankshaft, you must keep the chain under tension
while the crankshaft is turned to bring two of the pistons to TDC
for cleaning. Remember to return the engine to its original
position.

After the valves have been removed, cleaned, ground-in and
re-fitted to the head, the carrier on the Maxi is dropped into
position, the tappets replaced in their original order and the carrier
lifted to allow the camshaft to be re-fitted. Bolt down the carrier,
fit the sprocket to the camshaft and use a spanner on the sprocket
centre bolt to rotate the camshaft and check each valve gap in
turn. Make a note of the gaps.

You now have to remove the camshaft and lift out each tappet
in turn to check the thickness of the shim underneath. On standard
Austin-Morris OHC engines, shims are available from .097 in to
.127 inches in steps of .002 in. Additional shims from .141 in to
.149 in cater for the HL twin carburettor engines. Austin-Morris
don't stamp each shim with its full thickness – just the last two
figures. So a .119 shim will be marked 19 and a .097 shim will be
marked 97. On other engines where the shims are not so clearly

66

marked, the thickness of the existing shims must be measured using a micrometer. If you cannot borrow or hire one, the local engineering shop will measure the shims for you.

Once you know the old shim thickness you can select a new one to give the correct clearance. The arithmetic is simple: A + B − C = the shim thickness required, where:

A = existing valve clearance
B = thickness of shim removed
C = correct clearance

Suppose for instance an inlet valve on a Maxi had a .010 in clearance. The correct rebuild clearance is .016 to .018 in. The shim under the maladjusted tappet is .115 in thick. On the A + B − C basis this gives 10 + 115 − 18 = 107. So the correct shim is .107 in thick.

Fit the shims into their tappets with a smear of petroleum jelly. You can either refit the camshaft to the head at this stage or fit the head to the block, then add the camshaft afterwards.

If the head is on the block, the camshaft should be reset in approximately the same position as it was before removal. First check that the engine is still at TDC on the firing stroke (check the timing marks and distributor rotor), if the camshaft and carrier are marked these can be aligned. If the markings are on the sprocket, fitting this temporarily to the end of the camshaft will give an approximate idea of camshaft position. If all else fails, set the cam so the valves of No 1 cylinder are closed and the two cam lobes form a shallow V above the No 1 tappets when viewed from the front. The reason for this performance is to ensure the valves don't hit the pistons when the camshaft is tightened down.

With the camshaft fitted, add the sprocket and turn it if necessary using the centre bolt, to align the camshaft markings. Remove the sprocket, fit the chain, refit the sprocket. It should engage easily with the camshaft driving dowel or keyway. Release the chain tensioner. Turn the engine one revolution in the normal direction of rotation by engaging top gear and pulling the car forward and re-check that the TDC marks and camshaft marks align at the same moment – if they do not the sprocket is most likely one tooth out on the chain – slacken the tensioner, remove the sprocket, re-fit it to the chain and camshaft and check again.

Toothed belt drives

Where a toothed belt is used to drive the camshaft, loosen the camshaft pulley fixing nut before removing the complete belt. Generally the belt just pulls sideways off the pulleys after releasing the tension of a jockey pulley. If the belt is to be re-used, mark its direction of rotation with a chalk arrow and refit it the same way. If the car has covered more than 40,000 miles, it's a good idea to fit a new belt.

One of the advantages when decoking a toothed-belt ohc engine is that with the belt removed the crankshaft can be turned to

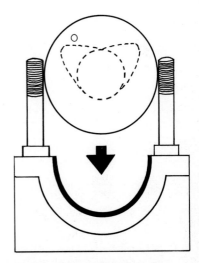

58 If the timing marks are on the sprocket, before you re-fit it, set the cam so the front two lobes form a shallow vee

67

bring each piston to TDC when scraping off the carbon. When re-fitting the camshaft to these engines, it is worth-while taking a tip from Vauxhall and turning the crankshaft back anti-clockwise about 90 degrees so all the pistons are about halfway down the bores. This prevents the valves hitting the pistons as the camshaft assembly is tightened and means the camshaft does not have to be pre-set.

Once the camshaft is on, rotate the camshaft and auxiliary pulleys until their markings coincide, *then* turn the crankshaft to align the TDC markings. Fit the belt, making sure the pulleys don't move and temporarily adjust the jockey pulley. Rotate the engine in its normal direction of rotation using a spanner on the crankshaft pulley nut until the TDC pointers align. Re-check the position of the camshaft marks. On Vauxhall engines belt tension is correct when the jockey pulley deflects the belt 0.3 in under a load of 10 lbs. The load can be checked with a cheap spring balance — as a guide a belt that is over-tightened will whine.

Indirect ohc engines

The most widespread ones in Britain are the overhead camshaft four-cylinder Ford engines. These have a camshaft supported by four cast-in carriers on the cylinder head. Strangely, to take the camshaft out it must be moved out rearwards towards the front bulkhead, so to change a camshaft the head must come off. Valve adjustment is covered in Chapter 2.

Water cooling systems are simple in theory but can be troublesome in practice. On the average car the cooling system comprises the radiator, water pump, cooling fan, thermostat, radiator cap or (on sealed systems) an overflow tank, a heater radiator and a few yards of hosepipe to link them all together.

Because it is extremely difficult to look inside a radiator or examine a water hose without cutting it in half, most manufacturers simply suggest that the water level and water pump drive belt (fan belt) are checked at regular intervals.

To do its job properly, the water must make a complete circuit from the engine water jacket through the radiator and back again. If the circuit is interrupted – by a blockage or because water has leaked out and air has got in, the water in the engine will be insulated from the cooling action of the radiator and will boil.

Drive belt

The most frequent cause of overheating is a broken drive belt. This stops the water pump which prevents water circulation, and the water round the engine boils.

Normally the same belt also turns the dynamo or alternator and an ignition warning light will glow when these stop turning. If you don't notice the light and do not have a water temperature indicator, the engine will begin to lose power and you will hear the rattle of pre-ignition and possibly catch the smell of hot rubber as it over-heats. Driving much past this point will cause the engine to seize up.

In theory, if you have been testing the tension of the belt at regular intervals a worn one will be spotted because it will have stretched to the point where all the adjustment is used up. If you are a bit forgetful about maintenance, carry a spare belt and the appropriate spanners so it can be fitted at the roadside.

Thermostat

A thermostat regulates the flow of water from the engine to the radiator. When the engine is cold, it cuts off the radiator entirely. The engine thus warms up fairly quickly because it only heats up the water around the cylinder head and block. At a pre-determined temperature (usually around 82°–88°C) the thermostat opens a valve and allows water to pass from the engine to the radiator.

Nowadays most cars use a wax-pellet thermostat. The way it works isn't of great importance, but when it is not working, it can cause problems because it fails in the shut position and the engine is isolated from the radiator. If this happens when the car is on the move, the water in the engine will boil pretty quickly.

In an emergency all you can do is wait for the engine to cool down, then get out a spanner and take off the thermostat housing (it is usually at the engine end of the top radiator hose). Take out the thermostat and refit the housing without it. If you are lucky, removing the thermostat housing won't damage the gasket. If

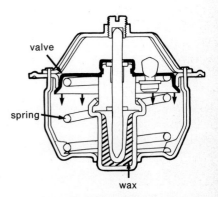

59 The small quantity of wax in a wax pellet thermostat expands against a fixed pin as the water heats it up. This causes the pellet casing and valve to move downwards, opening the valve against spring pressure

69

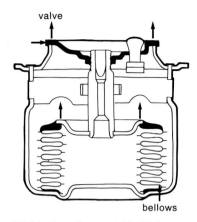

60 A bellows thermostat holds the valve shut when it is cold due to a vacuum within the bellows. At the appropriate temperature the vacuum disappears, the bellows expands, opening the valve upwards

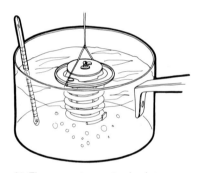

61 The accurate way to check a thermostat is to suspend it in a saucepan of water and heat it up. The thermostat should begin to open at the temperature marked on the casing

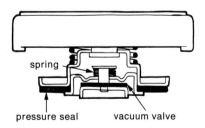

62 Besides the large rubber ring which forms a pressure seal in the filler neck, the radiator pressure cap also has a vacuum valve in the centre. Check that the small spring is working by pulling the valve gently downwards

the gasket is broken, you will need a small piece of card and a penknife to manufacture another one. Top up with water before driving off. If a thermostat is removed on a Maxi or ohc Allegro engine, water circulation in the head suffers. Drive gently until a new thermostat can be fitted.

Not so common now is the instance of a thermostat jammed open. This happens if a bellows-type thermostat fails. These are pressure-sensitive and are only fitted to systems pressurised at levels below 7 lb/sq in so they are likely to be found on older cars. A jammed-open thermostat will not require any immediate action as it will only delay the warm-up. Thermostat action can be checked by starting the engine from cold and resting a hand on the top hose while it ticks over. After a few minutes the thermostat should open and the hose will warm up quite quickly. If the hose heats up very slowly, the thermostat is jammed open – or has been removed.

If an engine has been overheated and it is not the fault of the thermostat, it is still a wise move to change a wax-pellet one. The reason is that over-heating will cause the wax to over-expand and some may leak out. This leaves less wax in the pellet to operate the valve next time. So the valve will not open so far, you will get over-heating, and if it is bad enough, more wax will escape. Eventually the thermostat will not have enough wax to open at all.

Radiator caps

These incorporate a pressure and a vacuum valve. The pressure valve allows the cooling system to build up a pressure as the engine warms up. Pressurising means that the water inside will have a higher boiling point than normal, and this is done to allow the engine to operate at a high temperature – where it is most efficient – without water loss.

The vacuum valve is fitted inside the pressure valve and lets air into the system as it cools down and the water contracts. Without the vacuum valve, the cooling water would suck in the radiator header tank and the hoses.

You can test a radiator cap at the same time as you check a thermostat. Warm up the engine from cold, and few minutes after the radiator has begun to warm-up, stop the engine and undo the cap half-a-turn. You should hear a slight hiss of escaping air as the pressure is released. Do not do this when the engine is fully warmed-up unless you have a piece of cloth protecting your hand – releasing the pressure in the system when the temperature inside is above 100° C will cause it to boil immediately.

A faulty cap will usually be showing some damage to the sealing ring which sits on the ledge round the inside of the filler neck. If the rubber is stretched or broken, fit a new cap. If the pressure seal looks in good condition, lift the vacuum valve, for if this is not seating properly, pressure will escape.

If there are no signs of damage, a suspect cap can be confirmed either by taking it to a garage and having it tested on a pressure tester or by checking for leakage from the overflow pipe. This pipe runs from the side of the filler neck to a discharge point alongside the radiator. If you can, get a jar under the end and check the contents after a run. With the radiator filled to within $\frac{3}{4}$ in of the bottom of the filler neck, there should be nothing in the container. If there is, the cap is faulty. If there is not space for a container, tie a balloon to the end of the pipe.

Water pumps

Broadly speaking there are three things which can go wrong with a water pump. It can stop working because its drive belt is broken (see drive belt). It may seize up, or it can leak water. Of the three, drive belt failure is the most common, followed by water pump leakage.

Leakage is caused by the failure of the seal within the pump. On most pumps the seal takes the form of a carbon ring which is spring-loaded on the face of the pump impeller. Wear in the pump bearings allows the spindle – and impeller – to run slightly off-centre which wears the seal unevenly.

Once water has got past the seal it passes through the bearing, washing away some of the grease in the process and setting up corrosion, and emerges from the spindle boss immediately behind the pump pulley.

Because it is masked by the pulley a leaking water pump isn't immediately obvious – the only sign you get is a mysterious drop in radiator water level. Things are complicated if the leak is a small one because water will only seep out when the engine is hot and the cooling system is pressurised. Once the engine has cooled and the pressure has disappeared, no more water seeps out. In addition, if the cooling fan is bolted to the water pump spindle, it will spin the leaking water elsewhere over the engine bay, further adding to the mystery.

If the pump seal is leaking there is almost certain to be some play in the pump bearings. On cars with a fan attached to the pump, slacken the drive belt, then grip the fan blades and rock the spindle from side to side. *Just* perceptible movement is acceptable, but if it is more than this you have most likely found a leaking pump. On cars with electric fans remove the drive belt and try to rock the pump pulley. Leaks can usually be confirmed by taking off the pulley and examining the spindle boss for traces of water.

In theory it is possible to repair a few water pumps using an overhaul kit, but bearing in mind that the parts cost nearly as much as a ready-built reconditioned pump with an as-new guarantee, most car manufacturers have given up repair kits and supply only new or reconditioned pumps.

Pump seizure is most likely to happen one cold morning if the cooling system is low on anti-freeze. Ice in the system holds the pump impeller rigid and the drive belt skids over the stationary pulley making loud shrieking noises and giving off a strong smell of rubber. Pouring a kettle-full of hot water over the outside of the pump usually cures this difficulty.

If the pump bearings seize, you will get the same symptoms and the only remedy is to fit a reconditioned pump; you should also fit a new drive belt.

To fit a new water pump, drain the cooling system first, then slacken and remove the drive belt. Where the fan is attached to the pump pulley, this comes off next. On what we fondly call 'orthodox' cars, this is simply a matter of reaching down between the radiator and the fan and dexterously using a small open-ended spanner. On some tranverse-engined cars, it may be necessary to remove the top radiator cowl and on a few cars it may be simpler to remove the radiator itself.

With the pulley released, detach the hoses from the pump, undo the four or five securing bolts (they are usually different lengths – note their position) and take it out. Unfortunately it doesn't always happen as easily as this because most pumps are located by small dowels and it is usually necessary to prise the pump gently from the block with a screwdriver to free it off. If the pump is to be scrapped you can, of course, tap it with a hammer to speed up the job.

Once the pump is off, carefully scrape the pieces of old gasket from the cylinder block with a penknife blade (take care not to gouge away any metal on aluminium engines) fit a new gasket and add the new pump. On some British Leyland engines a small by-pass hose connects the pump to the cylinder head. This should be clipped to the pump and wriggled on to the stub on the head at the same time as the pump is aligned on its dowels.

With the pump fitted, reverse the rest of the dismantling sequence, not forgetting to re-tension the drive belt and top up the system with water. Run the engine and check there are no leaks from the pump or hoses.

Water pumps sometimes squeak when the engine is idling. This is caused by the carbon seal inside and is not necessarily an indication of trouble. Providing the pump doesn't leak, the squeak can be ignored. If you cannot stand the noise, speeding-up the tick-over a fraction usually silences it.

Hoses

Most hoses seem to last for around 40,000 miles without sudden failure although after this they can cause problems. The worst calamity is a burst hose and the one which is most likely to go is the top radiator hose because it has to withstand higher temperatures and generally a bit more vibration than the others. Other than this, any leakage is likely to be confined to the joints where hoses are clipped to metal stubs, or junctions where a small-bore heater hose may be moulded into a radiator hose. Old heater hoses sometimes collapse internally and interrupt the flow of water. This is most likely to happen at sharp bends and if you squeeze the hose at this point it will feel squashy.

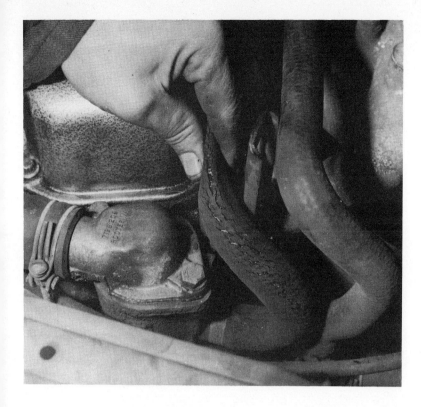

On paper, to renew a hose you simply drain the water from the system, unclip the hose, pull it off the stub at each end and clip on a new one. The first operation – undoing the clip – is pretty straight-forward except where a clip is fitted which is tightened by rotating a split pin. This can be loosened by turning the eye of the pin with a small screwdriver, but sometimes it won't re-tighten happily, and I always replace these with screw-up worm drive clips.

If the hose has spent several years on the same stub it will not be too keen to part from it, so cut it off with a sharp knife if it sticks. Clean the stub of any corrosion using a wire brush, smear it with a little soap and slip on the new hose.

Air locks

If you renew all the hoses at once, when you have refilled the cooling system there is a good chance of an air-lock in the heater. On cars without bleed valves in the cooling system, air is bled out as follows. Open the heater tap then warm-up the engine with the radiator cap off. Stop the engine and loosen the return pipe from the heater where it joins into the water pump or bottom hose. Restart the engine and while it is idling, and taking care not to push your hand in the fan, ease the heater pipe off the stub. Push it back on as soon as a steady stream of water flows through – usually a matter of seconds. Top up the radiator. As an alternative,

73

undo the heater hose at its highest joint and top up the system by pouring water in through this hose using a funnel.

Some cars have bleed valves. The Hillman Imp, for instance, has a valve in the pipe-work from the water pump next to the radiator. To remove air-locks remove the radiator cap, switch the heater to 'hot', and connect a length of transparent plastic pipe from the bleed valve to the radiator filler neck. Open the valve while the engine is started from cold and run at a fast idle. Top up the radiator if necessary, and when bubbles cease to appear in the bleed pipe, close the bleed valve.

Semi-sealed systems

Some cars do not have a pressure cap in the radiator. Instead the radiator is sealed and the expansion and contraction of the water is allowed for by connecting an overflow pipe from the radiator to an expansion tank or bottle.

The tank will have a pressure cap or valve in the top which acts in the same way as a radiator cap, but unlike a radiator the expansion tank is not filled to the top. Most of them are intended to be about half-full when the system is cold and are transparent so the level of the water can be checked against a mark.

When filling these systems an anti-freeze mixture must be used and the usual practice is to loosen the expansion tank cap (essential if the system is hot) then take out the filler plug which

64 Using a bleed valve to exclude air from a Hillman Imp cooling system

will be at the highest point in the system, maybe in the radiator or perhaps in the top of the thermostat housing. Fill the system to the top of the plug hole and fill the expansion tank to the level marked. Refit the plug and the expansion tank cap. Run the engine at a fast idle for about half a minute. Now undo the filler plug and add more water if the level has dropped. Refit the plug, start the engine and run it until the thermostat opens. Stop it and allow it to cool. When cold, top up the expansion tank to the required level.

Some cars with semi-sealed cooling systems have series of bleed valves at various points. The idea is that all the bleed valves are opened before filling up with the appropriate anti-freeze mixture, and as soon as neat fluid begins running out of each valve it is closed off. In theory this should exclude all air bubbles from the system.

Adding anti-freeze

Semi-sealed systems should always have an anti-freeze solution in them and on these it is best to use a fairly expensive anti-freeze – the car manufacturer will suggest one – because the expensive ones contain longer-lasting inhibitors to discourage internal rusting and corrosion.

On a non-sealed system on a cast iron engine, if you just want to stop the water from freezing, you can simply add about 20 per cent methylated spirit to it. You have got to remember, of course, not to check the radiator level in the dark with a match! The same applies to most of the cheaper anti-freeze mixtures which rely on methanol – which also gives off inflammable vapour – to discourage the water freezing. A cheap anti-freeze should not be used on aluminium engines.

If the car has a cooling system that is in reasonable condition and you intend keeping it, one of the more expensive 2- or 3-year anti-freezes is best. Some are coloured and the colour changes when they begin to lose their effect.

All anti-freeze has a searching action and can get through tinier holes than plain water. So after adding it, check all the hose joints after the engine has warmed up – you will most likely find a slight leak somewhere. If the hose is in good condition, tightening the clip a little will cure the leak.

Radiators

Two things go wrong here – the radiator may be holed, or it may become blocked internally.

Tiny holes can be cured by adding a proprietary compound to the water. Most of these work on the principle that they remain in suspension in the water until they find a small air hole. Once they leak out the hole, they begin to solidify on contact with the air and seal the leak. They work well when the leaks are small, but big holes or small ones which are under stress and can dislodge the sealer, will need different treatment.

If there is a large hole in the core of the radiator it will be difficult to repair because unless you cut away a considerable number of cooling fins, it is unlikely you can even get to the holed section. A radiator repairer would normally scrap a damaged core and solder a new one on to the existing top and bottom radiator tanks. You may be able to seal a small leak in a core if you drain the radiator, allow the core to dry, and squeeze a wodge of plastic body filler into the affected area. In theory this is not to be recommended for permanent repairs because it blocks a number of fins and tubes and will slightly reduce radiator efficiency. On the other hand it sometimes works and it is cheaper than a new radiator, so it is always worth a try. Leaks in the top (header) and bottom tanks are usually restricted to the area where the stub pipes emerge. The top hose in particular can put a lot of strain on the stub and sometimes this cracks where it meets the tank.

If you have a very powerful soldering iron, it may be possible to solder up the damage on a copper or brass tank, but you will need a lot of heat because the radiator will conduct so much away from the iron. As an alternative, if the radiator is removed from the car, a blow-torch will heat the stub sufficiently to melt the solder, but here you have to be careful you don't apply too much heat, otherwise other soldered joints in the vicinity will come apart. On balance, if you are familiar with soldering techniques, this sort of repair is possible, but for all others, I would suggest having the repair professionally done.

Internal blockages are usually due to a build-up of rust flakes in the bottom of the radiator. Most of these can be flushed out if the bottom hose is removed at the radiator and water from a garden hose connected to the mains is poured into the filler neck (on semi-sealed systems, feed in the water through the top hose). In severe cases, take out the radiator turn it upside down and hose water into it through the bottom hose stub. This back-flushing often clears stubborn debris caught in the matrix.

At the same time as the radiator is cleaned, flush the engine block by taking out the thermostat and hosing water into the thermostat housing until clean water emerges from the bottom hose connection.

In time the exhaust emission regulations will make carburettors untouchable for the home mechanic. Already some cars are fitted with carburettors which are pre-set at the factory and cannot be re-adjusted on the car. One of the advantages claimed for this sort of carburettor is long life. We shall see.

Meantime, there are millions of cars running with old-fashioned carburettors which (one manufacturer tells us) wear out after 40,000 miles. But before you chuck a worn carburettor away, it might be worth considering an overhaul. Spare parts are available reasonably cheaply for virtually all non-emission carburettors either from your local garage or from the carburettor manufacturer's agents. The manufacturer can also supply a technical information sheet if you require it.

Obviously in one chapter I cannot detail the overhaul of every different carburettor. But four of the most popular ones are shown here and although the details are different, the dismantling principles apply to all other types.

First, let us consider the symptoms of a worn-out unit. It guzzles unwarranted quantities of fuel, robs the engine of power and makes it difficult to start. When this happens, before jumping to any conclusion, it is wise to check two items – the air cleaner element, for if it is clogged with filth it will give the above symptoms, and the choke linkage which will also encourage the above behaviour if it is mal-adjusted.

The make-or-break test for a worn carburettor is to check the wear on the throttle spindle. The spindle is the carburettor shaft which is rotated by the cable or rod linkage when you press down the accelerator pedal. Once you have located it (quite often you must remove the air cleaner to see it), check it for side play by trying to waggle it.

Just the tiniest amount of movement is the sign that all is well. But if you can feel and hear the spindle rattling in the casting and can see it moving as well, the carburettor had better be scrapped, for a worn spindle will nullify any other good work you may do on the rest of the unit.

To overhaul the average fixed-choke carburettor you need a set of new gaskets, a float valve, a set of new jets, accelerator pump diaphragm and spring, economy valve diaphragm and all the necessary rubber O-rings and packing washers. On a variable-choke carburettor you should fit a new needle and jet, gaskets and float valve and, on the Stromberg CD, a new diaphragm.

The illustrations show the carburettors off the car. Removing the average carburettor is remarkably easy once you have uncovered it by taking off the air cleaner. Then all you have to do is disconnect the fuel pipe, vacuum pipe and (where fitted) the crankcase breather pipe, then disconnect the choke and throttle linkages. When this stage is reached, undoing the nuts securing the carburettor flange to the intake manifold will release the unit. When re-fitting, use new gaskets between the carburettor and intake manifold.

Solex fixed-choke

The PSEI-type carburettor shown in the illustrations represents a typical simple fixed-choke unit. It has two castings. The float cover casting houses the choke flap and float valve, while the lower casting incorporates the jets, diaphragm-type accelerator pump, float, throttle assembly and economy valve.

Because the float and float valve are in separate castings, a special tool is needed to check the fuel level. If fuel consumption seems high, fit a new float as well as a new valve, using the same thickness washer under the valve.

Jets should be unscrewed and cleaned. Each one is numbered, and to make sure it goes back into the correct hole, make a sketch on a notepad. Blocked jets should ideally be blown clear with a garage airline, but you can do just as well at home if you gently probe them clean with a nylon bristle. Since carburettor jets are calibrated to the nearest 1/10,000th of an inch, it's not a good idea to clean them with stiff wire as the slightest enlargement can ruin the fuel consumption. On this particular carburettor there is a ball valve beneath the accelerator pump spout which is retained by a spring. Do not try to take it out – just check it is free-moving by shaking the carburettor.

Zenith IV fixed-choke

This is more complicated than the Solex and breaks down into three sections – the cover which houses the economy valve, choke flap and linkage, the base which has the throttle spindle and float chamber bowl cast in it and the emulsion block which is bolted to the cover and houses the float valve, a piston-type accelerator pump and most of the jets.

Over the years it can develop faults. Early versions had composition floats which absorbed petrol and sank a little, giving an over-rich mixture. The cure is to fit a later type float assembly with hollow nylon floats. On these the float level, with the top casting inverted, is 31 mm from the base of the float to the gasket. See page 80 for the overhaul sequence.

SU HS series

The most widely used SU unit, it has a reputation for fuel economy and reliability. For some reason, it rarely suffers from severe spindle wear although over a long mileage the fuel consumption may deteriorate due to wear in the float valve and the jet.

If a new jet is fitted, a new needle should be fitted at the same time. All needles are marked with a code number or letters and the marking is on the side of the thickest section and can only be seen after the needle has been removed. Make sure you get a new needle of the same type.

Most of the SU's in circulation have their needles clamped firmly to the underside of the vacuum piston. On these, the jet must be re-centred after fitting and the procedure is shown in the illustrations. The latest HS carburettors use a needle which is spring-loaded to rub against the side of the jet and these do not need recentring. See page 81.

Solex fixed-choke *(figs 65–75)*

65 The Solex PSEI carburettor has what seems to be a complex external linkage. There is no need to dismantle this, but when refitting the top section, hold the spring-loaded choke flap vertical while the castings are re-united

66 Undo five screws and the top casting comes off. You can check the float valve if you suck on the fuel inlet (arrowed) while holding the valve plunger (A) shut

67 To renew the valve just unscrew it. Fit the same thickness of washer under the new valve

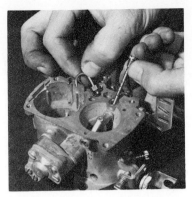

70 The emulsion tube (right) and accelerator pump spout come out of the top. Make sure they are both clear

73 The economy valve diaphragm is in a separate housing which is detached from the carburettor body by removing three screws

68 In the bottom casting the float and its spindle simply lift out. If you can hear petrol inside the float when it is shaken, fit a new one complete with a new spindle

71 Later carburettors have a small gauze filter over the end of the idling jet to discourage blockage

74 Undo two more screws to separate the halves of the housing and remove both diaphragm and spring

69 Remove a plug in the float chamber wall and you can unscrew the main jet. If the carburettor has done more than 20,000 miles, fit new jets all round

72 The accelerator pump diaphragm comes apart like this. On re-assembly the spring is entered first, then the new diaphragm, cylindrical section outwards, and lastly the cover

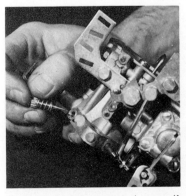

75 Check the volume control screw. If it is ridged or waisted, fit a new one, or idling adjustment will be difficult

76 The economy diaphragm is on top of the carburettor. Undo three screws, lift the top cover and remove a coil spring to get this far. Fit a new diaphragm and spring using new gaskets above and below the diaphragm edge

78 Off comes the top casting bringing with it the twin floats (A) emulsion block, accelerator pump and jets. Renew the 'O' ring (B) before re-assembly

80 Unscrew the valve and two other screws and the emulsion block can be lifted off. As it is lifted the accelerator pump piston will drop out. Check the telescopic action of the pump piston, if it is sticking after cleaning in petrol, fit a new one. Remove the jets from the emulsion block and check the mating face for truth with a straight-edge. Distorted blocks can often be trued up by rubbing them on a sheet of fine abrasive paper laid on plate glass

77 Before further dismantling make a sketch of the linkage. Then undo the accelerator pump and choke joints (arrowed)

79 Push out the pivot pin and the floats can be lifted off. The float valve (arrowed) helps secure the emulsion block

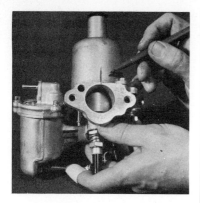

81 First mark the vacuum chamber for correct re-assembly

84 Fit a new needle with its shoulder flush with the base of the piston and tighten the screw

87 Undo the old float valve with a box spanner and fit a new one. Refit the float

82 At the top of the vacuum chamber unscrew the damper cap and pull the damper out. Then undo the fixing screws and lift off the chamber, the coil spring, piston and needle

85 Undo three screws, remove the float chamber lid complete with float

88 Turn the float lid upside-down and check the gap shown. If it isn't approximately $\frac{1}{8}$ in, renew the float and pivot pin

83 Loosen the grub screw at the side of the piston and pull the needle out

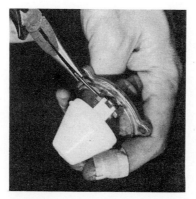

86 Detach the nylon float by pulling out the pivot pin with pliers

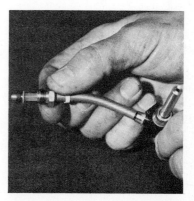

89 A new jet comes complete with a flexible length of pipe and a union for joining it to the base of the float chamber

90 To get out the old jet, disconnect the fast idle connecting link by removing a small screw and spacer (don't lose the spacer) undo the fuel pipe at the float chamber and pull out the jet. At the same time remove the jet adjusting nut (arrowed)

92 Loosen the jet locking nut (arrowed). Rest the carburettor on the jet base and press down the piston hard on to the jet using a pencil through the damper hole. Maintain this pressure while you re-tighten the locknut

94 Once the jet is centred, remove it, refit the jet adjusting nut and refit the jet. Reconnect the fast idle link and the fuel pipe at the float chamber

91 Refit the piston and needle, spring and vacuum chamber, insert the new jet and loosely connect its flexible pipe to the float chamber

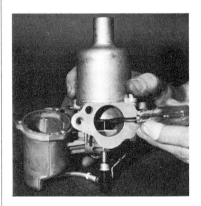

93 Lift the piston up $\frac{1}{4}$ in and let it drop. If the jet is correctly centred it will hit the jet bridge with a sharp click. If it doesn't, repeat the sequence in fig 92.

95 Screw the jet adjusting nut fully up, then undo it $2\frac{1}{2}$ turns. Top-up the damper hole to the top of hollow piston rod with engine oil and refit the damper

Stromberg CD

Similar in principle to the SU, the Stromberg CD uses a flexible diaphragm to raise and lower the needle in the jet instead of a close-fitting piston. Possible wear spots are the rotary choke valve, needle/jet assembly and float valve.

When the diaphragm is first taken out, if it is coated with petrol on the underside, it will distort. If you dry it out and leave it for half an hour it will regain its shape. Needle fitting and centring data is as detailed for the SU except that jet centring is carried out with the adjusting screw fitted and screwed fully up. The float level is 16.5 mm to 17.0 mm measured with the carburettor inverted from the base of the float to the gasket flange with the gasket in place. Some Strombergs have their damper retained by a cap on the air valve spindle – a sharp tug will release it.

Fuel pumps

It is quite simple to check whether a fuel pump is working; Disconnect the pipe to the carburettor, and if the pump is a mechanical one, have a helper rotate the engine on the starter while you hold a jam-jar under the open end of the pipe. There should be a healthy spurt of petrol from the pipe at every *other* engine revolution. The electric pump is even easier to check. Use the jam-jar procedure again, but just ask the helper to flick on the ignition – petrol should gush from the pipe the instant the switch is turned on.

Mechanical pumps

There are two types made by AC and SU. The more recent models cannot be dismantled for overhaul because the upper and lower halves are locked together during manufacture and if you try to part them, the pump will break. Earlier AC and SU pumps are held together by a ring of bolts and these can be overhauled and a new diaphragm and valves fitted. Overhaul kits are available fairly cheaply from garages or AC and SU stockists.

Stromberg CD *(figs 96–106)·*

96 Some Stromberg CD's have a retainer which holds the damper in position (arrowed). Unscrew the damper and give it a sharp tug to get it out. On re-assembly push the valve fully up after refitting the damper to the vacuum chamber cover – this re-positions the retainer

97 Undo four screws securing the vacuum chamber cover (mark the cover first). Remove the cover followed by the spring, diaphragm, air valve and needle

98 Four more screws hold the centre of the diaphragm to the top of the air valve. The lug (arrowed) engages with a recess in the air valve on re-assembly

99 Underneath the carburettor, undo this large screwed retainer to get at the jet assembly

100 This is the jet assembly in the order in which it is fitted. Renew the jet and all 'O' rings

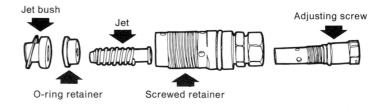

Jet bush

Jet

Adjusting screw

O-ring retainer

Screwed retainer

101 Don't forget this 'O' ring situated inside the jet bush

103 Renew the float valve, fitting a new packing washer of the same thickness as the old one. Check the float level (see text)

105 Re-assemble the carburettor, fitting a new needle as detailed in fig 84 for the SU. Engage this outer lug of the new diaphragm with the carburettor body casting, and make sure the lip on the diaphragm edge sits in the recess machined into the edge of the casting

102 Remove the float chamber from below, and make a note of the position of the float so it can be re-assembled correctly. Prise out the pivot pin to get out the twin floats

104 Two screws secure the rotary choke valve used on this CDS carburettor. The rubbing surfaces should be smooth and the drillings clean

106 To centralise the needle, turn up the adjusting screw until the jet is level with the jet bridge at the base of the choke tube, loosen the screwed retainer a fraction and press the air valve on to the jet using a screwdriver through the damper hole. Retighten the retainer (arrowed). Check centring as on the SU. Slacken the adjusting screw 3 turns, top-up and refit the damper

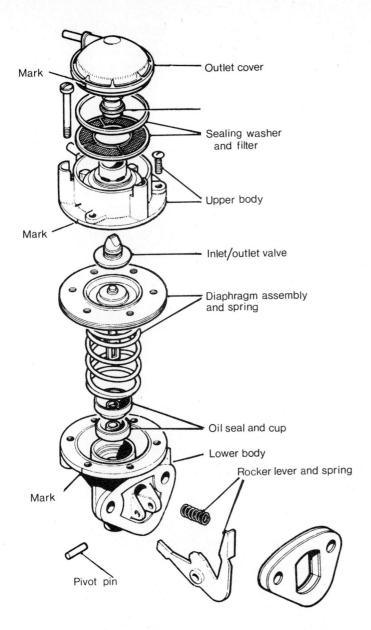

Mark — Outlet cover

Mark

Sealing washer and filter

Upper body

Mark

Inlet/outlet valve

Diaphragm assembly and spring

Oil seal and cup

Lower body

Rocker lever and spring

Mark

Pivot pin

107 SU Mechanical pump

To dismantle, first mark the outlet cover, upper and lower bodies with a file for correct re-assembly. Undo three long screws holding the outlet cover and remove it, with its sealing washer and filter. Remove three short screws and lift off the upper body. From the top, push out the flexible inlet/outlet valve. In the lower body, hold the rocker lever against spring pressure, push out the pivot pin, draw out the rocker arm and spring – this will release the diaphragm assembly and its spring. Oil the crankcase oil seal to prevent damage as the diaphragm rod is pulled out through it. The oil seal rarely needs renewal – a damaged one will allow oil to coat the underside of the diaphragm. If the seal has to be renewed, tap the top edges of the cup inwards and ease it out with pliers. Lever out the old seal, fit a new one, and use a vice to press the cup back into the casting. The casting is slightly distorted to secure the cup and sometimes it may be necessary to *gently* tap it straight to get the cup out, and to carefully squeeze it out of shape when the new seal is fitted. Take care here as the castings are brittle. A new inlet/outlet valve is a push fit in the upper body – take care not to damage its fine edges and ensure its groove has registered with the housing. Oil the new diaphragm rod before inserting it through the oil seal; insert the rocker, with its spring so the rocker end enters the stirrup on the diaphragm rod, and refit the pivot pin. Line up the outer holes in the diaphragm with the holes in the lower body, depress the rocker so the diaphragm is pulled down flat, and fit the upper body using the three short screws fitted finger-tight. Fit the filter, washer and outlet cover, holding them with the long screws. Tighten all screws evenly

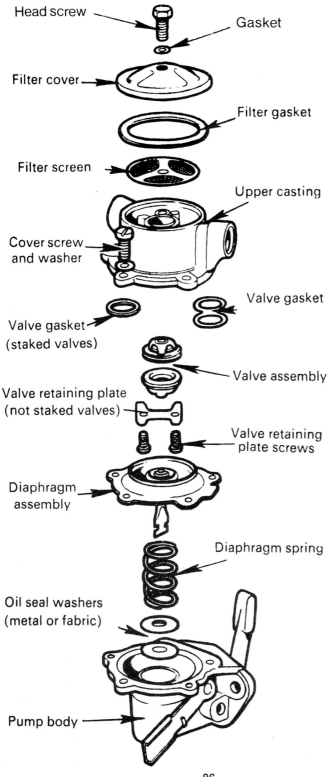

Head screw

Gasket

Filter cover

Filter gasket

Filter screen

Upper casting

Cover screw
and washer

Valve gasket

Valve gasket
(staked valves)

Valve assembly

Valve retaining plate
(not staked valves)

Valve retaining
plate screws

Diaphragm
assembly

Diaphragm spring

Oil seal washers
(metal or fabric)

Pump body

108 AC Mechanical pump

As with the SU pump, mark the pump bodies before separating them. In the top casting will be two valves, one facing upwards, one facing down. Make a note of their positions. The valve may be secured by a screwed-on plate. If so, undoing the screws will release them. Alternatively the casting may be staked – or distorted – to retain the valves and on these, scrape any irregularities out of the valve housings in the casting using the side of a screwdriver blade. Then lever the valves out (this breaks them of course). To disconnect the diaphragm, press it down and turn it through 90 degrees to unhook it from the rocker arm. To renew staked valves, fit a new gasket into the housing then get a short length of metal tube with an outside diameter of $\frac{3}{4}$ in and a bore of $\frac{9}{16}$ in – a piece of old-fashioned electrical conduit pipe is ideal. Use this in a vice to squeeze the new valves into their housings. Once they are in, use a small hammer and a $\frac{1}{8}$ in pin punch and tap the top edge of the valve housing in three places to stake the new valve in. Fitting valves secured by a screwed plate is a reversal of dismantling. Fit a new oil seal if necessary (see fig. 109), oil it and insert the diaphragm rod through it so the rod end passes through the rocker arm. Turn the diaphragm through 90 degrees to hook it on the rocker arm. Hold the diaphragm flat using the rocker arm while the two castings are re-united

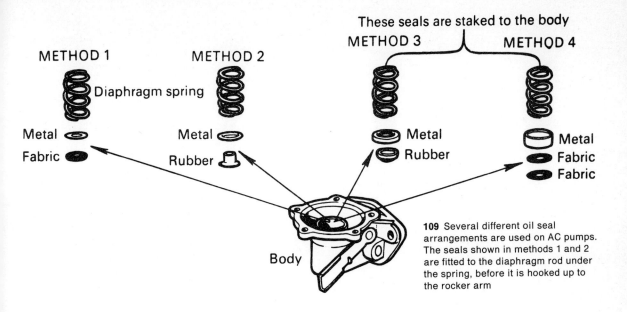

METHOD 1

Diaphragm spring

Metal

Fabric

METHOD 2

Metal

Rubber

These seals are staked to the body

METHOD 3

Metal

Rubber

METHOD 4

Metal

Fabric

Fabric

Body

109 Several different oil seal arrangements are used on AC pumps. The seals shown in methods 1 and 2 are fitted to the diaphragm rod under the spring, before it is hooked up to the rocker arm

Electric pumps

The most widely used one is the SU pump which uses the action of a solenoid to operate a diaphragm. Unlike the mechanical SU which is impressively reliable, the electric version is apt to stop working without warning and you cannot ignore it because when the pump stops, the car stops too.

I am not saying you cannot overhaul an SU electric pump, but I must confess I have never obtained a meaningful success rate. The last electric SU I overhauled operated reasonably cheerfully so long as I stood next to it and gave it a clout each time it stopped, but on its own it would not provide enough fuel for more than 100 yards motoring at a time.

The difficulty is that adjustment of the throw-over points under the bakelite end cap is fairly critical and so is the centralising of the diaphragm. It is usually a lot less bother to exchange the old one for a reconditioned pump which carries an as-new guarantee.

If an electric pump fails in the middle of nowhere, remove the bakelite end cap and check the contacts (admittedly this isn't easy on an early Mini where the pump is under the car just inboard of the rear nearside wheel, but do your best). Ideally you should remove the top contact, but if it is difficult to reach, try and get a thin file (a nail file) under it to scrape the contact surface. This may get it working again. Check the live feed with a test lamp (connected between the feed and earth, the lamp should light with the ignition 'on') and check the connections of the earth cable – sometimes this comes adrift and it will stop the pump if it does. If the power is there, tapping the outside of the pump with a screwdriver handle or something similar often persuades it to work for a mile or so.

110 On all mechanical pumps it is important that the rocker arm bears correctly on the camshaft and to prevent the rocker being inadvertently fitted *under* the camshaft, try this: Press in the rocker arm and cover the pump outlet with your thumb. Now with the arm held up by vacuum, place the pump in position. Tighten the fixings only half-way, then push the pump towards the block and release it. You should feel the spring-loaded rocker try to push the pump outwards and you'll doubtless hear a sucking noise which indicates the pump is working. If there were any distance pieces between the pump and block, the same number must be fitted on re-assembly

87

Chapter seven
Transmission

Strictly speaking the transmission includes all the components which transmit the rotation of the engine into rotation of the driving wheels. On what we used to call an 'orthodox' car with a front engine and rear wheel drive, the transmission, reading front to rear, consists of the clutch, gearbox, propeller shaft and back axle.

On cars with both the engine and driving wheels at the same end, there's no need for a propeller shaft, and on these the order of things is clutch, gearbox, final drive (usually housed within the gearbox casing) and thence via two drive-shafts to the wheels.

Gearboxes and back axles are not easy items to overhaul. The back axle requires special equipment like dial gauges when assembling the crownwheel and pinion, and because of this few garages, let alone do-it-yourself mechanics, rebuild them. It is simpler, and sometimes just as cheap to obtain a manufacturer's reconditioned unit from the dealer.

The average manual gearbox is much more complicated internally than a back axle, but it is possible for an expert home mechanic to overhaul one because special tools can either be avoided or made up from simple bits and pieces. But because gearbox overhaul is strictly for the expert I have not included it here. A workshop manual covering the gearbox in question gives all the information an experienced mechanic needs. Automatic transmission overhaul is best left to the specialists.

Fortunately not all transmission troubles involve the final drive and gearbox. We will begin with the most common failure points:

Propeller shaft universal joints

Most propeller shafts have two, sometimes three Hardy-Spicer-type joints. Modern ones tend to be 'sealed for life' with no provision for greasing, but centrifugal force being what it is, quite often the grease is thrown out over a period and the worn joint begins to make its presence known by emitting a loud knock when the clutch is engaged when moving away from a standstill. A suspect joint should be checked from under the car by trying to lever the two yokes apart. Any movement indicates that the internal roller bearings are worn.

Once you have detected a worn universal joint, look at the yokes very carefully. If the joint is located in them by circlips, an overhaul kit consisting of a new spider coupling, end cups and roller bearings can be bought and fitted. On some cars, the universal joints are staked into the yokes by distorting the metal. These cannot be overhauled because you cannot get the old joint out without damaging the yoke, so on these you need a new shaft which is at least ten times more expensive than an overhaul kit. Manufacturers use staked joints because they say they reduce vibration. Happily not all manufacturers use them.

To overhaul a joint it must be taken to the bench, but before the prop-shaft is taken off the car, it should be marked so that it can

Universal joint overhaul

111 A universal joint overhaul kit contains a new centre spider, four roller bearing caps and four new circlips

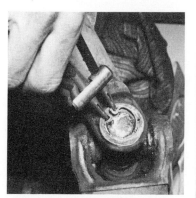

112 Put the joint in a vice, squeeze up the circlips with circlip pliers and take all of them out

113 Rest one yoke on the vice jaws, and hammer the other one downwards – if you wish shielding the bearing with a large socket – until the bearing cap begins to come out

114 You will soon reach the stage where the bearing cap and its rollers can be removed

115 Repeat the operations in 113 and 114 on the opposite bearing cap and you will be able to disengage the spider from one yoke. Treat the other two bearing caps in the same way

116 Take the bearing caps off the new spider. They should be packed with grease. Make sure there is plenty of it packed into the rollers

117 Enter one bearing into a yoke eye and fit the spider into it from the other side. Squeeze in the bearing using a vice

118 With all the bearing caps fitted flush with the surface of the yoke eyes, recess them using a hammer and drift until each circlip can be fitted into its groove to retain them

be returned to its original position. On a one-piece shaft the flanges where the shaft is bolted to the nose of the back axle should be scored with the corner of a file before unbolting them.

When taking the shaft out it is best if the rear of the car can be supported on prop-stands with the wheels clear of the ground. Then the handbrake can be let off and the shaft turned to give easy access to all the flange nuts. Once the flanges are parted, the shaft can be withdrawn from the splines on the gearbox tail-shaft.

Two-piece prop-shafts have three universal joints and a centre bearing bolted to the underside of the car. After parting the flanges, mark the bearing carrier before unbolting it from the floor pan. The picture guide shows how the joint is overhauled.

Rear drive-shaft joints

Rear wheel drive cars with independent suspension often use the same Hardy-Spicer-type joint as detailed for the propeller shaft. The overhaul procedure is the same except that getting the shaft out will not be so easy. In some instances the rear hub assembly must be disconnected from the rear suspension and this can be difficult – check the workshop manual before starting the job.

Some drive shafts have a doughnut joint. This is a thick rubber ring which looks like its namesake and is bolted between two yokes to make a flexible coupling. It can be renewed without taking out the drive shaft.

A worn doughnut will flex too much. As the car rolls when cornering, and the drive shaft articulates, the yokes sometimes come in contact, making a substantial knocking sound. A damaged doughnut can easily be seen – the rubber is usually torn and the metal inserts which house the mounting bolts are sometimes loose in the rubber.

New doughnuts are sold with a metal band round them to discourage distortion. To fit one, raise the rear of the car, unbolt the old doughnut and fit the new one in its place, using new bolts and nuts. Lastly, cut away the metal band with tin-snips. If a sound doughnut joint has to be removed, it should be clamped before it is unbolted. A clamp can be made using two large worm-drive hose-clips. Undo the screws, open up the clips and insert the serrated end of one clip to the worm screw of the other, making one long clip. Put the clip round the doughnut and tighten the screws to compress it.

Front drive-shaft joints

Front-wheel drive cars use constant velocity joints which are greased and then protected by a rubber gaiter. If a gaiter breaks and dirt gets in the joint wears. The first sign is a knocking sound on full lock, but in time the knocking will get worse unless the joint is renewed.

119 A doughnut joint links two three-pronged drive flanges on this Hillman Imp. If a sound doughnut is removed it should be compressed as shown using two worm-drive hose clips linked together. New joints are sold compressed with a metal band. The band is cut off after fitting

Constant-velocity joints

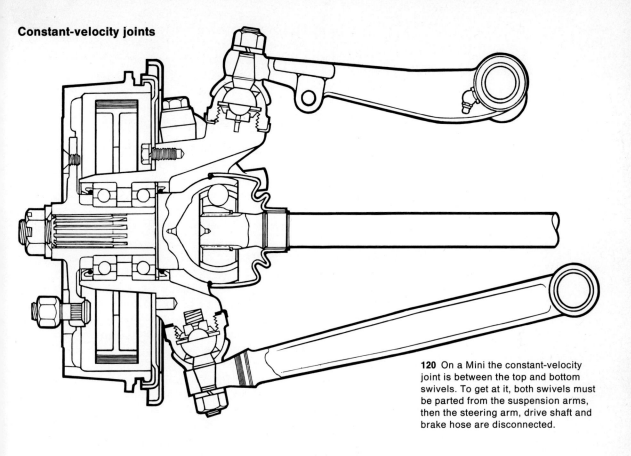

120 On a Mini the constant-velocity joint is between the top and bottom swivels. To get at it, both swivels must be parted from the suspension arms, then the steering arm, drive shaft and brake hose are disconnected.

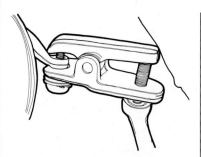

121 With the car on its wheels, remove the bump stop and insert a block of wood in its place. Then, jack up the car and remove the road wheel. Loosen both swivel nuts and the steering arm nut and use a taper breaker to loosen the joints. Remove the joint from the steering arm

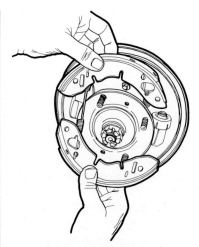

122 On older cars, the hydraulic pipe may break if the upper end of the brake hose is disconnected. If the joint is difficult to undo, the hose can be undone at the other end. First mark and remove the brake shoes

91

The most widely used British front-wheel drive-shafts are those on the British Leyland Minis and 1100/1300's. To renew the outer joint, the shaft must come out and the procedure is shown in the drawings. Most other front-wheel drive cars have a similar arrangement. Regrettably space does not allow me to go into all the differences, so if you are the least bit unsure about changing a front-wheel drive-shaft joint, check with a garage or the workshop manual.

Once the Mini drive-shaft is out, the old joint is knocked off with a hammer before fitting the new one. In theory it is possible to fit new ball bearings and a new bearing cage into these joints, but as a general rule a worn joint is best replaced with a new one.

At its inner end the Mini drive-shaft has another joint. The design has recently been changed, but the one in greatest circulation is a rubber-encased spider which looks like a rounded-off Maltese Cross and is attached to two yokes using a total of four U-bolts.

When one of these fails it is usually because of a small oil leak on the rear side of the Mini block. In time the oil rots the rubber, the joint becomes squashy, the drive-shaft runs off-centre and eventually clouts the gear-casing, making knocking noises on acceleration and deceleration.

A worn joint can often be levered out (after removing the U-bolts) using a heavy screwdriver. But to get the new one in, the outer yoke must be pulled away from the inner one a little to give enough clearance for the new joint.

The usual method is first to remove the front suspension rebound stop and with the weight of the car on the suspension, insert in its place a block of wood about one inch thick. This prevents the suspension drooping too much. The car is then supported on the front subframe and the appropriate wheel removed. You can then slither underneath and undo the U-bolts to release the old coupling.

If the screwdriver trick will not prise it out, undo the nut on the bottom suspension swivel and use a taper-breaker to separate it from the lower suspension arm. Separate the steering ball-joint from the steering arm in the same way. You can now lift the hub assembly out of the lower arm and swing it outwards to pull apart the drive-shaft yokes. If you are lucky the old joint will drop out and you can fit the new one.

As soon as the new joint is in position, refit the bottom swivel in lower arm then fit and tighten the U-bolts until the same amount of thread – about $\frac{1}{8}$ inch – protrudes through each nut. The rest of re-assembly is the reversal of dismantling.

Wheel bearings

There are two principal varieties – ball bearings and taper roller bearings. Both exhibit the same sympton when they are failing – a rumbling or moaning noise which alters in intensity on left- and right-hand corners.

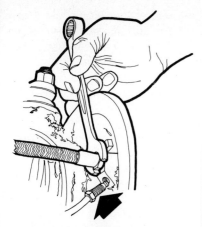

123 Put a hose clamp on the hose to prevent loss of fluid, then loosen it from the back of the wheel cylinder. Undo the bridging pipe union (arrowed) as well

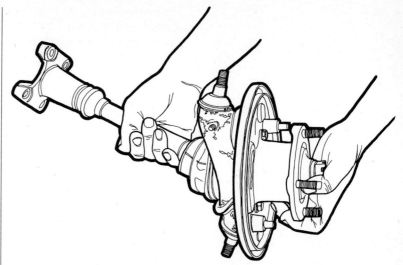

125 Undo the four nuts nearest the road wheel at the drive shaft inner coupling and prise out the U-bolts. Remove the nuts and disengage the upper and lower swivels from the suspension arms (lever the bottom one down with a length of wood if necessary) and take out the drive shaft and stub axle

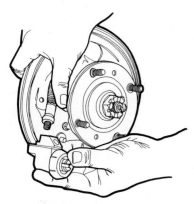

124 Unbolt the wheel cylinder from the backplate and pull a short length of the hose through the hole in the backplate. The cylinder can now be spun off the hose. Put it where dirt will not get into the opened ports

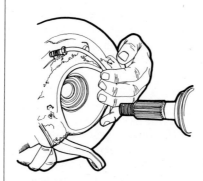

126 Grip the drive shaft tightly in a vice, remove the split pin and use a large spanner or socket with a long extension to undo the hub nut – it is tightened to 60 lb ft

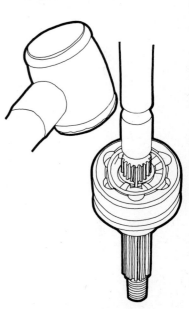

127 Use a screwdriver blade to snap the metal band or wire securing the gaiter to the joint and shaft and peel it back out the way. Hold the drive shaft vertically with the joint at the bottom. A sharp tap with a mallet will knock it off the shaft

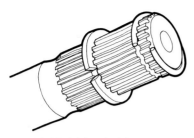

128 The Mini drive shaft has a square section circlip which the joint butts up against, and a round-section spring ring at the end. Renew the spring ring, smear a new rubber gaiter with special grease and slide it up the shaft

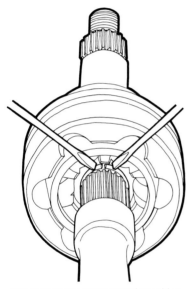

129 New joints come complete with a small sachet of the appropriate grease and a gaiter. Lubricate the joint using all the grease, then hold the drive-shaft in a vice so it points up at about 30 degrees. Somehow you have to squeeze up the spring ring so it begins to enter the centre of the coupling

130 Tap on the joint with a mallet – the spring ring will expand when it's fully home and prevent it sliding off. Fit the gaiter. There are two metal securing clips in the kit, but they need special pliers to tighten them. In cases of difficulty use soft binding wire, twisting the ends away from the direction of forward rotation. Reverse the dismantling procedure, tightening the hub nut to 60 lb ft, then on to the next split pin hole

To change wheel bearings the hub must come off. This is a job which normally requires a hub puller and sometimes a very large spanner to undo the hub locking nut. On a lot of cars the hub must be re-tightened to a specified torque, so a torque wrench is needed as well. If you are a bit uncertain about the job, ask the local garage storeman if you can see the Parts catalogue – this will give an exploded view of the hub assembly so you can see what's involved.

The drawings show how a set of rear bearings was changed on a Mini. At the front, the job involves taking out the drive-shaft. To avoid repetition, I have not detailed how the drive-shaft and hub were taken out and dismantled as this sequence is already shown in Figs 120 to 130.

Clutch renewal

The clutch is a friction device and a little of it wears away each time it is engaged. Fitting a new one at home can be a ticklish job, but on many cars it is by no means impossible, so if you enjoy a challenge it is worth having a go. But if you are not fascinated at the prospect of lying on your back supporting a heavy gearbox on your knees, ring round the local garages for a few quotations to have the job professionally done. You may be surprised to find that the costs are not alarmingly high – the high incidence of clutch failures means professional mechanics get plenty of practice and on most cars they can renew the clutch quite quickly and in the garage trade a quick job is a cheap one.

Of course there are exceptions. On some cars – the MGB and Austin 1800 for instance – the engine must come out before the clutch can be dismantled. A garage will not do this job quickly, but then neither can the average home mechanic. A few cars, like the British Leyland Minis, 1100's and 1300's need special tools to overhaul the clutch, but these can be hired.

On our orthodox front-engined rear-wheel drive car, the clutch assembly is bolted to the rear face of the flywheel and consists of a spring-loaded pressure plate and a friction-faced disc which is sandwiched between the plate and the flywheel. The clamping load on the disc is released when you push on the pedal by an arm which presses a thrust bearing on to levers or a diaphragm spring in the centre of the pressure plate.

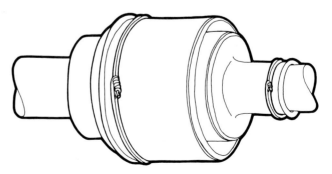

Wheel bearings

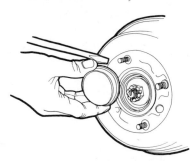

131 Remove the wheel and prise off the grease cap. The hub assembly is immediately behind the brake drum – take the drum off

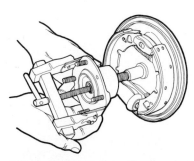

132 After removing the split pin and hub nut (some cars have a left-hand thread on the nearside rear nut) a puller is used to draw the hub off

133 The bearings are inside the hub. On ball-races, the inner cone is driven out with a punch. On a roller race, the inner cone and rollers will drop out of their own accord

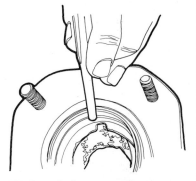

134 Once the inner cones have gone the outer cone can be driven out. This hub (and most others) has cut-aways, so a punch can be brought to bear directly on the cone. Hammer it out

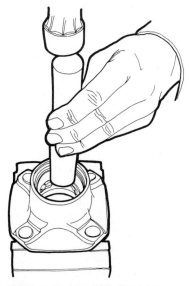

135 The new bearing is fitted the same way round as the old one. On ball-bearings this means the thinner edge of the outer cone faces out of the hub. The same applies to roller bearings. Lightly tap in the outer cone using a large drift and working all round the edge to keep it square. Make sure it is fully up against the register in the hub

136 Ball-races usually have a spacer between them. Insert this before fitting the second bearing, then fill each bearing with grease. Don't pack the complete hub – allow some room for expansion

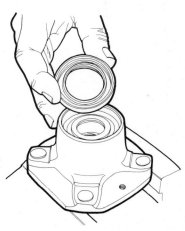

137 There will be an oil seal on the inside of the hub. Position it with its spring-loaded inner lip towards the bearing. Place a flat piece of timber on top, then drive it in by hammering on the timber

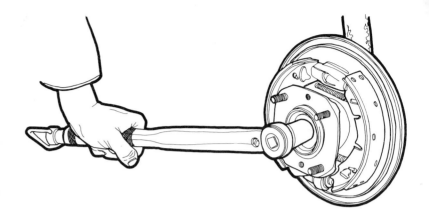

138 Refit the hub and tighten the nut to the required torque– this one goes to 60 lb ft, then on to the next split pin hole

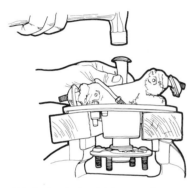

139 On front-wheel drive cars the driving flange must be removed before the bearings can be reached. Here the stub axle is supported on two wood blocks while the flange is drifted out

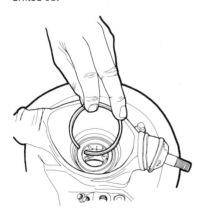

140 Removal and refitting of the bearings is the same as detailed for the rear ones, but watch out for any spacer rings – these are sometimes fitted between the inner bearing and the drive-shaft

When a clutch is worn it begins to slip. The slip generates heat and can cause the clutch spring or springs to lose their strength. Therefore when a clutch is renewed it is customary to renew the pressure plate assembly (or the springs if they are sold separately) and the thrust bearing, as well as the clutch disc.

The illustrations show how this is done on a Triumph Herald. The Herald is slightly unusual because the gearbox is taken out from inside the car after removing the transmission tunnel.

On other 'orthodox' cars the gearbox has to be taken out from below. The usual procedure here is to raise the car securely at the four corners, remove the propshaft and then use a pillar jack to support the rear of the engine while the gearbox rear mounting or cross-member is undone.

After taking out the gear lever or linkage, the speedometer drive cable and disconnecting the clutch cable or hydraulics, the bolts round the bell-housing are undone. Quite often the topmost bolts are difficult to reach because they are tight up against the bulkhead, and on some engines it is a help to drain the radiator and remove the top hose so the rear of the engine can be lowered on the jack to tilt the bolts into a more reachable position.

Before parting the gearbox from the engine, it is important to have some idea of what you are going to do when it comes free. If the 'box is bulky and heavy it can often be supported on a rope slung through the gear lever hole in the floor while you swing it clear of the engine. The rope sling means you will only have to support one end from under the car. Once this is lowered, the remainder of the 'box can be lowered using the rope. The same method is used in reverse when hoisting up the gearbox on re-assembly.

Smaller gearboxes are best supported if you lie on your back with your head towards the back axle. The system is to support the bell-housing on your knees and use your hands to hold up the tail-shaft. Moving the whole assembly rearwards means you are more-or-less evenly laden as it comes free. Incidentally, if you haven't drained the oil, tie a plastic bag round the end of the tail-shaft – it stops the oil dribbling into your face when the gearbox is tilted down at the back.

The only special tool you need on this sort of clutch job is a device to centralise the clutch disc while the pressure plate assembly is tightened up. The disc runs on the gearbox input shaft and if it isn't centrally located, the gearbox will not go back on. Professional mechanics use an input shaft from an old gearbox. Unless you have renewed umpteen clutches before you will not have one, but clutch mandrels (for that is what they are called) can be bought from accessory shops, or one can be made from a short length of $\frac{1}{2}$ in wooden dowel.

The dowel must be a snug fit in the hole in the centre of the flywheel. If necessary, enlarge it by winding round sticky tape until it fits. Push it into place, slip the clutch disc over it, and mark the position the clutch hub occupies along the length of the dowel. This section must be enlarged – again using sticky tape – until it fits snugly into the hub.

Use the dowel to hold the clutch disc against the flywheel (make sure the disc is right way round – see the picture guide), and then the pressure plate assembly is fitted and tightened. Now all you have to do is refit the gearbox.

A gearbox sometimes slides into position first time, or it may take a fair bit of jiggling before the spines on the input shaft can be persuaded to slip through the hub of the clutch disc. One of the problems is that it's very difficult to align the gearbox accurately while you are supporting its weight, so a helper alongside the vehicle shouting instructions is useful. What you must not do is try to force the gearbox home. A lot of force will damage the clutch disc and I've seen a car swaying precariously on axle stands as an irate mechanic tried (unsuccessfully) to kick home a reluctant gearbox. Providing the clutch disc is centralised and the gearbox is correctly aligned, it should slide easily into position.

Clutches needing special tools

On some cars with transverse engines the clutch can be renewed without removing the engine or gearbox from the car. The most common example is the clutch on the British Leyland Mini, 1100 and 1300 range. On these the clutch disc and pressure plate are on the engine side of the flywheel so the flywheel must be taken off, using a special puller, to renew them.

Because of the large number of these cars the special tools are readily available for hire. With the correct equipment, the clutch overhaul can be completed on a Saturday morning providing there are no serious snags.

The picture guide shows how the coil spring clutch is dismantled on an 1100. Besides the flywheel puller, you also need a centralising tool for the clutch disc (a disposable paper cup can be used in emergencies) and a torque wrench for tightening the flywheel securing bolt to 110–115 lb ft.

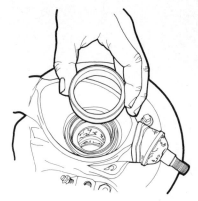

141 Lastly in goes the oil seal. A block of wood cannot be used here to drive it in, so one of the old outer cones from a discarded bearing is laid on top and this is lightly hammered to drive in the seal

Clutch renewal

142 On the Triumph Herald, the gearbox comes out from above, so the first job is to remove the gear lever knob, then the detachable transmission tunnel

143 Two bolts hold the clutch operating cylinder to the bell-housing. After releasing these the cylinder is parked out of the way

144 On the side of the gearbox is the speedometer drive. Undo the knurled nut and it comes out

147 Six bolts secure this diaphragm spring pressure plate to the flywheel. Undo them and it comes out, complete with clutch disc. Note the position of the hub boss (arrowed) on the disc

150 The clutch operating lever, which houses the release bearing, pivots on this pin. The pin is driven out here using an old six-inch nail

145 The prop-shaft flanges are marked with a file to ensure correct re-assembly before undoing the fixing bolts

148 It's a good idea to check the fit of the new disc on the splines of the gearbox input shaft before fitting it to the engine – file off any burrs if necessary

151 In this case the release bearing was jarred off the centre shaft by placing a socket over the shaft end and tapping it with a hammer while supporting the bearing

146 The rear of the engine is supported on a jack and the rear mounting nuts and bell-housing bolts have been undone. The gearbox can now be removed

149 A mandrel – in this case an old gearbox input shaft – centralises the new clutch plate as the pressure plate assembly is refitted to the flywheel

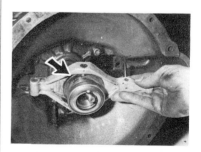

152 To fit a new bearing, tap it on the centre shaft with a soft mallet, making sure it is square. Then refit the operating arm and its pivot pin. Grease the sleeve (arrowed)

There are one or two golden rules for this particular job which you should know in advance. It is essential that the engine is set with No 1 piston at Top Dead Centre before the flywheel is taken off. The reason is that a C-washer secures the primary gear behind the flywheel, and if by evil chance No 1 cylinder is at Bottom Dead Centre, this washer can drop down and jam the flywheel as you try to take it off. The other rule concerns re-assembly. The clutch pressure plate, spring cover and flywheel are all marked with the letter A in one position near the edge, and they must all be assembled so their A-marks coincide to preserve correct balance.

155 Disconnect the feed wire and two bolts and remove the starter motor

Clutches needing special tools

153 On the BMC 1100, the battery box is removed to make a little extra room. You need a helper because the securing nuts are in the wheel arch and the bolt heads are in the engine bay

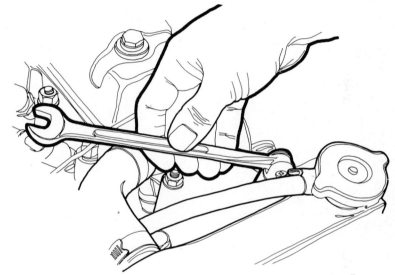

156 At the radiator, take out the two bolts from the top triangular steady plate

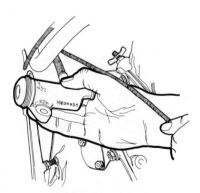

154 Remove the clutch slave cylinder which is held by two bolts and tie it out of the way

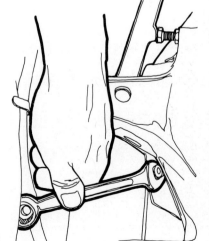

157 From inside the offside wheel arch undo the two nuts securing the engine mounting. If the bolts begin to turn, jack the engine up just enough to jam the bolts

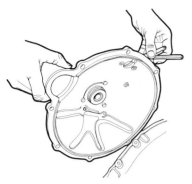

158 Raise the offside of the engine gently, watching that the fan doesn't contact the radiator. You should now be able to undo the ring of bolts holding the clutch cover and remove it. If you need more room, disconnect the exhaust down pipe before jacking further, but try to avoid doing this if possible

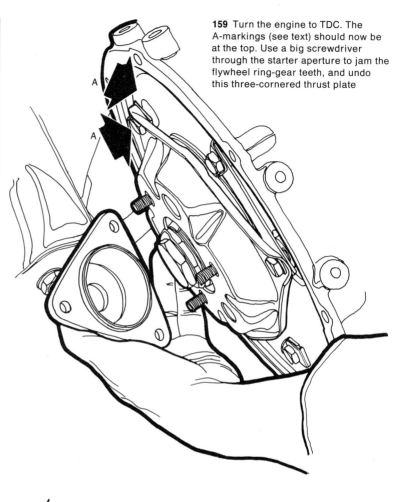

159 Turn the engine to TDC. The A-markings (see text) should now be at the top. Use a big screwdriver through the starter aperture to jam the flywheel ring-gear teeth, and undo this three-cornered thrust plate

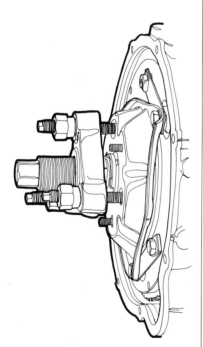

160 Using a 1½ in AF socket and long bar, undo the flywheel bolt about three turns after knocking back its lock washer, then assemble the puller as shown. Tighten the centre bolt as hard as you can and the flywheel should come free. Tapping the centre bolt with a hammer encourages tight ones

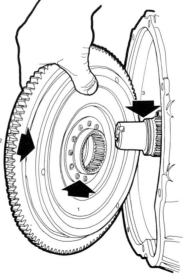

161 Out comes the flywheel. The disc (1), pressure plate (2) and all-important C-washer (3) are arrowed

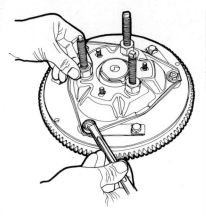

162 Coil spring clutches should be compressed using part of the special tool or three long $\frac{3}{8}$ in UNF set bolts and nuts. The nuts are tightened down to the cover before the outer bolts are taken out

163 Once the bolts are out, the pressure plate and clutch disc can be taken off. Here the three bolts which compressed the spring cover have been removed as well, showing the spring arrangement. If you are not renewing the springs, this item can remain clamped to the flywheel

164 The disc is assembled with the large boss on its hub facing the pressure plate. Renew the pressure plate if it is deeply scored

165 This is the official centralising tool which aligns the new disc. The spring cover should be compressed again when re-fitting the disc, then released to clamp it in position. The assembly can now be re-fitted to the engine and the flywheel bolt tightened to 110–115 lb ft.

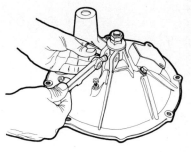

166 On the cover it's sound sense to renew the thrust bearing. First remove the split pin and knock out the pivot pin to release the lever..

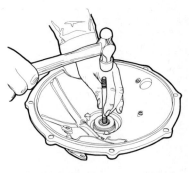

167 Support the cover on wood blocks and punch the throw-out plunger from the centre of the bearing

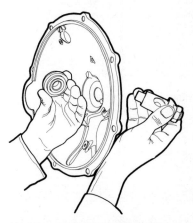

168 This is how the new bearing and throw-out plunger go together. Support the plunger on timber and drive on the bearing with a hollow piece of pipe

101

Chapter eight
Suspension and steering

Regardless of whether your car suspension uses coil springs, leaf springs, torsion bars, rubber cones, or some complex hydro-pneumatic system to soak up the bumps, all of them wear out in the same places – where they bend, slide and swivel. So most mechanical work involves the renewal of worn-out ball-joints, bearings and bushes.

All suspension systems have some sort of damping action built in to discourage the springs from continually bouncing the bodyshell up and down. On British Leyland cars with Hydrolastic or Hydagas suspension, damper valves are incorporated internally, but most other suspension systems use external telescopic or lever-type dampers to iron out the bouncing. External dampers wear out in time and need renewal.

Because even small saloon cars weigh close to a ton, steel suspension springs contain a lot of pent-up energy, even with the vehicle weight off them. It is important that this energy is not unleashed suddenly or haphazardly for an uncontrolled spring can cause injury. Fortunately quite a lot of work can be carried out without disturbing the spring. If the spring has to be removed, it is important that detailed information is obtained from the appropriate workshop manual before the job is started.

169 Telescopic rear dampers are the easiest to renew. Reverse the car up on ramps and undo the bottom fixing

170 At the top – usually inside the boot – is the upper mounting, in this instance it's a stud and two nuts. Hold the stud with grips or a small spanner, undo both nuts . . .

171 . . . and lift the mounting rubbers off to release the damper. Dampers which make knocking noises have usually worn out the mounting rubbers

Dampers

These can be checked with the car stationary simply by pushing down hard on each corner of the car in turn. The car should rebound and return to the static position – call it one-and-a-half bounces if you like. If the car bounces more than this, the dampers are worn.

Dampers do their job by moving a piston in a cylinder filled with fluid, and the main reason they give up the ghost is because one of the seals which is meant to keep the fluid in fails and lets some of it out. With less fluid there is less resistance to the movement of the piston and the damper action accordingly becomes weaker.

Leaking seals are not replaceable, and most dampers cannot be topped up. On those where you can replenish the fluid, a leaking seal will soon allow it to escape again, so the only cure for a leaking one is to chuck it away and fit a new one. Dampers, like brake linings, should be fitted in pairs on the same axle.

Sometimes a damper gives off knocking noises. This is because the rubber bushes which insulate it from the fixing bolt or nut have worn out and metal-to-metal contact is being made. New bushes are generally easily fitted.

The pictures show how lever type and telescopic dampers are renewed.

MacPherson Struts

A lot of cars use this type of front suspension in which the stub axle assembly is carried at the base of a long strut which also incorporates the coil spring and damper. When the damper on

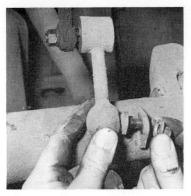

172 Lever dampers are normally linked to the rear axle by an articulating rod. Undo the bottom joint

175 Disconnect the steering by removing the ball joint at the steering arm

178 On the Triumph Herald, the damper also forms the mounting for the coil spring. First remove the three outer nuts at the top

173 Then unbolt the damper body from the chassis and draw out the complete assembly. Separate the articulating joint on the bench

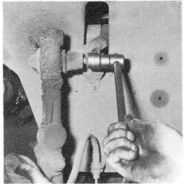

176 Undo the top joint where the arm from the lever damper meets the stub axle

179 Raise chassis front on stands, remove road wheel and disconnect anti-roll bar – if necessary raising bottom wishbone with a jack. Allow wishbones to droop and remove the bottom bolt

174 At the front, lever-type dampers often form part of the suspension linkage. Remove the wheel and support the bottom suspension arm

177 Remove the damper body from the car bodyshell. Fit the new one and tighten it to the top stub axle joint

180 Take out the coil-spring damper unit. Compress the spring and undo the top nut on the damper to get it out. This job must be done using spring compressors – see fig. 184

181 Some cars like the Viva HB have a separate damper in the centre of the front coil spring. On these, drive the car up on ramps

182 At the top of the spring housing undo this nut and push out the transverse bolt securing the top of the damper

183 At the bottom, undo the damper carrier from beneath the bottom wishbone and draw down the damper. Fully extend the new one when re-fitting the top bolt

one of these wears out, the spring must be compressed and the strut dismantled so the defective damper assembly can be taken out and replaced by an overhaul cartridge. The job involves using a set of spring clamps or adjustable compressors as shown in the illustrations.

Hydrolastic suspension

British Leyland use this 'float on fluid' system on the majority of their front-wheel drive cars. Fluid is contained in four displacers which take the place of the spring at each wheel. A pipe links the offside front and offside rear displacer and the same system is used on the nearside. This interconnection means that when a front wheel hits a bump and rises, fluid is squeezed from the front displacer and is forced into the rear one, expanding it and raising the rear of the car. In theory, the car remains level under most conditions.

If the system springs a leak, the car settles down on its bump stops. Most leaks seem to occur at the valves used for topping-up the system, and where the flexible hoses connect to the displacer units.

When the fluid has leaked out, the system must be refilled under pressure using special equipment which British Leyland dealers have. A Hydrolastic or Hydragas car which has lost all fluid can be driven unladen at speeds up to 30 mph. Since the car has to be taken to be pumped up by a dealer the fixing of defects on this system is more conveniently left to the professionals.

Steering ball-joints

The ball-joint which joins the end of the steering arm at the wheel hub to the end of the steering track-rod is one of the more common failure points on the steering system. Nowadays these joints are sealed for life, and their lifetime is dependent on how long it takes the grease to leak out. The rubber seal is easily damaged by careless removal of the joint and when this happens, water gets in, rust starts, and the joint develops a lot of free play.

A worn joint will allow the steering to wander as the car edges against white lines in the road or when it hits small bumps. It's best to check the joints with the front wheels up on ramps. Have a helper move the steering wheel back and forth while you hold the suspect joint. Any free play will be felt as a knock from within the joint.

To take off a ball-joint, the tapered pin which secures it to the steering arm must come out. The body of the joint can then be unscrewed from the steering arm.

When the joint is removed, it helps if the lock-nut on the steering arm is left in its original position as this indicates the position of the old joint and allows the new one to be fitted in the same place. In theory if this is done, the front wheels should be perfectly aligned but bearing in mind that a small error in front wheel alignment can cause accelerated tyre wear, it is always advisable

Fitting a strut cartridge

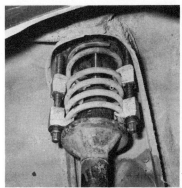

184 With MacPherson struts, raise the car under the chassis and use compressors or spring clips to hold down at least four coils

185 From under the bonnet release the three bolts securing the strut upper mounting to the bodyshell. Don't touch the centre nut at this stage

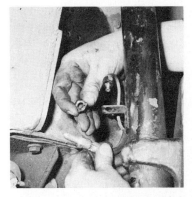

186 Under the wheel arch, disconnect the brake pipe (clamp the hose to prevent fluid loss) undo the steering ball joint then the bolts securing the track control arm to the bottom of the strut

187 Lever down on the track control arm and the strut, complete with stub axle and brake assembly (careful, it's heavy) can be taken out

188 On the bench, remove the top nut, take off the upper mounting, then the spring mounting plate and spring. Note the position of any washers

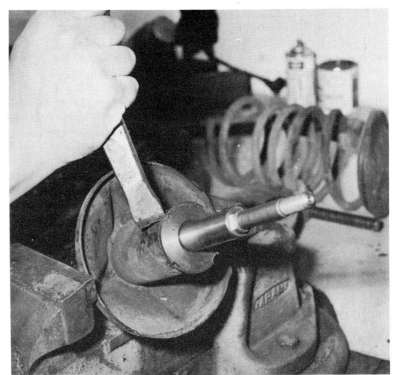

189 There is a gland nut at the top of the damper tube. If you don't have the special spanner needed to undo it, tap it round using a hammer and cold chisel. Pull out the strut spindle and old piston assembly. Tip out the fluid

190 Ideally the threads at the top of the damper tube should be tidied up with a thread-cleaner before slipping in a new damper cartridge

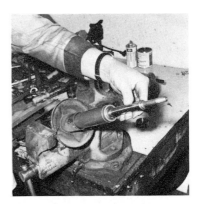

191 In goes a cartridge complete with its new spindle. Fit the gland nut, replace the spring and upper mountings then release the spring compressors and refit the strut to the car – a reversal of dismantling

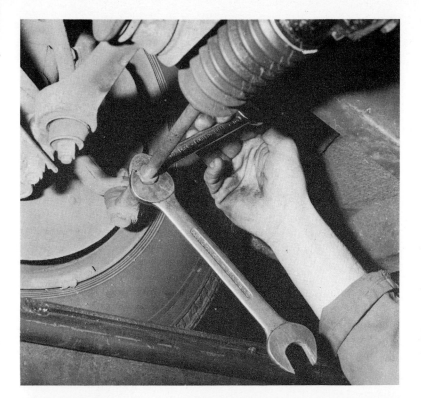

Steering ball joint renewal

192 First step when renewing a steering arm ball joint is to loosen the nut locking it to the track rod

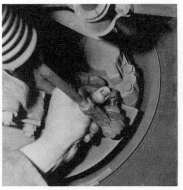

193 Next undo this nut locking the pin to the steering arm

194 Use a taper breaker to push out the ball pin

195 Hold the track rod to prevent it turning while the old ball joint is unscrewed

196 Screw on the new joint until it meets the locknut. Enter the tapered pin in the arm and tighten its nut. Re-tighten the lock nut

to have the front wheels tracked on a garage gauge after fitting a new steering ball-joint.

Steering column joints

In the interests of safety, steering columns are now made with universal joints which are intended to jack-knife on frontal impact, preventing the column from spearing the driver. Two main types of joint are used: a miniature version of the Hardy-Spicer universal joint similar to those fitted on the prop-shaft, and a flexible coupling which in its simplest form is no more than a rubber composition disc with four holes in it and a two-pronged spider attached to each side.

The joints are normally used on the intermediate steering shaft – a short shaft which connects the steering rack and pinion unit to the column which carries the wheel. When the joints wear, the flexible type coupling can be renewed, but the Hardy-Spicer type universal is normally replaced complete with a new shaft.

Wear in universal joints can be checked in the same way as for ball-joints. Any wear in the Hardy-Spicer type betrays itself by a knocking sound which can be felt as well as heard. Flexible couplings distort when they are loaded. Put the front wheels on ramps and watch for this while a helper turns the wheel back and forth. A worn flexible coupling can also be felt from the steering wheel as it will give the steering a soggy uncertain feel. A worn universal will rattle in sympathy with the smallest amount of wheel imbalance.

The easiest intermediate shaft to renew is one with a flexible coupling at one end and a universal at the other. All you do is drive the car up on ramps, set the steering in the straight-ahead position, and unbolt the shaft from the coupling and swing it sideways out of the way. Now undo the universal joint pinch bolt and pull it off the column.

On re-assembly, roughly align the intermediate shaft spider with its holes in the coupling, then fit the universal joint on its splines. Check that the holes in the spider line up with those in the coupling. If they do not refit the universal on its splines until they do. Bolt everything up and you have finished.

It would be nice if all intermediate shafts were as easy to fit as this. But some cars use an intermediate shaft with a splined universal joint at both ends and on these the steering column must be taken off and pulled away from the shaft to disengage the splines. The amount of work obviously varies from car to car, and a workshop manual is really needed.

Renewing a rack bellows seal

In the interests of lightness, most steering racks are lubricated with oil – usually EP 90 grade – and this is prevented from leaking out by a rubber bellows unit which seals each end of the rack housing to the track-rod. If the bellows breaks or is damaged, it must be renewed before grit can get into the rack and damage it.

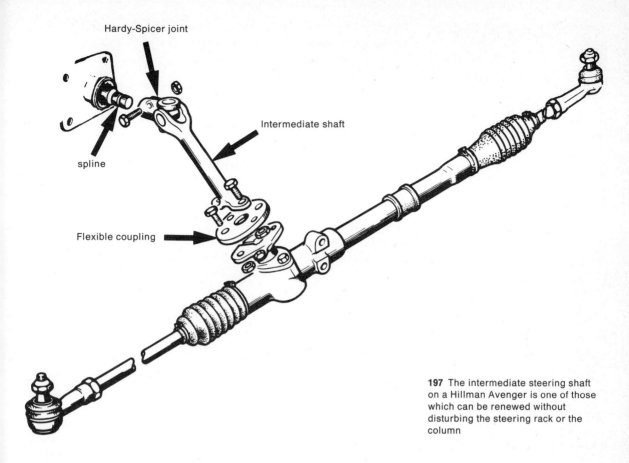

Hardy-Spicer joint

Intermediate shaft

spline

Flexible coupling

197 The intermediate steering shaft on a Hillman Avenger is one of those which can be renewed without disturbing the steering rack or the column

Most steering rack housings have a slightly larger diameter at one end than the other, so it is important when ordering a new bellows unit to specify which end of the rack it has to fit.

To get the old bellows off, the ball-joint at the end of the track rod must be disconnected from the steering arm and unscrewed. This has already been detailed.

In addition the ball joint locknut must be taken off the track-rod, and to ensure it goes back in exactly the same place you can either count the number of turns required to unscrew it, or clean the track rod behind it and put a turn of sticky tape round the rod with its edge against the nut to act as a marker.

Undo the clips securing the old bellows and peel it off. Grease the seating surfaces of the new bellows and slide it into position, clipping the outer end in the slight recess in the track rod. Assemble the inner end into the recess on the steering rack, but do not fit the clip yet – instead use an oil can to inject the correct quantity of EP 90 oil (usually $\frac{1}{4}$ pint) into the bellows. Fit the clip after lubricating, then re-assemble the locknut, ball-joint and taper pin. Have the wheel alignment checked professionally.

Chapter nine
Brakes

Most drivers give the brakes an easy time. When they stop they press the pedal gently, allowing plenty of space to pull up. It is an admirable habit because the brake linings and tyres last a long time. But it has one draw-back. For if you continually use only about one-third of your car's potential braking power, the braking system can deteriorate without you noticing it.

So occasionally it is a good idea to use the brakes really hard just to make sure the remaining two-thirds will work well in a crisis. All you need is a dry day and a short stretch of deserted flat road. Drive the car at a steady 20 mph, select neutral, check there is nothing behind, and do an emergency stop. In tip-top condition the brakes should pull up the car in about 16 feet. In fact we are not primarily interested in the stopping distance — mainly we are looking to see what happens to the car while the brakes are applied.

In theory it should pull up smartly in a straight line. If it pulls to one side, try again — you may have put a wheel on a loose patch. If it persistently pulls to the same side, check the tyre pressures, for if they are unequal on the same axle the car will pull in the direction of the softer tyre. If the pressures are right, something is amiss in the braking system.

It would be nice at this stage if I could tell·you exactly what the trouble was. Alas it is not this easy. On a drum-braked car, uneven adjustment can pull the car off line. But the same trouble can also be caused by a seized disc brake piston, a seized or leaking drum-brake wheel cylinder or something silly like a pair of brake linings assembled the wrong way round.

Just to complicate matters, car manufacturers do not standardise much on their braking systems and this means that at best I can only give a guide to the maintenance and trouble-shooting on the more popular systems and show some examples of how various jobs are done. For serious dismantling, a workshop manual is essential.

It may sound as though the braking system is a continual source of trouble. It is not, of course, but because it is invariably used gently and cannot be easily heard or felt to complain, it tends to be overlooked for very long periods. In fact, providing the system is checked and maintained at the recommended intervals — usually every 5,000 miles — maladies which beset neglected brakes such as worn-out linings and pads, and seized adjusters, never get a chance to develop.

Fitting disc pads

Pads should be renewed when the friction material has worn to within $\frac{1}{8}$ in of the backing plate, or when the electrical pad thickness indicator light comes on.

On most British cars, removing the pads involves jacking up the car, removing the road wheels, and detaching a couple of pad retaining pins before pulling the pads from the caliper. Any exposed pistons are then cleaned, and retracted into their bores to make room for new, thicker pads. On this sort of layout it should be possible to change both sets of front wheel pads (pads should only be fitted in sets of four) within an hour.

Not all cars are this simple. On some the caliper must be removed from the disc to fit new pads. Where this involves undoing mounting bolts, take care that it is the mounting bolts you are undoing and not the bolts holding the two halves of the caliper together. It is never necessary to split a caliper to fit new pads, and if this is inadvertently done, the caliper should be rebuilt by a brake specialist using new high-tensile bolts tightened to the appropriate torque. The old bolts tend to stretch in service, and once disturbed you cannot guarantee the two halves will re-unite without distortion or leakage if they are re-used.

While the pads are being changed, check the surface of the disc. It is normal for this to be scored a little, but deep scores – which will cause accelerated wear of the mating pad – call for a change of disc.

Originally all disc calipers had two pistons – one to push a pad on to each side of the disc. But rising costs have driven manu-facturers to the use of cheaper calipers having one piston or two pistons in the same cylinder. On these the opposite pad is drawn on to the disc by a yoke attached to the back of the rear-most piston or by a swinging plate.

Girling and Lockheed produce the majority of British disc brakes. In essence most of them are similar from the pad change point of view except for the type of dust cover used to keep dirt from the caliper bore.

Girling use an expanding bellows-type rubber dust cover. Providing this is undamaged, the piston can be retracted without further attention – but make sure the bellows is not pinched as the piston is pushed back into its bore, for this is now they get broken.

Lockheed use a dust excluder seal like a second hydraulic seal at the mouth of the caliper bore. Once the chromium plated piston has passed through this seal it is open to the atmosphere and collects its share of dirt and moisture. So when Lockheed pads are changed, it is essential that the exposed section of the piston is cleaned with a piece of cloth dipped in fresh brake fluid, then inspected for corrosion. Providing it is not rusty or pitted it can be coated with Lockheed disc brake lubricant and then pushed back into the bore.

Sometimes there are snags. A piston which is seized will refuse to retract. Before new pads can be fitted, the seized piston must be got out and a new one fitted. This operation is covered later.

On the Girling swinging caliper brake used at the rear of the Rover 2000 and Ford Zephyr/Zodiac Mk 4 range, a special tool is needed to wind back the piston. On these it is easy to damage the mechanism if the special tool is not available, and these are best left to the professionals.

Renewing pads

198 Split pins retain the pads on this Lockheed two-piston caliper

199 Withdraw the pins and take out the retaining plate. Pull out the pads using pliers if necessary. As each pad comes out, check behind it for shims. Any shims must be re-fitted in the same position

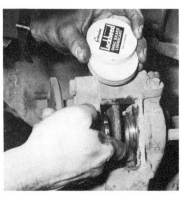

200 Clean the exposed pistons with brake fluid then coat them with Lockheed disc brake lubricant

As the illustrations show, pad changing involves the loss of a little fluid. After new ones have been fitted, it is important to press the brake pedal a few times until the normal pedal 'feel' is obtained, then top up the fluid reservoir.

Fitting new brake linings

New drum brake linings are needed when the old ones have worn down to within $\frac{1}{32}$ in of any one rivet head or, on bonded linings, when the surface has worn to within $\frac{1}{16}$ in of the shoe face.

Once, relining brakes meant chiselling the old friction material from the shoes and riveting on new strips of lining material. Nowadays it is a lot easier and quicker to fit ready-lined shoes which are accurately ground to conform to the shape of the drum. Fitting new shoes involves five basic steps:

1 Jack up the wheel, remove it, back off brake adjustment.
2 Remove the drum.
3 Lever out the old shoes.
4 Clean the backplate, lubricate sparingly.
5 Fit new shoes, refit drum and wheel, adjust brakes and test.

It looks all straight-forward and logical, and sometimes it is. But because of the lack of standardisation on braking systems, what is easy on one car may be difficult on another. The best way to appreciate the snags is to look at the five steps in more detail.

Adjustment

In order to get the drum off it is normally necessary to adjust the linings away from the drum and your car may have any one of ten different brake adjusting systems. There is not space to include them all here although the system your car uses will be detailed in the handbook.

The most widely used manual adjusters consist of a small square-headed screw which pokes through the under-car side of the brake backplate. On most cars turning this screw anti-clockwise (looking at the head) moves the linings away from the drum.

The only difficulty you might encounter is if the screw is rusted up and seized. Somehow you have to get at the protruding threads with a wire brush and scrape away the rust, and then dose the screw with penetrating oil. Do not use an open-ended spanner on a stiff adjuster – get one that's good and strong and surrounds the square head of the screw completely. Turning it clockwise a fraction often breaks the hold of the rust. Once it has moved, it can be unscrewed.

A few adjusters are meant to be stiff. These rely on their friction to give a self-adjusting action to the shoes and must not be lubricated. They usually have hexagon heads and there will not be any thread protruding from the backplate.

Automatic adjusters are used on the back brakes of a lot of cars. If all goes normally, the drum should come off without any de-adjustment being necessary. But occasionally people get the

201 Use a squeeze-bottle to suck fluid out of the master cylinder reservoir, or open a bleed screw at the caliper

204 Top up the reservoir with new fluid and press the brake pedal a few times to position the new pads

207 Support the caliper so it won't stretch the hydraulic hose, undo two securing clips and pull the pads out

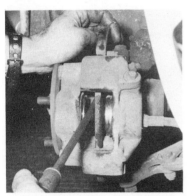

202 Press each piston fully back into the bore, taking care not to tilt and jam it. If the bleed screw has been opened, close it while the piston is still under pressure

Lockheed heavy duty caliper
205 On this one the pads can only be removed after taking the caliper off

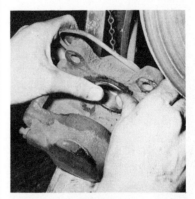

208 Siphon fluid from the reservoir or open a bleed screw, clean the piston and push each piston back

203 Clean any dirt from the pad aperture, fit new pads complete with a new retainer and split pins

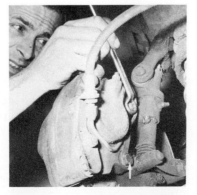

206 It has two retaining bolts on the stub axle side. Turn back their lock washers, remove them and the caliper comes off

209 Clean the recess, fit new pads, securing them with the clips (arrowed)

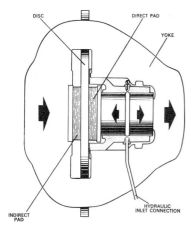

DISC — DIRECT PAD — YOKE — HYDRAULIC INLET CONNECTION — INDIRECT PAD

Girling A-type caliper
210 This caliper uses two opposed pistons in a single bore to push the pads on to the disc

211 Pads are retained by two pins and the pins are in turn kept in place by two wire clips. Withdraw the clips, pull out the pins and the pads come out – note the position of any shims for re-assembly

212 Fit new pads one at a time. First open the bleed screw (arrowed) and lever the yoke towards the wheel stud side of the disc. Close the bleed screw then fit the outer pad

213 Open the bleed screw again, and press in the piston like this. Close the bleed screw and fit the other pad. It is not necessary to clean Girling pistons when they are shrouded by a bellows-type rubber seal

114

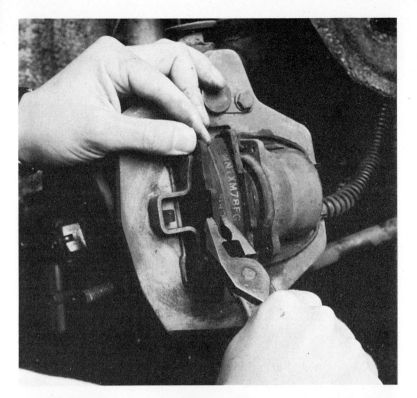

Lockheed swinging caliper
214 On this single piston caliper, new pads are wedge-shaped and as they wear they gradually become parallel with the backing plate. First remove the split pins and retaining plate

215 Pull out the pads

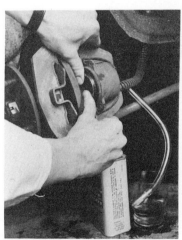

216 Clean and lubricate the piston, open the bleed screw, retract the piston, then close the bleed screw

217 A new pad (right) compared with a worn one

218 Fit the pads, a new retaining plate and new split pins. Top up the fluid reservoir and check the pedal action

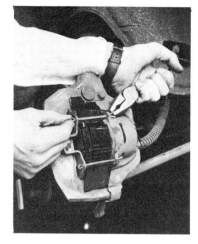

219 Loosen this screw and have someone lightly press the pedal to hold the pads in contact with the disc. Tighten the screw to 6 lb ft to re-align the caliper swinging plate (far right)

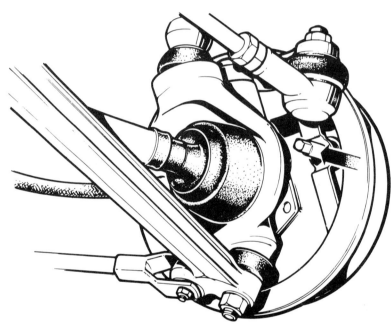

220 Most adjusters on drum brake systems have a square head and are turned anti-clockwise to move the linings away from the drum

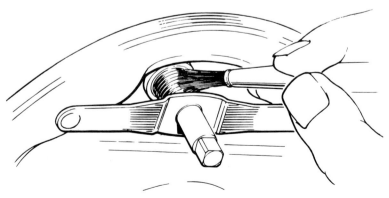

221 Stiff adjusters can sometimes be freed if the protruding threads are cleaned then brushed with penetrating oil

idea that self-adjusting brakes are also self-servicing and never bother to check the linings. In time the linings wear down to the rivets and the rivets begin to carve grooves in the drum and you end up with the drum and lining interlocking together so the drum cannot be pulled off. All current self-adjusting systems have a built-in arrangement which allows the shoe to be de-adjusted a little to cope with a sticking drum. But it will not be enough for a well interlocked drum and the only way to get this one off is to cut it off with a hacksaw. If it is any consolation, a scored drum must be renewed anyway.

Removing the drum

If the drum has one or two small locating bolts or screws on the face adjacent to the wheel studs, when these are removed the drum should pull straight off. The same applies to drums which are located by a centre boss protruding through them. On all these, if the drum sticks, a few gentle thumps round the inner edge with a nylon mallet will get it off.

Some brake drums are made in one piece with the hub assembly. On cars with taper roller wheel bearings, getting the drum off involves prising out the bearing grease cap with a big screwdriver, then undoing the split pin and taking off the centre hub nut. The drum is then removed complete with bearings.

British Leyland 1100's and 1300's need a special puller to draw off the rear drums, and because these use ball-bearings there's a real chance that the inner bearing may come apart, leaving the inner cone jammed on the stub-axle and spilling balls all over the floor. When this happens in theory you need another puller to draw the inner cone off the axle. The puller in question is relatively rare outside British Leyland garages, but quite often the inner cone responds if it is heated with a blow-lamp and gently tapped forward using a thin chisel behind it.

A separated bearing on an 1100 can easily turn what should be a half-hour job into a frustrating all-day marathon, so if you are the tiniest bit quick-tempered it is better to leave this one to a dealer. With the appropriate special tools it is quite a quick job.

Removing the shoes

Once the drum is off you will be faced by two shoes, at least two pull-off springs and most likely a variety of levers, push-rods and perhaps a small wheel with teeth on.

The first task is to make a note of what the assembly looks like before you touch it. Scratch arrows on the shoe webs to show the direction of forward wheel rotation and mark them 'top' and 'bottom' or 'front' and 'rear' depending on their position. Draw the shape and position of the pull-off springs on a note-pad noting particularly which holes they fit into in the shoes. Some springs are assymetrical so they miss a rotating hub or tension an adjuster wheel – it is important to note these peculiarities too.

Each shoe will most likely be held against the backplate by a

222 The easy brake drums to remove push over the wheel studs. This one has a single retaining screw (arrowed) some drums have two bolts or screws to retain them

223 To remove the drum, undo the retainers and pull it off the studs

117

steady spring. Take these out and use a large screwdriver to lever the shoe tips from their abutments. As they swing clear, the springs will pull them together and then drop out of their holes. Disengage the shoes from any levers and remove them.

The backplate

Check the wheel cylinder by peeling back the rubber cover and look underneath for brake fluid. It should be packed with rubber grease, but if fluid seeps out, fit a new cylinder. Some wheel cylinders are intended to slide in the backplate. Check they are free-moving, if necessary lubricating the sliding base of the cylinder under the protective rubber cover using a feeler gauge coated with brake grease.

Check the action of manual adjusters. Where the adjusting screw separates two wedges, remove the wedges and the screw and coat all moving surfaces with a high melting point grease sold by the brake manufacturers.

Clean the backplate surface with methylated spirit, then lightly coat any surfaces that the shoes rub on with brake grease. Before fitting the shoes, check the shoe-tips and file off any burrs, then lightly coat them with brake grease. Keep grease away from the hydraulic rubbers in wheel cylinders.

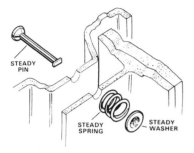

224a This seems the most popular type of brake shoe steady spring

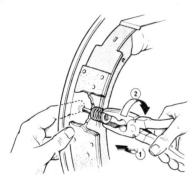

224b To release the shoe, support the head of the pin behind the backplate, press down on the washer and turn it through 90 degrees

225 This typical two leading-shoe layout shows the importance of marking the shoes before removing them. Note how the return springs are biased to avoid the wheel cylinders and adjusters. The linings are not placed centrally on the shoes as you might expect – they appear to have slipped in the direction of forward wheel rotation. Fitting them back-to-front would reduce efficiency

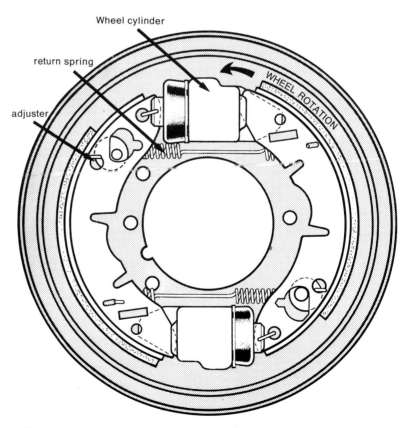

New shoes

Refitting is a reversal of dismantling, but take care that grease or oil doesn't contaminate the lining surface. Back off all adjustment before attempting to refit the drums. Re-adjust the brakes.

The hydraulic system

Assuming you have been maintaining the car at regular intervals, any trouble here should be picked up long before it becomes serious. The main problems are:
  *Old or contaminated brake fluid.
  *Air in the fluid.
  *Fluid leakage.
  *Damaged flexible hoses.
  *Corrosion of hydraulic pipes.
  *Seized hydraulic piston.
  Most of these troubles are inter-related. For instance, old brake fluid will contain water which will have caused rusting inside the system – and this will eventually cause a piston to seize up.
  Before any hydraulic component is dismantled it is important that the working area and your hands are clean. Brake fluid is a mixture of vegetable oil, alcohol and various additives and if the areas in contact with fluid are contaminated with engine oil, petrol, paraffin or carbon tetrachloride, the hydraulic seals will be permanently damaged (they usually swell up) and will all have to be changed. Only clean brake fluid, the brake manufacturer's cleaning fluid or methylated spirits should be used for cleaning hydraulic components.

Changing the fluid

The brake manufacturers recommend this is done every 18 months or 24,000 miles, to get rid of fluid which has absorbed water.
  To do this job you really need a helper, a large can of new brake fluid, a glass jar, a 12 in length of flexible rubber or plastic tube and a spanner to fit the bleed screws on the brake backplate or disc caliper. On most cars the bleed screw can be reached if the wheels are run up on ramps. If you do not have ramps, use the car jack and remove the wheel to reach the bleed screw – but do not get under the car while it is just supported on the jack.
  Fit the spanner on the bleed screw, push the tube on the end and put the other end in the jar, open the screw half a turn and have your helper pump the brake pedal until all the fluid has vanished from the master cylinder reservoir. On cars with dual line braking systems which have a split reservoir, this process will only empty half of it. If the screw you have been using is a front one, close it and open a rear one to drain the rest of the reservoir or vice-versa.
  Once the fluid is out, throw it away (never re-use brake fluid) and close all bleed screws. All you have to do now is refill the system with fresh fluid, and then bleed it.

226 Off comes a steady pin prior to removing the brake shoes. The rubber covers on the wheel cylinders have already been peeled back to check for fluid leaks

227 Lift the shoes against spring pressure and ease them off their abutments. In this instance a Girling brake shoe removing tool is being used, but a big screwdriver is almost as effective

228 Fitting new shoes is a reversal of the dismantling procedure. Lightly lubricate the shoe tips and the places where the shoes contact the backplate with brake grease, and before refitting the drum, gently tap the ends of the shoes to centralise them

Bleeding the hydraulics

Brake bleeding is only necessary if the hydraulic system has been emptied or has been dismantled. It is not a normal service operation. The idea of bleeding is to remove any air bubbles from the fluid for if they are left in the pipe-work they will have to be squeezed up before the fluid can operate the brakes. In severe instances the pedal can be pushed down to the toe-board without much reaction from the brakes.

The order in which bleeding is carried out depends on the braking system. On cars with drums all round, begin with the wheel farthest from the master cylinder (usually the nearside rear) and finish with the nearest one. If the car has discs at the front and drums at the rear, bleed the discs first (starting with the one farthest from the cylinder) then bleed the drum brakes. On dual-line systems, the Girling layout is bled as for an all-drum set-up, on the Lockheed dual system both offside brakes are bled together (two jam-jars, two bleed tubes) then both nearside brakes. On cars like the Vauxhall Viva which have only one bleed screw at the back, this is opened when bleeding both sides.

Once you have sorted out the method, the actual mechanics of the job are simple. First fill the reservoir to the top (try not to spill any brake fluid – it is a good paint stripper). Pour about an inch of clean fluid into the glass jar, attach the spanner and pipe to the first bleed screw and immerse the other end in the fluid.

Open the screw half a turn and get your helper to pump the pedal. On Lockheed brakes, he should push the pedal down slowly and allow it to return fast. On cars with the cast-iron Girling CB master cylinder the pedal is pressed slowly and allowed to return slowly, while the aluminium Girling CV cylinder, the pedal is pushed down fully once, then given three quick jabs before allowing it to return quickly.

Besides operating the pedal, the helper should ensure that the reservoir remains topped-up, for if the level falls too much, air will be drawn in and you will have to start again.

At the bleed screw, prepare to close it when clean fluid free from air bubbles is seen coming from the tube. Your helper should hold the pedal fully down while the screw is closed. On the Lockheed two-at-once divided line system, close one screw, then give one more pump at the pedal, then close the second one while the pedal is held down.

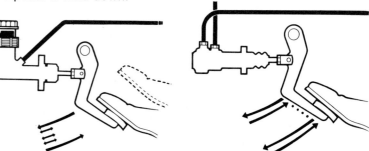

229 The different pedal techniques used when bleeding brakes with a Girling CV master cylinder (left) and CB master cylinder

Air in the fluid

From the driving seat you will know there is air in the fluid because the pedal will feel spongy. If bleeding does not give a permanent cure, check the system for leaks and renew parts as necessary. Sometimes you will not find a leak because in its early stages, air can leak into the hydraulic system without hydraulic fluid leaking out.

Girling have produced a device called a hose clamp which is used to detect the source of the leak when faced with the above problem. The clamps are designed to squeeze up the flexible hoses, blocking off the supply to the appropriate wheel.

Suppose there is air in the system and you do not know where it is. It will be either in one of the wheel cylinders or calipers or the master cylinder.

Our average car has three flexible brake shoes, sometimes four. You need one hose clamp for each hose. Fit them in position and clamp up all the hoses. Now the pedal should feel firm without a trace of sponginess. If it feels spongy as before, the master cylinder is the cause of the trouble.

From this point, release the hose clamps one at a time. When the sponginess suddenly returns you have uncovered the line with the air in it – renew the offending wheel cylinder or change the seals in the disc caliper.

Leaks

The most likely place for hydraulic fluid to leak is at one of the wheel cylinders, disc brake calipers or the master cylinder. What usually happens is the bore or piston which the soft rubber hydraulic seal rubs against gets roughened up – usually by rust –

230 When a wheel cylinder has sprung a leak as bad as this, don't bother to try repairing it – fit a new one

121

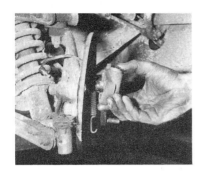

231 Remove the top of the master cylinder, place a square of polythene over the filler neck and re-tighten the cap. Undo the brake pipe behind the wheel cylinder and remove the cylinder – this one is bolted on

232 Clean the backplate, fit a new dust seal and fit the new cylinder in exactly the same position as the old one. On this one the large threaded ports accept the hydraulic pipe and bleed screw, the other holes are for the mounting bolts.

233 Some wheel cylinders are intended to slide in the backplate and are generally secured by spring clips. The clips can usually be tapped out using a screwdriver and a light hammer

and tears the seal, allowing fluid to weep out. The cause differs depending on the component involved.

On wheel cylinders and the master cylinder, water in the brake fluid can cause rusting within cast-iron cylinder barrels, and corrosion within aluminium barrels. This is avoided if the fluid is changed every 18 months.

The first sign of leakage is an accelerated drop in the fluid level in the master cylinder reservoir. If the leak is at a wheel cylinder, fluid will drip into the brake drum and lubricate the linings. You will notice that the car pulls to one side when you push the pedal because the fluid-filled brake drum is not providing as much retardation as the good drum on the same axle so the car pulls away from the leaking side. A leaking master cylinder will drip fluid on to the pushrod from the brake pedal from where it usually runs down the pedal shaft, gets under the rubber pad and eventually causes it to slide off.

Assuming the bores of the wheel cylinders and master cylinders are sound (which they rarely are) the leak can be cured by fitting new hydraulic seals in place of the old ones. In my experience this is rarely successful if the car is more than two years old and it's better to spend a bit more and fit a new master cylinder or wheel cylinder in place of the leaking one. One brake manufacturer reckons a one-in-three chance of failure when fitting new seals.

Disc brake calipers do not work in the same way as a wheel cylinder. Here the piston which presses the pads against the disc is smooth and the seal mounted in a groove in the cylinder.

As disc pads wear, each piston emerges a little more from the caliper, automatically taking up the adjustment. Since the piston is only travelling in one direction, the only time the seal is likely to be damaged is when the pads wear out and the piston is forced back through the seal to make room for the thicker ones. The illustrations show how new seals are fitted to a Girling caliper. Lockheed calipers need a special tool to fit the dust excluding seal.

Damaged hoses and pipes

Hydraulic brake hoses are immensely tough, but in time the outer surface may begin to perish or crack and if the hose has been twisted during fitting, it may be chafed by part of the suspension, and if this has happened the hose must be changed.

It is preferable to retain as much fluid in the hydraulic system as possible when the hose is disconnected, and the easiest way is to remove the lid of the fluid reservoir, stretch a piece of polythene sheet over the filler neck, and replace the lid. You will lose a little fluid as the hose is undone, but the polythene diaphragm stops air getting in and the flow soon stops.

At its inner end, the hose is attached to the metal pipe by an acorn nut. Undo this first. Now undo the locknut which secures the inner end of the hose to a mounting bracket. There is a hexagon section on the hose to prevent it turning. Lastly unscrew the hose from the caliper or wheel cylinder.

234 Out comes the old sliding cylinder. The mounting ahead of the open bore is a handbrake lever pivot

235 Clean the area on which the wheel cylinder slides with emery cloth

236 Lubricate the backplate with brake grease, pop in the new cylinder and engage the handbrake lever

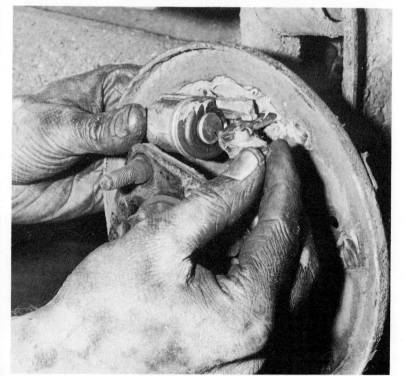

237 This is how the clips are assembled which secure the cylinder to the backplate. Push them together and they will lock in position. Quite often the clip side of the cylinder is shrouded by a rubber cover. Fill it with rubber lubricant and fit it before re-connecting the brake pipe and handbrake

Changing Girling caliper seals and pistons

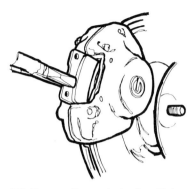

238 Remove the road wheel and take out the pads, noting the position of any shims

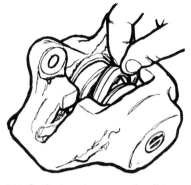

241 On the bench, remove the dirt-excluding seals and pull out the pistons – for seized pistons, see text

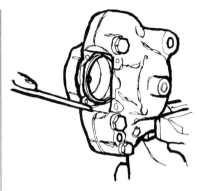

244 Clean any dirt and rust from the pad abutments on the caliper

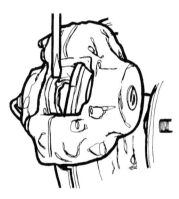

239 Once the pads are out you might find a cause of leakage or seizure – such as this break in the dirt-excluding seal protecting the piston. Press the brake pedal to push the pistons fully out (on to the disc)

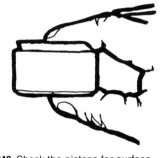

242 Check the pistons for surface damage after cleaning them with brake fluid. If the chromium plated surface is rusted, pitted or peeling, fit new pistons. Only un-marked pistons should be re-used

245 Wash the caliper in Girling cleaning fluid or methylated spirit. Dry it with a clean nylon cloth

240 Prevent air entering the master cylinder using a polythene diaphragm and remove the caliper from the stub axle

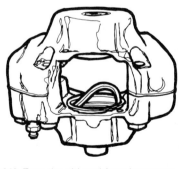

243 Ease the old seal from its groove in the caliper bore using a small blunt-nosed screwdriver. Using the same tool, carefully scrape any rust from the bore, use a strip of nylon cloth to clean out the seal groove

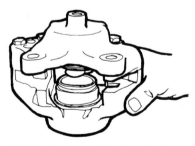

246 Coat a new seal in clean brake fluid, fit it in its groove by hand, then dip a new piston in brake fluid and insert it through the seal

When fitting a new hose, make sure you get the correct one for the car (some have metric threads) and renew any washers that are fitted with it. Replacement is a reversal of dismantling, but make sure the hose is held securely while the fixing nut is tightened on the inner bracket – if the hose twists it may chafe.

Metal hydraulic pipes cannot be made up at home – they must be supplied by a dealer or brake specialist who will ensure they are the correct length with the right flares and fittings on the ends.

The most common reason for renewing brake pipes is that the old ones have rusted. If inspection shows any rust on the pipes it means the protective plating has deteriorated and the pipe should be renewed. Take the old one with you when you have the new one made so it can be used as a pattern for the new pipe. The new pipe can be shaped by bending it carefully by hand, but avoid bends with a radius of less than 1 inch and take care the tube isn't flattened when it is bent. When fitting new pipes put a twist of sticky tape over the ends to prevent dirt entering the bores and remove the tape just before they are fixed at each end.

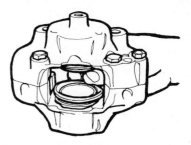

247 Before pushing the piston fully into the bore, fit the new dust excluding seal to the end. Fit a new piston and seal in the other caliper bore

Seized piston

On a drum brake system, a seized piston will not do its fair share of work and the car will pull slightly to one side. To check which piston is jammed, remove the brake drum, take out the brake shoes and use a screwdriver in the slotted end of each piston and try to turn it. The piston which does not budge is the seized one. Renew the complete wheel cylinder.

When a disc brake piston seizes, usually only the piston has to be renewed. But first you have to get it out. The best way is to use the car's hydraulic system to push it out. First try removing the pads and stamping hard on the brake pedal. This should push both pistons out as far as the disc. If the caliper is now removed from the hub, it is quite likely the piston can be taken out by hand. If it will not shift, leave the caliper off the disc, but keep it connected to the brake hose (tie it up so it doesn't hang on the hose) and use a clamp such as a valve spring compressor to hold down the un-seized piston while you press the pedal again. This will usually pop out the piston, accompanied by much brake fluid, after which the hose can be clamped, the caliper unscrewed and moved to the bench and the bore examined.

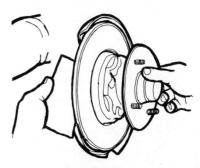

248 On the car, clean any rust off the edge of the disc with coarse emery cloth. Re-fit the caliper, insert the pads, reconnect the brake hose or pipe, remove the PVC diaphragm from the master cylinder reservoir and bleed the brakes

The mouth of the bore between the seal and the outer edge is likely to be rusted. If this is all the rust there is, scrape it away gently with a blunt-nosed screwdriver, clean it thoroughly in cleaning fluid or meths, fit a new seal and a new piston and all will be well. If the rust has got into the groove which locates the hydraulic seal, there's a chance that the damage will allow fluid to leak round the back of the seal, and in these circumstances, a new caliper is the only sure remedy. Incidentally, some car manufacturers do not sell individual pistons as spare parts, preferring to sell a complete caliper instead at considerably greater expense. If you hit this snag, contact the Sales and Service

249 It is advisable to renew hydraulic hoses at 40,000 mile intervals or when cracks are apparent in the outer surface when they are bent like this

Department of the brake manufacturer – it is best to telephone them – and ask for the name of your nearest brake specialist. He should stock individual pistons.

250 When new hoses are fitted, connect the outer end to the wheel cylinder or caliper first. Thread the inner end through its mounting bracket then prevent the hose from turning (and twisting) using a spanner on a hexagon A while locknut B is tightened. Finally tighten the tube nut C. Reverse this process when taking off a hose

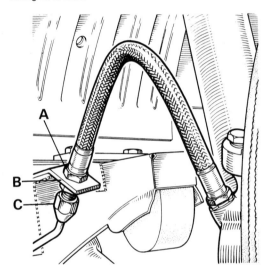

251 In the early 1970's British cars began to switch from Unified to Metric brake pipe unions. It is important that these are not interchanged since the threads are not compatible. The drawings show the physical differences. In addition, metric unions are stamped M and are black. Metric threads in wheel cylinders or calipers are not counterbored as unified ones usually are. If in doubt, check that the bleed screw and hose will screw fully home by hand. If they won't, or are unduly slack, the threads may not be compatible

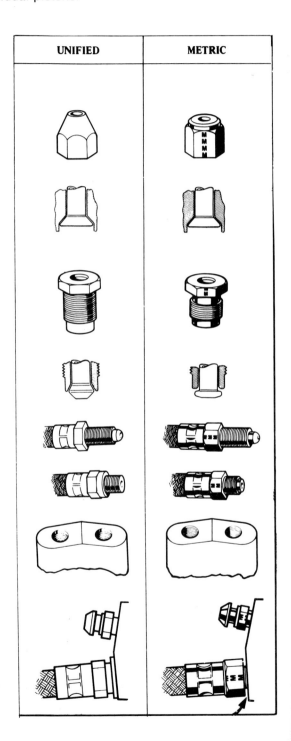

UNIFIED	METRIC

Unlike the household electrical system where two wires carry the feed and return current to each electrical item, a car uses just one cable to connect each electrical component to the battery live terminal. The return circuit is taken through the steel bodyshell and the other battery terminal is connected to the bodywork to complete the circuit.

The battery is the heart of the car's electrical system. Most people know it needs topping-up with distilled water from time to time, and when they do, it is customary to put in too much water. As a result the electrolyte sprays out of the vent holes when the battery is fully charged.

As a guide, batteries should be topped up to the point where the distilled water just covers the top of the separator plates – you can see these if you look down the vent holes (don't use a naked flame to look in the hole – battery gas is inflammable). On batteries where you cannot take off the vents – such as the Lucas Aqualok – the topping-up level will either automatically set itself or you will be able to see the level of the electrolyte through the semi-transparent battery case. Incidentally, plastic-cased batteries don't seem to need topping-up so frequently as the rubber-cased ones.

Besides keeping an eye on the electrolyte you should keep the top of the battery clean and dry. This is not easy on some of the cut-priced batteries where the top is littered with separate filler caps and lots of inter-cell connectors, but do your best. You can discourage corrosion by spraying the top with one of those rust-preventative fluids used to stop rusting inside chassis box sections. The more expensive batteries tend to have smoother top faces and are easier to keep clean.

The terminals should be given a birthday once a year just before winter starts. Separate the terminals from the battery posts and clean the mating surfaces to bright metal with glasspaper or a wire brush. Lightly coat them with Vaseline and refit. Do not use ordinary grease – it is a good insulator. At the same time clean the earth connection where the earth terminal bolts to the bodyshell.

If the car is not used for a period, the battery may lose its charge. It can be rejuvenated if you have a trickle-charger, but remember to connect like terminals – the plus lead on the charger goes to the plus lead on the battery and vice-versa. If you get the connections the wrong way round, the charger will blow its fuse or if no fuse is fitted will burn out. A battery with the wrong polarity will (among other things) wreck any transistorised radios or tape players you have in the car. On batteries with irremovable tops keep the top shut when charging, otherwise air-locks will push out the acid.

If the battery seems permanently flat, you can get an idea of its condition by checking the specific gravity of the electrolyte with a hydrometer. The higher the specific gravity reading (in other words the greater the strength of sulphuric acid) the better it is.

A hydrometer is simply a sampling tube with a small float inside.

Chapter ten
Electrics

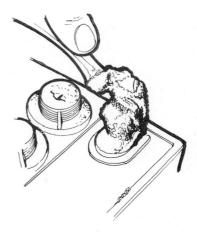

252 Over-filling or neglect allows battery terminals to corrode. Clean them and coat the mating surfaces with petroleum jelly to restore a sound connection

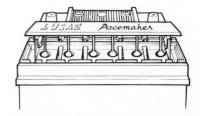

253 On Lucas Aqualok batteries the top won't come off. Keep it shut down when charging

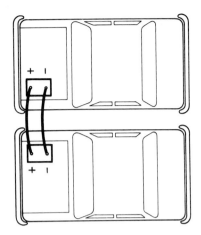

254 The right way with jumper leads – connect like terminals on both batteries

Electrolyte from the battery is drawn into the tube using a rubber bulb, and the specific gravity is read off on the calibrated float. As a guide, at 15° C (60° F) a fully charged battery gives a reading of 1.270 to 1.290, a half-charged one indicates 1.190 to 1.210 and a flat battery shows 1.110 to 1.120. All cells should be within 0.040. If they are not, the battery is failing and due for renewal.

If you want to take a hydrometer reading and the battery needs topping-up, run the car for at least 30 minutes after adding distilled water before checking the specific gravity.

Emergency starts

Most garage breakdown men carry a set of heavy gauge jumper leads for starting cars with weak batteries. If you have a set of these and a friend (or a second car) with a fully charged battery, you can always start a car with a flat battery by linking the sound battery to the flat one using the jumper leads.

There is one rule. As with the charger, connect-up *like* terminals – plus to plus, minus to minus. If you do not there will be substantial spark when you join up the last terminal, and if one car has an alternator, there is a risk of damaging its transistorised output stage. Where cars are positive earth in one case and negative earth in the other, do not let the bodyshells or bumpers touch.

If the jumper leads seem to have little effect, check the connections – the warm one will be the one that's making poor contact. If all seems well, where applicable, check the connection of the battery posts on the terminals – corrosion between a post and terminal cap will cause a bad connection.

If you have a flat battery and no jumper leads, there is a trick which can be tried on cars with dynamos, but must *never* be used on cars with alternators.

What you do is substitute a good battery for the flat one, start the engine, and while the engine is kept running at around 3,000 rpm, the good battery is disconnected (the engine will keep going using current from the dynamo) and the flat battery is re-fitted. Now providing you can motor for about 20 miles, the dynamo will charge up the flat battery.

The reason why you must not do this on a car with an alternator is because the alternator will blow the transistors in the output stage if it is run on an open-circuit. This sort of damage often calls for a new alternator.

The charging circuit

On paper the alternator is much more efficient than a DC dynamo. In theory the alternator is also likely to be more trouble-free because it has sealed-for-life bearings and its brushes carry a far smaller load than a dynamo. On the other hand, if something goes wrong with the transistorised output stage of an alternator, although spare parts are available, they are expensive and few garages want to be bothered fitting them, so the usual answer is a new or reconditioned unit which is quite expensive.

The DC dynamo is a simpler device which passes its current to a separate control box. If anything goes wrong, spares are cheap and easily obtained and it's usually possible to fit them yourself.

Most dynamos seem to need a new set of commutator brushes after about 40,000 miles.

You will know something has gone wrong with the charging system because the dashboard warning lamp will come on or the battery condition indicator will give lower readings than usual. The most usual trouble is a broken drive belt (see Chapter 5). If this is not the cause, check the security of the cables or plugs at the back of the unit, and if there is still no charge, the next step is to look at the condition of the brushes.

The ubiquitous Lucas dynamo has two oblong brushes in box-like holders and the brushes should be renewed when they are worn to the point where the top surface of the brush is $\frac{1}{8}$ in below the top of the holder. If you take the dynamo off the car, you can see the tops of the holders if you peer through the air holes in the backplate.

As the illustrations show, getting the dynamo apart is theoretically easy – all you do is unscrew two through-bolts and the whole thing pulls apart. The only snag is that the through-bolts are sometimes very tight and refuse to undo when attacked by a screwdriver. The answer is to grip the reluctant bolt-head in a vice and turn the dynamo body to loosen it. A screwdriver will then undo it the rest of the way.

New dynamo brushes

255 Remove the dynamo from the car, undo the two through-bolts and pull them right out

256 Pull off the end plate which carries the brushes

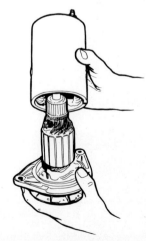

257 Draw the casing off the armature. It is not normally necessary to dismantle further

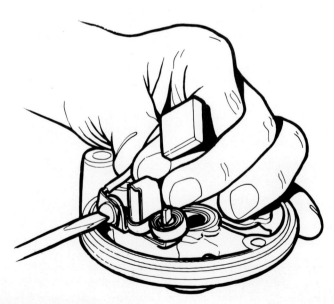

258 Disconnect the wires on the old brushes from the terminal tags. Fit new ones in their place

259 Push up the new brushes until the ends are flush with the bottom of the holders. Rest each clock-spring against the side of its brush to hold it up

260 If the commutator is dirty or glazed, clean the surface with fine glasspaper

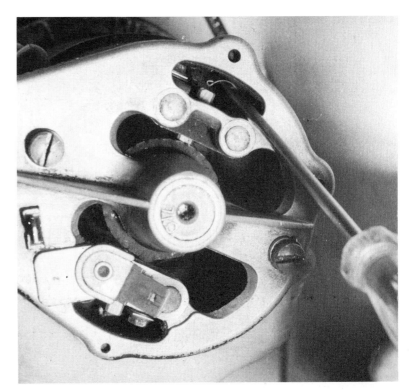

261 Reassemble the dynamo then use a screwdriver through the holes in the end plate to lift the clock springs so they bear on the end of each brush

Besides worn-out brushes, dynamos sometimes wear out the porous bronze bearing in the centre of the end plate. At first sight this bearing – which is pressed into the end plate – looks difficult to get out. Happily it is pretty soft and if you nibble at it by tapping the edge using a light hammer on a small screwdriver you can chisel a groove down one edge. The bearing can then be prised inwards and drawn out with pliers. A new bearing should be pre-lubricated before fitting. The best way to do this is to stand it on your thumb and fill it to the top with engine oil. Now place your finger on top of the bearing and squeeze. You will see oil come through the outer walls of the bearing.

The best way of fitting the new bearing is to use the dynamo armature – which turns in the bearing – to push it into place. Lay the end plate, with the bearing resting on the mouth of its hole, on the bench. Insert the armature end into the bearing, hold it vertical, and tap the nut in the centre of the dynamo pulley gently with a soft mallet to drive in the bearing.

Sometimes the armature on an overworked dynamo burns out, and if you cannot buy a replacement, the only alternative is a reconditioned unit. Your old dynamo will be taken in part exchange for the reconditioned one, but it is worth knowing in advance that reconditioned dynamos come minus the drive pulley, locating key and fixing nut. To get the old one off, loosen the pulley nut and un-screw it about five turns. Support the dynamo by holding the pulley in your hand and smite the pulley nut a hefty blow with a copper mallet. This will jar the pulley which can then be taken off the shaft after removing the nut.

262 Pre-lubricating a dynamo rear bearing bush

263 Using the dynamo armature to insert the new bush

Fitting alternator brushes

264 Disconnect the alternator cables (usually plugged into the back) remove the alternator from the car and detach the rear cover. The cover is sometimes secured by recessed screws which must be reached using a box spanner

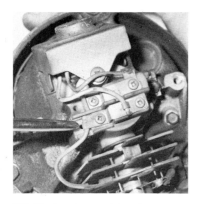

265 The brushes on this unit are under the metal strips. To avoid mixing-up the connections, it's best to renew one brush at a time

266 This is what the brushes look like – they are much smaller than dynamo brushes and come complete with a coil spring

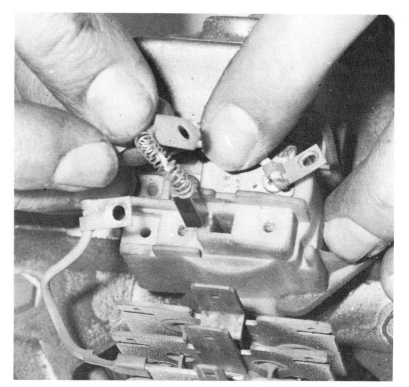

267 Thread each new brush carbon into the square hole and screw down the metal strip – not forgetting to reconnect the wires

Alternators do not have plain bearings and because the brushes do not carry all the output current as on a dynamo, brush wear is a lot slower. But alternator brushes do wear eventually, and the illustrations show how the brushes on a popular alternator are changed.

Starters

These are very heavy duty electric motors which are wired to produce maximum turning effort from a standing start. When cold starting a medium car engine it is not unusual for a starter to draw 200 amps from the battery, and the wiring layout within the motor means that the average starter uses four brushes.

Although one is a generator and the other is a motor, from the practical aspect there are similarities between the dynamo and starter.

As on the dynamo, most starter motors are held together by two through-bolts. Undo these and the nuts on the rear terminal, and the end plate, carrying the four brushes can be drawn off.

It is here you will notice the first difference. Starter motor brush wires are soldered, not screwed to their terminals. What's more, two brushes will be fixed to the end plate and two will be connected by longer wires to the two ends of the field winding inside the casing.

Because starter motors only operate for perhaps five or ten seconds at a time, they are not so liable to brush wear as dynamos. If the brushes have to be replaced, snip the wires from the old ones, leaving about a $\frac{1}{2}$ in length of the old cable still attached to the field windings. The wires from the new brushes are soldered to the short pieces of old cable. The reason for doing this is because the field windings are invariably made of aluminium and the copper brush wires cannot be soldered directly to them.

During re-assembly it is important that the screw terminal which protrudes through the backplate is insulated from it. It is usual to insulate it with a nylon sleeve. Make sure this is in position when the terminal nuts are re-fitted, otherwise operating the starter will cause a substantial short circuit.

At the other end of the starter will be a pinion which engages with the ring gear round the outside of the engine flywheel. There are two ways of engaging this pinion with the ring gear. Inertia starters use a system where the pinion runs along a screw thread and is thrown into engagement with the ring gear as soon as the starter begins to turn. Obviously the action of a rotating pinion crashing into engagement with stationary ring gear teeth causes some wear on the teeth.

A pre-engaged starter carries a solenoid piggy-back style on the top of its casing. When the starter is operated, the first thing that happens is the solenoid moves the pinion into engagement with the ring gear. Most of the time when the pinion is fully home, the starter turns. Occasionally the pinion and ring gear meet tooth-to-tooth. When this happens, a spring loads the pinion

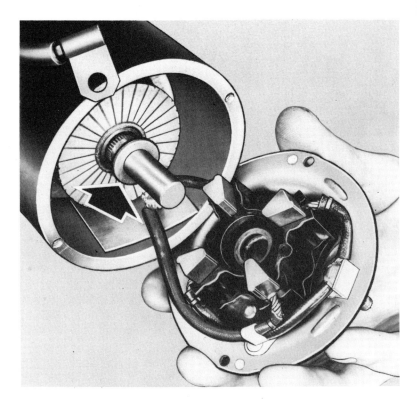

268 Starter motors have four brushes. This one has a face-type commutator and the brushes are housed in plastic holders in the end-plate. This motor doesn't use through bolts – small screws secure the end-plate. The arrow shows a thrust washer – make sure this is re-fitted on re-assembly

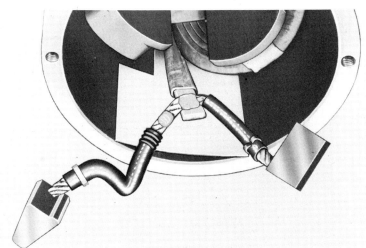

269 When fitting new brushes to starter field windings, leave about ½ in of the old brush cable in position and solder the new brush wire to this

towards the ring gear so that the instant the starter begins to turn, it slips into mesh.

On an inertia drive, the pinion is automatically thrown out of mesh once the ring-gear teeth begin travelling faster than the pinion teeth. On a pre-engaged unit this doesn't happen, so the pinion is carried on a one-way clutch to prevent the engine from driving the starter and over-revving it. The solenoid retracts the pinion when the starter switch is released.

Because it leads a fairly violent life the inertia starter pinion is more likely to give trouble and when something goes wrong you will be faced with the following symptoms when you operate the starter.

Complete silence: Most likely electrical trouble. Did you leave the side-lights on all night and flatten the battery? Check by putting on the headlamps. If they are dim or non-existent, check the battery connections and the connections in the heavy duty cable between battery and solenoid, and solenoid and starter and the earth braid between the engine and chassis. If all is well check the battery with a hydrometer.

If the hydrometer shows the battery is fully charged, the starter solenoid may be faulty, or the starter mounting bolts may be loose, providing a poor earth return. If the bolts are tight, check the solenoid – some have a manual button; give this a push to close the contacts inside. If there is no button, remove the rubber covers on the terminals and bridge them with a spanner or screwdriver – sparks here indicate the battery is working but the solenoid isn't. With a helper to operate the choke and accelerator, you should be able to start the car between you by bridging out a faulty solenoid.

Pinion engages then silence: Most likely the starter motor has worked loose and the pinion teeth have climbed up the tips of the ring-gear teeth and jammed against the casting of the bell-housing. In this state the engine seems to have seized up and push starting often results in the car coming to a shuddering halt when the clutch is released. The cure is to remove the cap from the centre of the starter motor end plate and turn the squared end of the armature to unwind the inertia pinion from the ring gear. Check the starter motor mounting bolts.

Starter turns – does not engage: Assuming the battery and connections are sound, there are two possibilities: the most optimistic one is that there is a trace of clutch dust on the thread that the pinion slides on and this is causing it to stick. Remove the starter motor, clean the thread with paraffin and refit the starter. Do not oil the pinion as the oil will attract more clutch dust.

The pessimistic possibility is that the ring gear teeth have worn away. A four-stroke engine tends to stop in the same positions and this means that on four-cylinder cars two sections of the ring gear – three on a six-cylinder engine – get all the hammering from the pinion. Sometimes fitting a new pinion (it will have worn teeth, as well) effects a temporary cure, but the long term answer is to remove the flywheel, chop off the old ring gear and have a new one fitted. This involves heat treatment, isn't an easy job and is best left to the experts.

Pre-engaged starters avoid most of this drama, but they can be a bit finnicky if they are incorrectly adjusted. To adjust the average 12v starter, the solenoid is connected to a 6v supply and

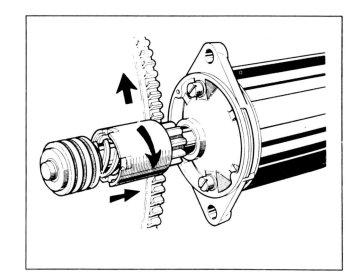

270a The action of the inertia pinion: shaft rotation causes the pinion to slide along the thread and into engagement with the ring-gear teeth

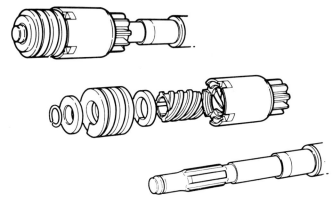

270b The pinion assembly is held by a small circular clip. Take out the clip and the complete assembly slides off the shaft

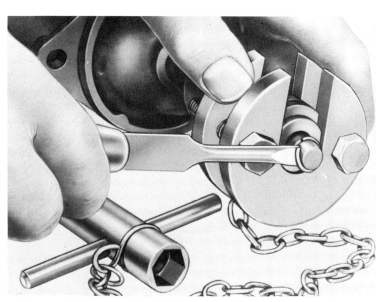

271 To get the clip off, the large buffer spring at the end must be squeezed up. This tool is built for the job. After fitting a new pinion assembly, compress the spring again to re-fit the clip

the other battery terminal joined to the starter casing. The lower-than-standard voltage from this circuit means the solenoid holds the pinion nicely in its running position but the motor does not turn and you can measure the gap shown with a feeler gauge.

Unfortunately, a lot of people do not have access to 6v batteries and try to do the same job with the 12v one. This makes the action of the solenoid much more violent and the clearance cannot be accurately measured. With the wrong clearance, all sorts of things go wrong – the pinion begins turning too early or the pinion gets fully engaged and the motor will not turn. Since different motors have different clearances, pre-engaged starter adjustment is best left to the professionals.

Distributor overhaul

The illustrations show the overhaul of the popular Lucas 25D distributor. Not all distributors are exactly the same, but there is enough similarity among the majority of them for you to use it as a guide.

As mentioned in the engine adjustments chapter, the test of a worn-out distributor is to see whether there is a lot of sideways play in the shaft. If the play is only just perceptible, the distributor can be successfully overhauled. A lot of sideways play in the shaft indicates the bearings are worn and these cannot easily be replaced, so in these instances it is better to fit a reconditioned distributor.

Before taking the distributor off an engine you must take steps to ensure it will be re-fitted in exactly the same position. Mark the distributor body and the adjacent engine casting and also note the position of the rotor arm in relation to the edge of the distributor body. When the unit is refitted, both the body and rotor arm must be in their original positions – this is particularly important on distributors which have a gear instead of an offset dog drive at the base of the shaft – on these the skewing of the gear teeth will mean the rotor turns as the distributor is pushed into position, so turn it back about 30 degrees before inserting the distributor to allow for this.

Control boxes

Cars with a DC dynamo have a control box which regulates the flow of charging current to the battery. Its two main functions are to limit dynamo output so it doesn't overload itself and burn out, and to break the circuit between the battery and the dynamo when the engine stops in order to prevent the battery discharging itself through the dynamo.

Over-charging causes the battery electrolyte to bubble and fizz out of the ventilation holes. The battery needs frequent topping-up and in severe instances may become quite hot. When this happens, the dynamo will be on the point of burning-out. Under-charging has the opposite effect – the battery gradually goes flat.

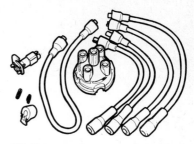

272 These are the new parts required for a Lucas distributor overhaul – a new cam, new springs, a rotor, HT cables and cap

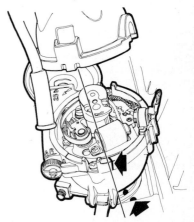

273 Before disturbing the distributor on the engine, number the HT cables, mark the body in relation to the engine casting and the position of the rotor in relation to the distributor body

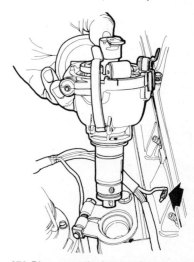

274 Disconnect the low tension wire (arrowed) loosen the distributor clamp and lift the unit out

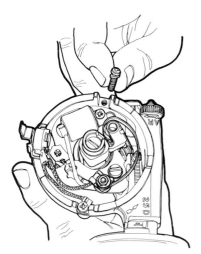

275 Two small screws hold the edge of the contact breaker base plate. Take them out (above)

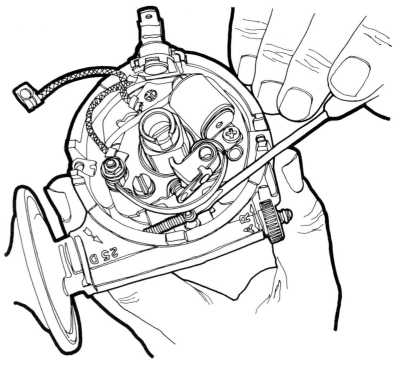

276 Unhook the spring connecting the plate to the vacuum advance diaphragm (right) ;

277 Lift out the base plate complete with the contact breakers and the distributor LT terminal (below right)

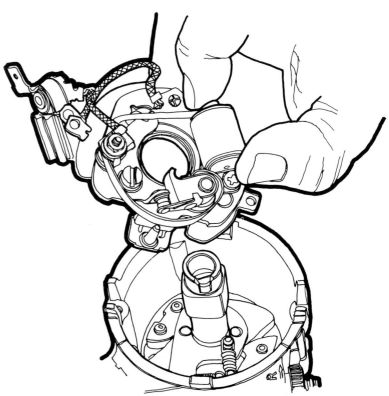

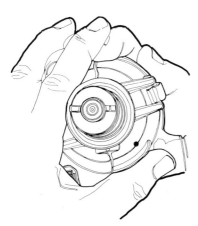

278 Before going any further, note the position of the offset driving dog at the bottom of the distributor shaft

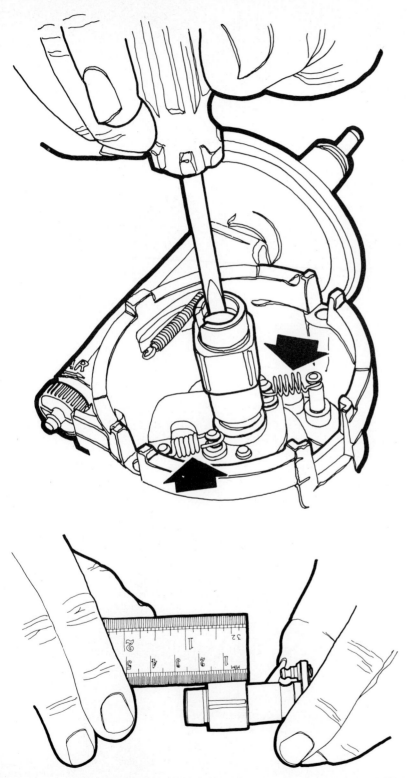

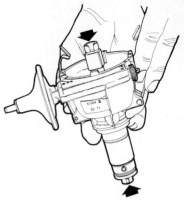

279 Identify with paint if necessary the side of the dog which aligns with the rotor cut-out above the cam (above)

280 Undo the centre screw to release the cam, lever the advance springs (arrowed) off their posts (left)

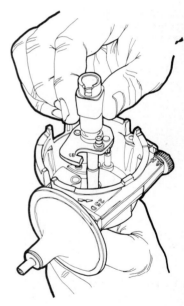

281 Lift out the cam

282 Wear in the cam lobes will give uneven contact breaker gaps – check with a straight-edge

283 Old cams tend to wear where the driving pins engage with the centrifugal advance weights. This affects a car's acceleration.

284 Upend the distributor to shake out the advance weights, then clean and oil the action plate (right)

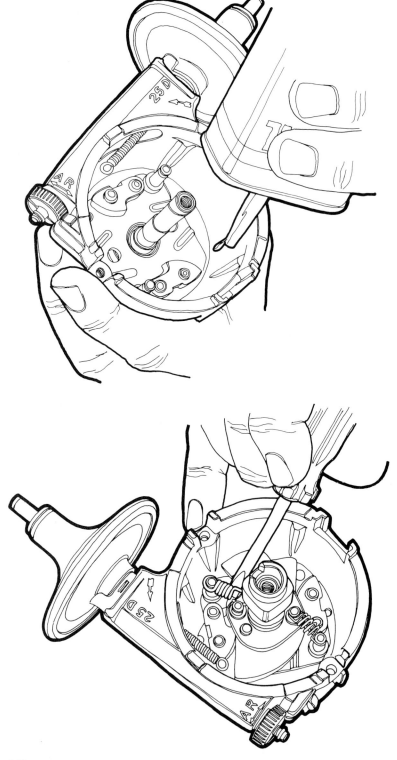

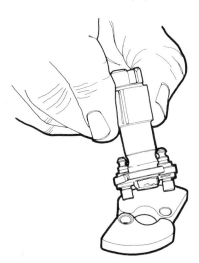

285 This is how the new cam engages with the advance weights. Put the weights on the action plate and fit the cam into them. Make sure the rotor cut-out aligns with the driving dog as in fig 279

286 With the cam engaged in the weights, fit new springs, taking care not to over-stretch them. One spring is usually intentionally loose. They can be fitted to either pair of posts

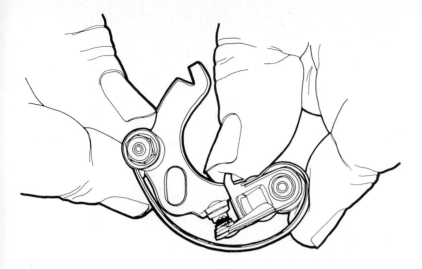

287 Clean new contact breaker points with a petrol moistened cloth before fitting – the contacts are coated in preservative which will burn them if it is left on

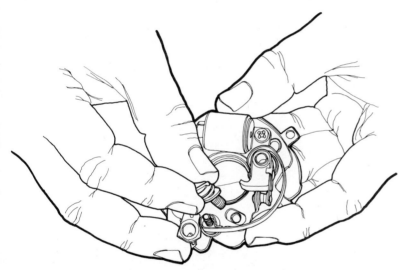

288 Fit the new contacts to the contact-breaker base plate

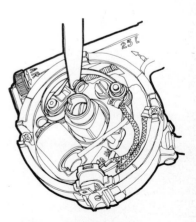

289 Refit the baseplate to the distributor (don't forget the earth wire under one fixing screw) connect-up the vacuum advance spring (see fig 276) and adjust the points gap

Of the two, over-charging is unquestionably due to a control box mal-function. Regrettably without an accurate moving coil voltmeter (expensive) and ammeter and the appropriate electrical manual, you can't check and adjust the control box yourself – have an auto electrician check it for you.

Under-charging may or may not be the fault of the control box. Before calling in the professionals, check the fan belt tension, dynamo and alternator connections, brushes and battery connections.

Wiring

Unfortunately for us laymen, the wiring diagram which your handbook should contain will bear little or no resemblance to the wires on the car. Because he has not the space to lay out all the cables

141

290 The ready-made HT cables are plugged into the new distributor cap using the old one as a guide

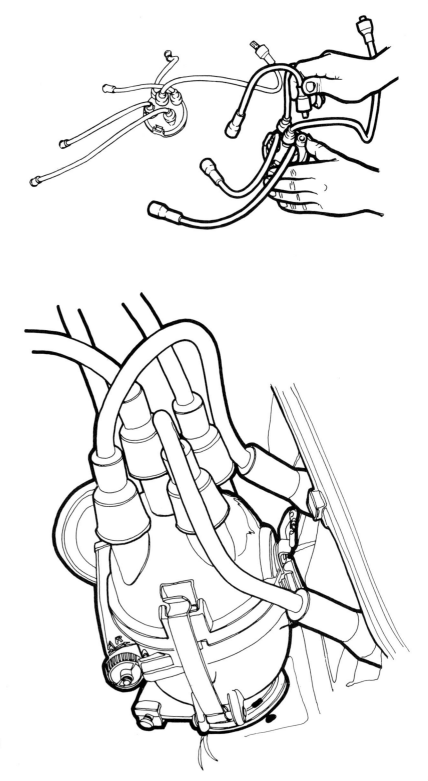

291 Refit the distributor, re-aligning the rotor and body with their respective marks – don't forget to add the new rotor before putting on the new cap. Check the ignition timing

in nice geometric patterns like the diagram shows, the car manufacturer bunches them together in a harness and tucks them out of the way as much as possible.

Happily, the cables are different colours and provided you know the colour code, individual circuits can be traced reasonably easily. The code in the table is the one used by the majority of British car makers.

WIRING COLOURS

A standard cable colour coding is used on most British-built cars, and the following are cables you are likely to find in the wiring harness:

Brown or red	Main feeds (battery to alternator; control box 'B' terminal, etc).
Blue	Headlamp main feed to dip switch.
White	Ignition coil feed; ignition fuse feed.
Purple	Direct accessory fused supply (interior light, horn, boot lamp, etc).
Green	Ignition-controlled accessory fused supply (gauges, stop lamp switch, wipers, etc).
Black	Earth.
Grey	Alternative coding for accessories.
Brown/white or red/white	Looped or parallel main feeds (control box to lighting and ignition switches, etc).
Red/green	Pilot and tail lamp feeds.
Red/yellow	Auxiliary lamps.
Green/brown	Supply, flasher switch to canister.
Green/blue	Engine temperature sensor to gauge.
Green/red	Supply, near-side flashers.
Green/white	Supply, off-side flashers.
Green/yellow	Supply, heater switch to heater motor.
Lt green/purple	Supply, indicator warning light.
Lt green/brown	Supply, indicator switch.
White/green	Ignition-controlled accessories, unfused.
Purple/white	Interior lamp return to courtesy switch.
Black/blue	Supply, heater switch to heater motor, two-speed versions.
Blue/white	Headlamp main beam.
Blue/red	Headlamp dipped beam.

If you are unsure about the wiring colours on any particular car (and they are not *all* the same) check with the wiring diagram for the model. This will always include a reference to colours, or give a separate colour code.

Fuses

When an electrical fault develops there are two ways you will know. Either the component at the end of the circuit will not work, or a fuse will blow.

A fuse is a deliberate weak link in an electrical circuit. In the event of the circuit being over-loaded the fuse wire or metal strip becomes red-hot and melts, breaking the circuit before any serious damage can be done.

Some cars have just two fuses, others have as many as 14 or more. Regardless of the number, when a fuse blows, it is important to establish the cause of the trouble before fitting a new one – otherwise that will blow again as soon as the circuit is switched on.

Fuse failure is caused by a short-circuit. The sort of thing that happens is that you omit to disconnect the battery when fitting your new radio and while you are groping under the dashboard a spanner touches the live feed to the ignition switch, there is a small spark and the fuse blows.

A fuse will also blow if engine vibration has caused the insulation round a live cable to rub off where it passes through the bodywork, and the wire touches the body metal. Similarly a live lead which has become disconnected and swings against part of the bodywork can cause a momentary short-circuit and blow a fuse. If we are honest, we will realise the last two are rarely the fault of the car manufacturer – usually wires get chafed or disconnected after someone has been tinkering with the car.

Once a fuse has blown you need to identify the faulty circuit. On cars with one fuse per circuit this is easy, but where a single fuse protects perhaps the fuel pump, direction indicators, heater blower, windscreen wipers and stop-lamps circuits, a blown fuse causes all these to fail simultaneously.

Often a little back-tracking will indicate the cause. If the fuse fails, say, when the direction indicators were used, fit a new fuse and use hand signals to get you home until you can check the direction indicator circuit.

If the circuits failed for no apparent reason and the fuse seems sound, clean the fuse contacts and those in the fuse box with fine glass-paper. Sometimes fuse contacts oxidise and give a poor connection.

The worst fault to trace is the intermittent one where a fuse may blow for no apparent reason after a week or so when everything operated perfectly. If all else fails, the only real way to find the cause is to fuse every circuit individually using line fuses. This sounds easy until you actually come to do it. Here is what is involved:

292 A line fuse and holder

First find the feed wire to the fuse box. This is the connection that's live when the fuse has been removed. Check it using a test lamp. Disconnect the battery, disconnect this live feed and fit a screw-on cable connector to the end — the sort do-it-yourself shops sell for household wiring. If there are four circuits to be tested, insert four short cables into the other end of the connector. We now have a feed wire with four branches.

Connect each branch to one side of a line fuse. Insert a fuse of the appropriate rating (see fuse ratings later on) and connect one of the four wires from the output side of the old fuse to the output end of each line fuse. The first fuse to blow will identify the faulty circuit.

Fuse ratings

It is important that the fuse you use to protect a circuit is of the right value. If it is too weak it will blow repeatedly, while if it is too heavy, damage may be caused before it blows.

When a circuit is to be fused, first find out the wattage of the component it feeds, divide this figure by the battery voltage and you have the fuse rating in amps. So in a 12v circuit a 60W lamp needs a fuse which will accept $\frac{60}{12} = 5$ amps.

All would be well if we could fit a 5 amp fuse and forget it, but some fuses are continuously rated – which means that one marked 5 amps will pass 5 amps but will blow when the current reaches 10 amps – whereas others are marked with the blow-out rating and in this case, fitting a 5 amp one would cause it to blow as soon as our lamp was switched on.

The confusion is clearing because Joseph Lucas, who make most of the blow-out rated fuses, are slowly switching to continuously rated ones. If you are using a blow-out rated fuse, fit one of double the capacity of the component.

Broken circuits

If a component does not work and the fuse has not blown you will obviously want to know whether it is the circuit or the component that is at fault. Where you can, remove a component, connect its live feed direct to the live battery terminal and earth the body of the component to the battery terminal connected to the bodyshell. If it does not work when connected up like this, it is faulty.

Quite often it is not convenient to bring a suspect component to the battery for testing.

Here you need one of those test lamps which looks like a screwdriver but instead of a blade has a sharp point at the end, a test bulb in the handle, and a length of cable coming from the top of the handle with a crocodile clip on the end.

Suppose the heater blower motor does not work. First use the car's wiring diagram to identify the colour of the live feed to the motor. You must now locate it under the dashboard and trace it back to the switch. If necessary, disconnect the switch from the facia and pull it out (see switches).

Clip the cable of the test lamp to a good earth point such as a bright bolt or screw head, turn on the ignition and put the probe on the input terminal of the switch. The tester should light. If it does not, the feed to the switch – from the ignition-controlled fuse – has a break in it. If the tester lights, move the probe to the switch output terminal and turn on the switch. If there is no light, the switch is faulty. If it lights up, the fault is further on.

The cable from the switch to the motor can be checked by inserting the pointed probe through the insulation into the wires inside. The bulb will light up if there is current in it.

If the feed cable is live right up to the heater motor, look to see if the motor has an earth cable. This can be tested for continuity if you stick a pin through the insulation to contact the wires inside and connect the crocodile clip from the tester to the pin. Stick the tester's probe into the live feed, and if the earth wire is making a sound earth as it should, the test lamp will light. At this stage, if the motor still does not work, it is the motor that is faulty.

293 Checking a circuit for continuity using a test lamp fitted with a probe (see text)

Switches

A switch is a means of joining up and breaking a circuit. The simplest ones have two cables going into them – we will call them the input cable and the output cable. You can test this sort of switch with a circuit tester or even more simply by disconnecting the two wires and joining them together. If everything works when this is done, but does not work when the switch is used, the switch is faulty.

The same principle applies to more complex switches, although on these the wiring diagrams should be consulted so the appropriate wires can be identified before joining them together. A typical example is the make-and-break switch that operates the flashing direction indicators. This is sealed in a canister and is frequently blamed for flasher irregularities, sometimes unfairly. It is tested quite simply.

First note the colour and position of the wires at the back of the canister, then disconnect them and join them together using a paper-clip to link the connectors or the ends of the cables. Turn on the ignition and select the offside flashing indicators using the column-mounted switch. The offside indicators and the pilot bulb should light up and stay lit. The same should happen when the nearside indicators are selected. If every bulb lights up, any irregularities *are* caused by the switch. But if a bulb fails to light it is most likely the bulb which has blown or its earth connection is poor.

It is not always obvious how some dashboard switches come out. The easiest to understand are tumbler switches which are secured by a screwed-on nut. Undo the nut and the switch tumbler can be pushed out through the hole in the facia. Switches with knobs on are also commonly held by a nut, but you cannot pull the switch through the hole in the facia until the knob is taken off. It is invariably located by a spring-loaded transverse pin. Look underneath and you will most likely see the pin head – press it inwards with a wire nail and the knob will pull off. Rocker switches are normally held by clips on the side of the switch body. These can be squeezed together by reaching behind the facia and the switch pulled out of its mounting hole towards the steering wheel.

The chassis earth-return system has the advantage of halving the number of cables required in a car's wiring harness. But it has disadvantages too.

When a car begins to go rusty, the corrosion can break the earth return and the component will not work. This happens quite often with lamps on older cars where the lamp body traps mud and dirt which corrodes the bodywork away. The lamp relies on the fixing screws holding its shell to the bodywork as an earth return. If this bodywork rots, the light goes out.

To cure it, fit some extra fixing screws into sound metal at another point on the lamp shell, or in severe instances, run a separate earth wire from the lamp shell to a nearby piece of sound body metal.

Chapter eleven
Minor body repairs

Sooner or later almost every car picks up the odd dent and patch of rust. If the rust is ignored, it will get worse. A dent does not get any worse, but it will not go away either. This chapter shows how to fix them.

Before we get down to detail, it is important that the methods shown here are not used on bodywork which is load-bearing. As a rule-of-thumb, external bodywork such as front wings, rear wings, the bonnet, boot and doors are not load-bearing, but certain sections of the floor and engine bay which support the suspension, engine, transmission and the box-sections which stiffen the bodyshell are. If you are in doubt consult a body repairer.

Paint damage

The most trivial of all body damage (although it may not seem so at the time) is scratched paint. If you are lucky (!) the scratch will not penetrate as deeply as the primer under the top coat and in these instances all you need is a soft cloth and a tin of cutting compound. Rubbing the scratch with the compound will smooth off the sharp edges and put a gloss on the damaged surface until it is virtually invisible. Scratches which have uncovered the primer or bare metal should be treated as detailed in Chapter 13.

Rust patches

The most likely place for rust to start is in the front wings. If the headlamps are in the wing, dirt thrown forward by the road wheel packs into the pocket between the headlamp shell and the top corner of the wing. At the back, dirt thrown rearwards collects in the top rear corner. In time, the salty solution which is sprayed on the winter roads to melt ice is absorbed by the dirt and this corrodes the metal from the inside outwards.

The first sign of trouble is the appearance of small blisters on the paint surface. Prick one of these with a pin and in its early stages, it will be full of water. At a later stage the pin will go straight through the bodyshell.

To repair the damage you need a body repair kit which contains resin, hardener, glass mat and a tin of plastic body filler. You also need something to support the glass-fibre repair while it is still wet, and most kits include some perforated zinc or expanded aluminium mesh for this purpose. Alternatively, good ironmongers sell it. Choose a dry warm place when carrying out the repair – resin and plastic filler do not cure well in a damp atmosphere.

The job can be split into three stages:
1 Remove the corroded metal.
2 Bridge the gap with glass fibre.
3 Smooth the surface.

Removing rusty metal

First clear the decks. If the rusty area is near a headlamp, for instance, take out the headlamp assembly so you can see exactly what you are doing. Wire brush away the accumulated dirt from under the area on which you are working.

Now comes the grim bit. Put a rotary wire brush or coarse abrasive disc in a power drill and start it spinning in the centre of the damage. As it scratches the paint off you will see the extent of the corrosion – usually the brush gouges out a much bigger hole than you had anticipated. If power tools are not available, use coarse emery cloth for this job.

Once the really soft metal has been removed, use tin snips to enlarge the hole until there is sound metal at the edge. Rub the edge with coarse emery cloth to remove the paint and roughen the bare metal underneath, so there is 1 in. of clean metal round the outside, then tap the edge inwards about $\frac{1}{4}$ in using the ball end of an engineer's hammer.

Bridging the gap

To give the repair strength, resin-bonded glass mat is used to fill the hole. This is extremely soggy when the resin is wet, so it needs some support and this is provided by filling the hole with perforated zinc or expanded metal.

The method you use depends on whether or not you can get behind the damaged panel. If you can, cut the mesh to shape and bend it if necessary to the correct contour. Now mix up a small quantity of plastic filler paste, using plenty of hardener so that it sets quickly. Press the mesh against the turned-down edge of the hole from behind, and knife on filler from the outside, so you 'tack' the mesh to the edge of the hole. On a warm day this will begin to stiffen up in a minute or so and you will be able to let go.

If you cannot get behind the panel, hook a piece of soft wire through the middle of the mesh, thread the mesh through the hole, and while you hold it with the wire, bend it to shape. Keeping the mesh firmly against the hole with the wire, apply the filler to the edge. Once the filler has set, unhook the wire.

You will now have a depression in the panel some $\frac{1}{4}$ in below the surface with a mesh floor. The next stage is to cover it with glass fibre. Mix the resin and hardener together and cut two patches of glass mat so they overlap the edge of the mesh by $\frac{1}{4}$ in. Fix one to the mesh with plenty of resin dabbed on with a paint brush. Try to avoid surplus resin running down the paintwork – it is difficult to get off once it has hardened, although it can be wiped off using a rag soaked in meths if it is attacked immediately. Resin the second patch on top of the first.

If all has gone well, when the resin has cured, you should have a depression in the panel about $\frac{1}{8}$ in deep with a glass-fibre floor. Check that the glass mat doesn't protrude above the contour of the panel. If any does, smooth it down with the sanding disc or emery.

149

Smoothing the surface

We now need some more plastic filler. Mix it with hardener and smooth it on with a flexible spreader so it is slightly proud of the surrounding bodywork.

When it has hardened, roughly shape it to the body contour using either coarse (80 grit) abrasive paper wrapped round a wood block, or an open-toothed file such as a Surform. Apply another thin layer of filler to smooth out any irregularities shown up by the rough-finishing. When this has hardened, smooth it with a finer grade of wet-or-dry paper – something around 180 to 220 grade is ideal – and use this paper wet, also wrapped round a wood block.

As the repair begins to smooth out you will notice a number of pin-holes. These are caused by air-bubbles in the filler. To get rid of them, dry the area and smear on a thin wafer of fresh filler. When this has hardened, finish the smoothing-down with progressively finer grades of abrasive paper used wet. The sort of progression to aim for is from 180 or 220 then to 340 and finishing with something very fine – around 400 or 500 grade.

When you have reached the stage when your hand ·cannot detect any difference between the contour of the repair and the contour of the surrounding metalwork, the next step is to paint it – see Chapter 13.

Repairs from the inside

In theory, if you can get behind the damaged panel, it is better to block the hole with polythene sheet taped over it and backed with cardboard, and then stick on two laminations of glass mat from the inside.

Unfortunately I have always found that rust holes rarely appear where it is convenient to use this method. But on the off-chance you find one, here is what to do.

Remove the damaged metal until you have an edge of sound bodywork. On the inside, clean a strip $1\frac{1}{2}$ in wide all round the edge down to the bare metal (quite a job if the car has a coat of underbody sealer) and rough up the exposed metal with a sanding disc or coarse emery.

Cut a sheet of polythene $\frac{1}{2}$ in larger all round than the hole and stick it on the outside with adhesive tape. Avoid wrinkling it and make sure all the edges are taped so that resin will not leak through and run down the paintwork. Cut a sheet of carton cardboard to roughly the same size as the polythene and tape this over the top to form a backing for the polythene.

Cut a patch of glass fibre mat so that it overlaps the hole by at least 1 in all round, and from the inside coat the edge of the hole and the polythene with resin and add the patch, gently stippling on more resin with a paint brush (do not press too hard or you will deform the cardboard). Add another layer of glass mat in the same way.

When the resin has cured, peel off the cardboard and then the

294 If you can get behind a dent hammer it out until it is just below the level of the surrounding bodywork

polythene. With luck, the patch will conform to the body contour very closely and only a small skin of filler will be needed to blend it with the rest of the bodywork.

Surface Rust

Where the corrosion has not actually eaten a hole through the metal, you can cut out the glass fibre process.

First use the rotary wire brush to scratch off the surface rust and try to remove what is left using emery cloth. Ideally you should remove all rust back to bare metal, although in practice it is extremely difficult to get rid of all traces.

Treat the bare metal <u>with</u> a rust-proofing fluid. Some of these contain hydrochloric acid and must be washed off a few minutes after application – follow the directions on the container. Dry the area thoroughly after washing down.

The next step is to build up any depressions in the metal. If the depressions are shallow you can use bare metal stopper – a putty-like version of cellulose primer – which is applied using a knife. Alternatively, plastic body filler can be used. Build up the damaged area so it is only fractionally proud of the body contour, and when it has hardened (leave stopper at least 24 hours) rub down with about 340 grade wet or dry paper on a wooden block used wet. Blend in with the surrounding panels with 400 grade before painting.

Dents

Small dents are best filled with plastic filler, but to cut down the amount of filler required, the dent should be made as shallow as possible.

There are two separate ways of doing this depending on how accessible the dent is.

If you can get behind it, tapping the edges of the dent with a rubber-headed mallet will push it out. Work from the outside inwards as the dent straightens out, but don't try to push it out entirely – leave a shallow depression for the filler.

If you cannot get behind a dent, it can be drawn out from the outside. Drill a small hole in the centre and insert a self-tapping screw. Now use a claw hammer to pull out the dent. Rest the hammer-head on a small wood block to prevent body damage as you lever the screw outwards.

Once the worst of the dent has been eased out, use a grinding disc on a power drill or coarse emery cloth to rub the paint down to the bare metal in the dented area and for about 1 inch round the outside edge. Use a sharp implement like the tang of a file to score a number of lines in the dented section – this helps the filler to grip well. Now just load on the filler as described earlier for rust repairs. Smooth it off and paint (see Chapter 13).

295 With the dent made as shallow as possible, grind the paint off until bare metal is exposed, then score the metal with the tang of a file to give a key for the filler

296 Mix plastic filler and hardener, following the instructions exactly. Load it into the dented area so it is proud of the surrounding bodywork. Work reasonably quickly. When it has cured smooth the filler to the exact contour of the body with a file, then progressively finer grades of abrasive paper used wet. Start with 180–220 grade, progress to 320–340 grade and finish with the fine stuff – around 400–500 grade

Chapter twelve
Bigger bodywork jobs

If you have an eight-year-old car with a rotting front wing it is unlikely you will want to pay a fancy price for it to have a professional body repairer fit a new one.

This line of thought has led to a big increase in the number of replacement body panels available for the more corrosion-prone popular cars. You can also buy what is loosely termed home welding equipment to fix on the new metal panels. If you do not like the idea of metalwork, as an alternative, glass fibre panels are available for many cars and these can be fitted using just a power drill and pop-rivets.

Regrettably cars do not only rust away on the outside. Corrosion also attacks load-bearing box sections and suspension mountings. All load-bearing structures should be professionally welded.

Welding

True welding involves heating two pieces of metal until they melt and fuse together. In practice it is usual to melt in a little extra metal from a filler rod to bridge any gaps.

It sounds straight-forward, and if you are welding together say, two lengths of angle-iron, it is. But car body metal is painfully thin – less than a millimetre thick on average – and if you apply too much heat to it you will burn a hole right through.

Body repairers use either oxy-acetylene gas welding equipment or a carbon-dioxide welding process to join panels. Both are ideal for welding thin metal, but both are highly priced for occasional home use.

Most cheaper home equipment is electrical, either powered by the mains or car batteries. A few butane or propane gas torches are available, but these cannot produce enough concentrated heat to weld body metal, although they can be used to braze together small components off the car.

Battery-powered welders

There are two types – carbon-contact torches, and a solenoid-operated arc welder.

A carbon-contact torch needs just a 12v car battery. One terminal on the battery is connected, using heavy-gauge cable and crocodile clips to the metal to be welded. The other terminal is connected by cable to a carbon holder. A carbon rod is clamped in the holder and when touched to the metal the resulting short circuit produces intense heat at the carbon tip. As with all welding operations it is essential to wear goggles or a mask to prevent eye damage.

The temperature at the carbon tip can be regulated by altering the distance between the clamp on the holder and the business end of the carbon rod. A short carbon will produce a higher temperature than a long one. Once the contact has been made, the carbon is held lightly on the metal until it reaches the desired

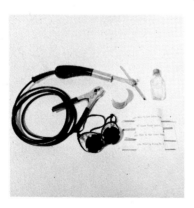

297 A battery-operated carbon contact brazing set

152

temperature and then is moved along in a series of small circles while the filler rod is fed into the joint.

To call this a home welder is really a mis-nomer. It *will* weld if the carbon is held in position long enough, but for non-load-bearing panels, brazing – in which brass filler rod is fed into a mild steel joint which has been made white hot – is strong enough. Because brazing does not need so much heat, it is easier on the battery and is better for amateurs because there is less chance of burning holes in the bodywork.

The limitation of carbon-contact brazing is the battery. If you do not mind tackling small areas at a time, it is possible to spot-braze a new wing or sill into place with this process, but it is unlikely you will finish the job without having to recharge the battery two or three times. In its favour a battery-operated carbon-contact set is the cheapest of all home 'welding' gear.

More expensive than a carbon-contact set, but cheaper than the cheapest mains welders is a solenoid arc welder now sold by Rawlplug and called the Welder's Mate. It requires at least two 12v batteries and uses ordinary arc-welding electrodes to make metal-to-metal joints.

Arc welding uses the same electrical hook-up as for carbon-contact work – one lead is connected to the metal being welded and the other goes to the electrode. But unlike carbon-contact, the electrode is also the filler rod. When it touches the metal it forms an arc and the electrode wire begins burning away and deposits itself on the metal being joined. To maintain the arc, the electrode tip is held slightly above the surface of the metal.

Normally arc-welding is too fierce a process for car body repairs. A mains-powered unit will blast a hole straight through as soon as the arc is made. The Welder's Mate unit somehow manages to reduce the ferocity of the arc and allows it to weld thinner metal. It comes with copious operating instructions and providing you read these, use two batteries in good condition and weld clean metal, it does work.

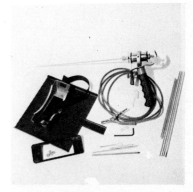

298a This battery-powered arc welder has a solenoid in the holder which helps maintain the arc

298b The connections for the battery-powered arc welder – it's essential to use two 12v batteries

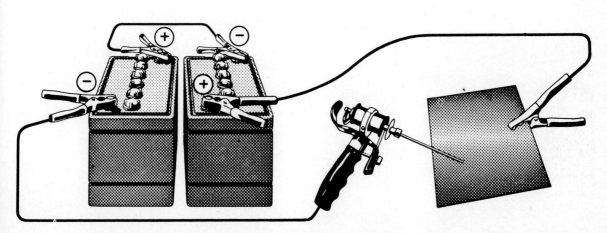

153

The limitation of the unit is the gradual decline in power of the batteries. As the power reduces, it becomes more difficult to strike an arc. With arc welding the arc is struck rather like striking a match, but if battery voltage is low, the electrode sticks to the work and glows red-hot throughout its length. All you can do when this happens is to wrench the electrode off and try again. If you are nearing the end of a job when the batteries begin to fail, cutting the electrode in half makes it easier to strike an arc – in fact I find it best always to work with half-length electrodes when using this unit.

Mains welders: A twin carbon torch

Although most mains arc welding equipment is too powerful for car body metal, an arc welding transformer can be used to power a twin carbon torch. A holder grips two copper-coated carbon rods and these can be adjusted so the tips meet at 45 degree angle. Two cables come from the torch and one is connected to the 'work' terminal on the transformer (the one normally connected to the metal being welded) while the other goes to the output terminal.

Once it is connected, touching the carbons together produces a brilliant arc of the sort produced by an arc lamp. Chemicals in the carbon rod produce a flame at the arc and this is used to heat the metal in the same way as a gas torch. The size of the flame can be adjusted within limits using a lever or slide on the handle to alter the gap between the carbon tips; a wide gap gives a large soft flame, a small gap, a more compact one. The arc emits a buzzing sound and I have found that the hottest flame coincides with maximum noise.

On paper the twin-carbon torch seems to offer the electrical equivalent of the oxy-acetylene torch. In practice it is not so versatile because there is little control over the temperature of the flame and the two carbons which have a large overhang towards the end of the holder make it rather cumbersome in tight corners.

Some cheaper twin carbon torch outfits use small air-cooled mains transformers which are not continuously rated. With these as the transformer heats up its efficiency drops and the arc at the torch gets smaller and more difficult to maintain. After about 10–15 minutes the torch will not operate properly and the transformer must be allowed to cool down – which can take an hour on a warm day. If you can stand this sort of frustration, they do a good job while they are working, although it is easier on the temper to pay a higher price and get either a fan-cooled or oil-cooled transformer.

Mains carbon-contact

Some arc welding transformers are built with an extra winding in them so they can be used with a carbon contact holder. With mains power behind them, these outfits can be used for true welding if you wish, but since we are only dealing with non-

299 Twin-carbon torch outfit with a small air-cooled transformer

300 This corrosion is typical of what you find on a car more than 6 years old

154

load-bearing panels, brazing will do and is quicker. It also means the carbons last a little longer. Carbon contact brazing cannot be performed from the ordinary terminals of the arc welder.

Welding on a new panel

First we have to get the old panel off. Where panels are not bolted on, car manufacturers spot-weld them. The distance between spot-welds varies depending on the strength required from the joint.

The tidiest way of removing the unwanted panel is to drill out the spot welds with a $\frac{1}{4}$ in carbon steel drill. Then, in theory the old metal is lifted off, the flange cleaned up with a coarse grinding disc and a new one welded on.

Alas it is rarely this easy. Spot-welds are very hard and you will need a lot of time and a fair number of new drill bits to do this. In addition, most old panels tend to be a bit rusty and weak, so it is quicker to use a sharp cold chisel and a 4 lb club hammer to chop the old panel away from the flange.

Once the panel is free, you are quite likely to find some of the metal underneath has rusted. If the rusting is severe and affects a load-bearing panel, have a professional put it right. If it is not load-bearing, you can patch it with some mild steel sheet.

Sheet mild steel is not the sort of item you can buy over-the-counter from your friendly ironmonger. Most body repairers have a little and may sell you some although they are not retailers and you cannot blame them if they say they have none to spare. The next best thing to a new piece of mild steel is a secondhand piece and this can be obtained from a breaker's yard. Most car bonnets are fairly flat and if you can find an unrusted one with a crunch at one end you should get it for scrap price. It is worth noting that a breaker's yard is the place to get panels for old cars where the makers have stopped producing spares.

Once you have got the mild steel, cut the rust away until you reach a sound metal, and clean the edge to bright metal with emery. Now cut the mild steel with tin-snips until it overlaps the hole by $\frac{1}{2}$ in all round. Drill a series of $\frac{1}{8}$ in holes round the edge and use pop rivets or self-tapping screws to temporarily fix the patch. If necessary remove a $\frac{1}{2}$ in strip of paint from the edge down to bare metal. It can now be tack-welded or brazed in place.

Regardless of the type of equipment you are using, if you have not tried brazing or welding before you will find the next stage quite difficult. You must wear goggles or a mask to be able to look into the arc. But until the arc has been struck, you will not be able to see a thing through the goggles. The best compromise is to place the electrode or carbon very near the spot before pulling the mask or goggles over your eyes. With luck, when you strike the arc or bring the carbon into contact, you will be very near the place you want to be.

Metal distorts when it is heated, so work as near to each self-tapping screw or pop rivet as you can. Put a ring of tacks

301 A club hammer and cold chisel make short work of removing the corroded metal

302 Under the rear apron, the vertical stiffening panel was corroded all along its lower edge

303 The ragged section was cut away with snips and new metal was cut to shape and pop-riveted on in its place

155

304 Using a twin-carbon torch, the new metal is spot-brazed to the remaining sound metal of the stiffening panel

305 The new apron is held on the fixing flanges by grips and self-tapping screws while the edges are spot-brazed

306 A glass-fibre replacement panel can often be used on a non load-bearing area when the existing metal panel has rusted. First remove the old metal

round the outside, and if further strength is required, put an extra tack in between each one. If the edge of the patch distorts away from the panel it can usually be tapped back with a hammer. In severe instances, drill another hole and screw or rivet it.

When you have finished, you will no doubt be horrified with the result. Few do-it-yourself brazing or welding sets give attractive-looking results in amateur hands, but where out-of-sight patches are concerned, it is the strength, not the appearance that matters. Before the area is closed off give the patch a coat of zinc-rich paint to discourage further corrosion.

The outer panel must be matched accurately with its mounting flanges before any attempt is made to fix it on. How accurately it aligns depends on what sort of a job you made of getting the old one off. The cold chisel method usually leaves a strip of the old panel behind. In theory you should chisel this off too, but if the car is old you must weigh up whether removing it will cause more damage – if it will, it is better to leave it on, tidy up the edge and grind any paint and rust off the face with a coarse sanding disc and fit the new panel over the top of it. The extra thickness of metal will, of course, fractionally mis-align the panel, but it is unlikely to be noticeable. On cars with sounder bodywork, remove all traces of the old panel and grind the flange until all dirt is removed.

Fortunately car makers either cover up exposed body flanges with trim strips or tuck them inside so you cannot see them. This means we do not need an immaculate finish, although the end result should not be too ragged otherwise trim strips will not fit over it.

Remembering that metal distorts when it is heated, the first essential is to borrow as many G-clamps or Mole wrenches as you can. Offer up the panel and clamp the edges into position. If you only have one or two clamps, drill holes and secure the panel with self-tapping screws or rivets at 12 in intervals.

We have already seen that the car maker overlaps the metal when he spot-welds it, but it is easier if you can weld or braze together the edges of the metal. Less heat is required to bring the edges to the required temperature and this means the job can be done more quickly, with less distortion and less heat-spread to damage surrounding paintwork. From the strength point of view, edge-joining is not quite so strong as a through-metal spot-weld, but remember we are not dealing with load-bearing panels, and so our only real requirement is that it does not fall off.

There are areas where you cannot get to the edges and through-metal weld is the only way. It helps the less powerful equipment if a $\frac{1}{4}$ in hole is drilled in the upper panel and the edge of this is tacked to the metal underneath.

Once the panel has been clamped in place, tack the corners and the seams at 12 in intervals. When the edges are heated, they tend to spread apart, so work only right alongside a clamp, screw or rivet. Once the panel is tacked in position, you can fill in the spaces with a series of spot-welds. Each time you make one, move the clamp alongside the area being treated to hold the metal tightly together.

Once the join has been completed, the seam will have a knobbly edge. If a trim strip has to cover it, grind off the worst of the lumps before fitting it. On out-of-sight edges, the grinding is optional, although here it is an idea to give the joint a coat of underbody sealer to discourage water seeping in.

Glass fibre panels

If your door sill has just rusted through or you have clouted a tree with the front wing of your Ford Escort, a glass fibre replacement sounds ideal. Glass fibre panels will not rust and if you remove the old panel down to the mounting flanges the plastic panel can be drilled and simply secured with pop rivets instead of using welding gear.

But there are snags. The first one is that a glass fibre panel of reasonable strength is at least $\frac{1}{8}$ in thick whereas body metal is less than 1 mm thick. So depending on how they are fixed some glass fibre replacements will not align very well when matched up to the body flanges. Also, glass fibre is not so rigid as steel, so a plastic replica of what is a perfectly rigid steel panel may flap in the breeze at motorway speeds. This can be overcome in the manufacturing stage by building-in stiffening ribs. In addition, you get what you pay for. Cheap plastic panels will have been made quickly. The surface finish may not be particularly good and there might be pieces missing where air bubbles have formed at sharp corners. If you want to, you can fill these flaws yourself with plastic body filler, but make sure you get a good discount for your trouble.

Sticking on panels

There are occasions when it is not convenient to weld a new panel in place. I recently came across one such instance, when a quarter-panel had to be fixed below the woodwork on a Mini Traveller. Once it has been in place a few years, this wood is difficult to get off without damage, so to avoid it being burnt by brazing or welding, the panel was stuck on with Devcon Plastic Steel. This epoxy adhesive has a putty-like consistency which fills any irregularities between the mating flanges. It is available in a fast-setting form which takes about four minutes to begin curing at 60° F. The slower-setting version (which is cheaper) will require the panel to be clamped in place until it dries.

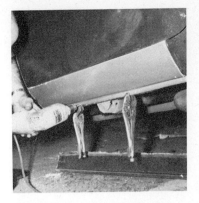

307 Clamp the glass-fibre panel in position and drill a series of fixing holes about 2 in apart

308 Secure the panel with pop-rivets and fill any gaps with plastic body filler before priming and painting

309 Sticking on a Mini Traveller rear corner with epoxy adhesive. Welding here would burn the woodwork

157

Chapter thirteen
Painting

The car's paintwork is one of its most vulnerable areas – stones thrown up by other vehicles can chip it, atmospheric pollution eats it away and it is the first thing to suffer in even the most minor collision.

Perhaps because of its vulnerability, accessory shops sell a vast array of cosmetics to clean, and brighten paintwork. They also sell various first-aid kits for healing the wounds.

You can buy colour-matched paint transfers which stick over a scratch and almost completely disguise it; there are small tins of touch-up paint with a brush under the lid like nail-varnish bottles; aerosol spray paints are intended for respraying slightly larger areas, while if you want to be more ambitious there are electric vibrator spray guns and compressed air spray outfits with which you can spray the complete car.

We will start with the small stuff.

Paint transfers

These are ideal for covering-up small scratches, where the primer under the colour coat has not been broken. If the scratch goes to the bare metal, seal it with a touch of brushed-on primer (even a layer of nail-varnish is better than nothing) before applying the transfer. The paint round the edge of the damage will blend better if it is cleaned with an abrasive compound before applying the transfer. Transfers will stick sufficiently strongly to resist normal washing, but they tend to peel if a rubbing compound is used on them.

Brush-on paint

It is possible to brush-paint a complete car, but despite what the advertisements say, it is extremely difficult to get rid of the brush-marks and the finished job never looks so good as a spray job.

For touching-in small chips a brush is ideal as in theory it can deliver a spot of paint accurately in exactly the right place. In practice paint brushes attached to paint tin lids are rarely of good quality and it is often better to dab the paint on with the end of a clean match stick. If the chipping has broken the primer coat, scrape it down to the bare metal with a penknife blade and re-prime. Applying touch-up paint to a deep chip, will make it look the same colour but when it dries it will still be below the surface of the surrounding paint. If you are fussy about such things, the answer is to buy a small tin of bare metal cellulose stopper – knife a thin layer of this into the chipped section to restore the level, leave it 24 hours to harden, then apply the touch-up using a good quality small brush.

Aerosol spray paints

At first sight these seem like the do-it-yourself answer to all paint problems – they are compact, colour-matched, and apparently easy to use. In theory, if you want to cover a small area you just buy one, if you want to spray the complete car, you buy a lot.

Unfortunately, aerosol cans of paint have their disadvantages, the chief one being that to get the paint through the nozzle with the fairly low pressure that is in the can, the paint has to be thinned considerably.

Thin paint poses a number of problems. For a start it does not cover very well, so there is a tendency to put a bit more on to try and give depth to the colour. Alas as soon as you do this, the build-up of too much thin paint results in it turning into tear-drops and running down the side of the car.

The other disadvantage of thin paint is that it does not shine very much. Again the temptation is to give an extra coat – after all, it looks shiny while it is wet! The result is as above.

There is still another unfortunate side-effect from using aerosols: because there is only a small quantity of paint in each can, most people restrict its use to a small area. No professional paint sprayer would contemplate spotting-in, say a three-inch diameter patch on a front wing with a quick squirt from a spray gun – he would clean off the complete wing, mask off the surrounding areas at the joins and spray the whole wing. The advantage of finishing the edge of the new paint at a natural body join is that any slight colour mis-match does not show. And he is also not bothered by a halo of foggy-looking paint round the edge of the repair.

If you aerosol spray in the middle of a panel you will produce this halo at the edge – it is caused by the paint droplets at the edge partly drying en route to the panel, so when they get there, they are not fluid enough to spread out and join up as the others do.

Happily there are ways round the difficulties posed by aerosol spray paints, but you will need a few extra bits and pieces first.

The materials add up to a sheet or two of fine (about 400–500 grit) waterproof abrasive paper. The best known is the stuff 3M make called Wet-or-dry. In practice it is very rarely used dry, because continually dipping it in a bucket of water prevents the paint clogging it and ensures it removes the paint surface evenly.

If the car has been wax polished regularly, you will need a wax remover or a little engine cleaner to remove the wax film, otherwise the new paint will flake and peel off.

Lastly, get some masking tape. Genuine masking tape is designed so it can be bent round corners reasonably easily and should not drag off the existing paint when you peel it off. It is tempting to think that any old sticky tape will do this job, but believe me, masking tape is the best.

The first rule when spray-painting is to prepare the surface. Remove any wax, then smooth the area to be treated with fine grade wet-or-dry paper used with lots of water. Pay particular attention to the edges of the old paint which should be feathered so they blend smoothly with the bare metal or the edge of a repair.

Ideally the edge of the new paint should be taken to a natural body join. But if the repair is a small one, and the panel is large, this can be inconvenient and expensive so try this.

Lay a sheet of newspaper on the roof of the car. Unroll a length of masking tape and stick it along the edge of the paper so that the tape overlaps the paper and some of it sticks to the roof. Gently peel the paper and tape from the roof and stick it alongside the area to be sprayed, leaving a minimum gap of about 1 inch between the edge of the repair and the edge of the tape. Mask off all four sides of the area in this way, and stick on any extra sheets of paper which may be necessary to protect the existing paintwork from spray drift.

Using a can of primer, shake it for as long as the instructions suggest and test it on the masking paper. Spray the area within the masking tape, starting the spray while it is over the masking paper and moving it across the panel and releasing the button when it is over the paper again – this prevents blobs of paint which sometimes occur when the button is pressed and released, from hitting the panel.

Apply two coats and remove the masking when they are touch-dry. You will now have a panel with a small square section painted in primer. Allow the primer to dry – this may take anything from an hour to 12 hours depending on the paint and the air temperature – and then rub the edge with 400 or 500 grade wet-or-dry paper and plenty of water until it can be felt with the fingers to blend with the surrounding paint.

If necessary the rest of the primer can be rubbed down *very lightly* if there are any 'nibs' on the paint.

The area can now be masked off again, but this time the tape edge is about two inches from the edge of the primer. Cover the surrounding bodywork as before and spray with top-coat. Gloss paint is more likely to form tear-drops and run than primer so apply the coats thinly – the first coat, for instance, should only just hide the primer. Allow each coat to touch-dry before applying the next and build up the coats until the colour matches the rest of the car. Do not worry at this stage if the finish is not very shiny.

Remove the masking tape and leave the paint to harden for about two weeks. At the end of this time, use 500 grade paper and plenty of water to gently feather the edge into the existing paint, then rub the whole area with a mildly abrasive polish – this will give the new paint a shine and blend it with the existing paint.

Vibrator spray guns

These are plugged into a mains electricity supply and force a jet of paint from the nozzle by the action of a vibrator on a small piston rod. Some vibrator guns are seven times more expensive than others and regrettably you get what you pay for – cheap guns require a paint consistency like water and are subject to block-ages, while the more expensive ones are more powerful and can handle a thicker mix of paint – the thicker the paint goes on, the fewer coats you need and the better the gloss you get.

Air-driven spray guns

Professional paint sprayers use a compressed air supply at about 60 lb sq in with a delivery of 10 cubic feet per minute to blow the paint on the car. The do-it-yourself equivalent has a small electric portable compressor which as a rule produces considerably less than 60 lb sq in at the paint nozzle and has a delivery rate of about $\frac{3}{4}$ cubic ft/min. Nevertheless it has sufficient puff to provide an atomised spray at the nozzle, although the density of the spray is not up to that of a professional outfit. The ones I have tried have been comparable with one of the better vibrator spray guns and can handle paint at about the same viscosity. As an alternative to buying a spray painting outfit, if you wish to do some major spray painting, it is worth considering hiring a spraying outfit for a weekend.

Local resprays

This is the name given by 'the trade' to the painting of part of a car – the front wing, bonnet top or a door – while leaving the original paintwork on the rest of the car. Experience shows this is the biggest paint job that most do-it-yourself men are willing to tackle. To do it you really need a large aerosol of paint or a vibrator spray gun or an air-driven outfit.

It is possible that you may run into some problems getting paint other than aerosols or touch-in kits as few car dealers sell paint and thinners in bulk over the counter. What you need is a paint supplier; the only snag is that these usually only deal wholesale and are limited to 'the trade'. In case of difficulty the local accessory shop or body repair man should be able to order the paint you need, or provide you with the necessary order form so you can go and get it yourself. Make sure you quote the paint specification you need (most cars carry the paint code number on the under-bonnet identification plate). If in doubt, quote the make, model, year and colour of the car – a paint specialist will be able to look it up on a colour guide.

Paint and primer is sold by the litre, and, allowing for a few mistakes, a litre should be plenty enough for four doors, or, say, the complete front of the car ahead of the windscreen. Buy the same amount of primer as paint (the colour of the primer varies with the colour of the top coat) and get twice as much thinners as paint.

The man who sells the paint will also have masking tape, abrasive paper and a highly useful item called a tack-rag which is a sticky cloth used to wipe the dust off a panel immediately before painting it. If you are planning to spray in an enclosed space, it is worthwhile buying a cheap mask to keep the spray out of your lungs. If spraying in the open try to do the work in the early morning on a warm day before there are too many insects about.

Prepare the surface as detailed for aerosol spraying.

Before it is used, spray paint must be stirred thoroughly and

310 It is best if new paint finishes at a natural body joint which will disguise any slight mis-match. Use proper masking tape

311 This viscosity cap is used to measure the thickness of the paint

312 On goes a coat of primer-surfacer. This will provide a good key for the top-coat

then thinned to spraying consistency. Stirring is important because most primers contain a filler which settles to the bottom during the paint's shelf life. With top coat certain pigments settle at the bottom and unless the paint is stirred thoroughly you will not obtain the correct colour.

The viscosity of the paint varies depending on the spray gun. Where a vibrator gun is intended for spraying paint the manufacturers will list a viscosity cup among the optional extras. This is rather like the upper half of an egg-timer. After you have mixed paint and thinners, you top up the cup with one finger blocking the outlet hole at the bottom. When it is full, unblock the hole and time how long it takes the paint to run through. Compare this with a chart from the spray gun manufacturer which will indicate the correct time for spraying car paint.

If you do not have a viscosity cup you must mix paint and thinners on a trial-and-error basis and put it into the spray gun and spray on to an old piece of card or hardboard. Start with a 50-50 mixture of paint and thinners and test the gun – a thin coating with a tendency to run easily off a vertical surface indicates the paint has been thinned too much. If the spray covers a narrow area and the paint appears as a number of blobs which refuse to flow into each other, the paint is too thick and is not being atomised correctly.

If you are not familiar with the gun you are using, the next check should be on the distance that the gun needs to be held from the work. On average, most do-it-yourself guns seem to work best with the nozzle 10 in–15 in from the panel being sprayed. This too should be verified on an old piece of card. Holding the gun too close causes a rapid build-up of paint and subsequent running; if the gun is too far, the spray droplets will partially dry en route and will be too far apart when they hit the surface – the result will be a matt finish.

Once you have the spray gun operating properly, you can top it up with primer and turn your attention to the car. If you are working on an unsealed concrete floor, spray some water on it to discourage dust, then wipe the area to be sprayed with the tacky cloth. Apply a coat of primer and let this dry. If you are unhappy with the surface, the odd 'nib' can be removed with fine abrasive paper when the paint is dry, or if you feel the result is completely beneath you, soak a rag with thinners, wipe the lot off and try again.

If you are going to stop spraying for a moment, the gun should be cleaned with thinners. The easiest way to do this is to have a small tin-lid – the lid of an aerosol can is ideal – topped up with thinners. When painting stops, remove the reservoir from the gun, dip the pick-up pipe in the thinners and operate the gun for a few seconds – this removes surplus paint and prevents it sticking up. On air driven guns, the thinners must be added to the reservoir.

Modern primers do not need copious rubbing down before the addition of top coat. All that is usually necessary is a few wipes with a dry piece of 500 grade wet-or-dry to remove any odd nibs.

Top coat is not so forgiving as primer, so make sure you are happy with the viscosity before you begin. As with aerosols, to prevent blobs, start and finish spraying over masking paper. I prefer to paint the edges first then fill in the remainder with horizontal strokes.

It is important that you can see the surface of the paint as it is being sprayed on, for this enables you to gauge the speed at which the gun should be moved. If the paint is hitting the surface as a series of individual droplets, the gun is moving too fast, and it should be slowed down until the paint can be seen to form a gloss as it hits the surface. This is where the real skill comes into spray painting, for the speed of the gun should be *just* fast enough to deposit a layer of glossy paint, but not slow enough to allow the paint to build up and form a run. If you are working inside under fluorescent lights, it will not be easy to do this, but putting an extra tungsten lamp alongside the work will allow you to sight along the paint and see the surface. If you have trouble gauging the amount of paint to put on, err on the side of putting too little – a poor gloss can always be improved by polishing later with a mild abrasive.

313 I spray the edges first then fill in the centre with horizontal strokes

Chapter fourteen
Fault finding

There is not a mechanic born who has not wasted hours dismantling something only to find that the component that he thought was faulty is, in fact, perfectly sound.

Fault diagnosis is a difficult art and because it can be time-consuming, car manufacturers and dealers are increasingly using electronic equipment to diagnose and pin-point trouble. The equipment is impressive and expensive and allows the engine to be checked while it is running. Its principal disadvantage is that it requires a skilled operator and because good garage mechanics tend to be 'poached' by rival garages, you cannot always be sure that the man working the machine is the one who originally attended the training course on how to use it.

There is also the cost. Running a full electronic check on an engine will cost a few pounds and if all that the engine needed was a new set of contact-breaker points, then this represents a very expensive way of finding out.

If you have a little time and apply a series of logical checks it is possible to track down most faults using only simple equipment. The check lists which follow cover not only the engine, but also the clutch, gearbox, rear axle, steering and suspension, brakes and electrics.

If, after checking the items I have mentioned, the fault still persists, then the time has arrived to give in gracefully and submit the car to electronic treatment. But with luck, on most occasions, you should find the trouble before this becomes necessary.

ENGINE

We begin with the assumption that it will not start. To establish whether the trouble is mechanical, in the ignition or fuel system, make these checks first.

Ignition. Remove one spark plug and, with its HT cable connected lay it on the cylinder head (not the rocker cover) so the plug body makes a good earth contact. With the ignition on, turn the engine on the starter. If there is no spark from the plug electrodes, it is ignition trouble.

Fuel. On some carburettors, it is easy to lift off the float chamber lid and check inside for petrol. If the float chamber is not very accessible, remove the air cleaner, pull the throttle linkage to open the throttle plate and peer into the intake. On an engine that has been cranked with the choke in use, you should see wet petrol in the manifold. Mechanical fuel pumps are tested by taking the fuel pipe off the carburettor and spinning the engine. The pipe should spurt petrol once for every two revolutions of the engine. Electrical pumps are easier to check. Disconnect the pipe and have a helper switch the ignition on and off. The instant the ignition goes on, the pump should squirt petrol.

Mechanical. An engine rarely breaks without making a noise so normally there is some warning. Have someone operate the starter and place a thumb over each spark plug hole in turn to feel for compression. If the engine will not rotate, see item No 8.

Engine

1

Engine turns but will not start.
*Ignition

Ignition switch not making contact; low-tension wiring connections dirty/broken; dirty or pitted contact-breaker points or points mal-adjusted; contact-breaker rocker arm sticking; rocker arm spring broken; spark plug HT leads leaking current; moisture on coil; faulty coil or condenser.

Switch on the ignition, detach the HT lead from the coil at the distributor, remove the distributor cap and while holding the coil lead about $\frac{1}{4}$ in from an earth point, flick open the contact breaker points and watch for a spark. If there is no spark from the coil HT lead or just a weak one, check LT connections for tightness, corrosion and bad insulation and rectify as necessary. In emergencies pitted points can be trued-up in situ with a nail-file and oily points can be cleaned by closing them on a slip of paper. A sticking rocker arm can be removed from its pivot and the hole enlarged using a small screwdriver. If the spring is broken, there's little that can be done except fit a spare. Wipe any moisture from the coil and tape up any suspect insulation on the HT leads. If there is still no spark, maybe the ignition switch is faulty – check by connecting a test lamp between the switch terminal on the coil and earth. The terminal will be labelled SW on some cars or + in negative earth and − on positive-earth models. The test lamp should light with the ignition on. If it does not the switch can be by-passed by taking a cable from the live terminal on the battery to the coil SW terminal. A faulty coil and condenser can only be checked by substitution.

2

Engine turns but will not fire, good spark at the coil.
*Ignition.

Most likely something amiss inside the distributor cap – centre brush or spring not making contact with the rotor arm; cracked cap, moisture inside distributor, cracked rotor arm; tracking inside distributor cap; leaking HT leads.

Detach one HT lead from a plug and with the ignition on and the gearbox in neutral, have someone operate the starter. A spark should jump from the end of the lead when it is held $\frac{1}{4}$ in from an earth point. If there is no spark, remove the distributor cap and check the centre brush – usually it can be pulled out a little to improve contact. A cracked cap must be renewed, so must one that is tracking. Moisture affects the ignition system mostly in winter when the car is left out overnight. Wipe any condensation from inside the cap and if you suspect water is getting in from outside, spray it with a silicone water-proofer. Cracked rotor arms must be renewed, leaking HT leads can be temporarily patched with tape but new ones should be fitted as soon as possible.

3

Engine turns but will not fire, good spark at the distributor.
*Ignition.

It looks like trouble at the plugs or in the plug HT leads. Check for damaged or dirty plug exteriors; plugs loose in the head; incorrect plugs fitted. Where an engine has just been reassembled, check that the HT leads are on the correct plugs and check the ignition timing.

Plug insulators should be wiped clean and dry on the outside and if the car is continually a poor starter because the rain gets in, fit some water-proof plug caps. A cracked insulator will cause mis-firing although on its own it is unlikely to prevent the engine starting. If the plugs are loose you will lose compression and the engine may not start. Sometimes short reach plugs are inadvertently fitted in a head designed to accept long reach plugs. When this happens the plug electrodes are pocketed and may not fire the rich mixture required for a cold start – fit the correct grade of plug. Check the position of HT leads by finding the firing order in the handbook and tracing the leads from the distributor cap. Most engines fire 1–3–4–2 or 1–2–4–3 or 1–5–3–6–2–4 and the rotor arm usually turns anti-clockwise. Ignition timing is checked with No 1 cylinder at TDC on compression. The timing marks should be aligned correctly at the instant the distributor points open.

4

Engine turns but will not start.
Ignition system working.
*Fuel.

Most likely lack of petrol. If the float chamber test shows it is empty or nearly so, check for a faulty fuel pump or a stuck float chamber valve.

To check electric pumps, disconnect the petrol pipe from the carburettor and have someone switch the ignition on and off quickly. You should see a spurt of petrol come from the disconnected pipe. On a mechanical pump the engine has to be rotated on the starter for a couple of revolutions to check the pump action. Electric pumps usually fail because the contacts are pitted and worn – frequently a sharp tap on the pump body with a screwdriver handle gets them going at least for a short period. Mechanical pumps rarely break down. If they do, the diaphragm may be split – a new one can sometimes be fitted using a pump repair kit, although some mechanical pumps cannot now be dismantled. Sticking float chamber valves can be freed after working the needle back and forth.

5

Engine turns but will not start. Float chamber is topped up with fuel.
*Fuel.

Something is affecting the fuel/air mixture. Check for incorrect idling adjustment; choke not working; faulty automatic choke; blocked slow-running jet; air leaks into intake manifold; leaking float; water in fuel; incorrect use of choke.

While the top is off the float chamber, make sure the float does, in fact, float. If it sinks, the mixture will be very rich. There is nothing that can be done except to renew it. As a next step, check the choke. For a cold start any choke flap should completely block the air intake (you will have to remove the air cleaner to check). On SU's make sure that the jet is lowered when the choke knob is pulled out fully and on Stromberg CD's see that the choke bar lifts the air valve or that the spindle which turns the metering disc on CDS carburettors is, in fact, turning.

Automatic chokes sometimes stick with the butterfly flap open. Waggling the flap often persuades it to close – oil the linkage to discourage it happening again. If the slow-running jet is blocked the car should start if you hold the throttle partly open but it will not idle. Providing you keep revving the engine the car should go. It takes a big induction leak to prevent starting – look for a disconnected emission valve pipe before blaming the manifold nuts for coming loose – check these if nothing appears to have fallen off. Water in the fuel can usually be seen in the float-chamber because like oil and water, petrol and water do not mix. Swab up the mixture with a cloth and take a sample (see section 4) in a glass jar. Water will sink to the bottom. You will have to drain the tank to lose the water altogether. If you pull the choke out fully when the engine is being re-started when it is hot, you will usually flood it. The remedy is to remove the spark plugs and wipe the raw petrol from the electrodes, then refit the plugs push in the choke and hold the accelerator fully down while you operate the starter. The fresh air through the intake will take the over-rich mixture down the exhaust system and with luck the engine will start.

6
Engine turns, but will not start. Carburettor has fuel, ignition is satisfactory.
*Mechanical.

It looks like valve trouble – valves not seating or sticking open; incorrect valve clearances; burnt valves; incorrect valve timing; leaking cylinder head gasket.

Sticking or leaking valves can be confirmed using a compression tester which will also show up a blown gasket. Valve clearances should be checked if the compression test doesn't indicate a fault – on pushrod engines you will be able to see a broken valve spring; on ohc layouts a broken spring is suggested by one over-large valve clearance. Valve timing will only be wrong if the engine has been dismantled – check this again.

7
Engine will not start, will not turn on the starter.
*Electrical.

Flat battery; corroded terminals; broken earth strap; bad connection or breakage in battery feed to starter; short-circuit in feed to starter; faulty starter solenoid, faulty starter or incorrect adjustment of pre-engaged-type starter. Faulty ignition/starter switch.

The classic quick test for a flat battery is to switch on the headlamps. If they are dim the battery is either flat in which case it should be re-charged, or corrosion on the terminals is blocking the flow of current. If you suspect the terminals, disconnect them, wire brush away any corrosion until the bright metal shows, and re-connect them after smearing the mating surfaces with petroleum jelly. Also check the joint where the earth terminal clamps to the bodyshell. If the headlamps work well examine the connections on the heavy duty cable which runs from the battery to the starter solenoid and from the solenoid to the starter – tighten any loose ones. A short circuit (happily rare) betrays itself by a crackling sound as the starter is operated. This should be insulated immediately before it can cause a fire. A faulty solenoid can be checked by removing the rubber covers over the terminals that link it to the heavy cable and bridging these with a screwdriver shaft. It causes some sparks, but does no harm, and if the starter works after this treatment, you know the solenoid is faulty. If the starter is faulty, cars with manual transmission can be push-started, although with an automatic, you will have to overhaul the motor before it will go. On cars with pre-engaged starters, where the solenoid is mounted on the back of the starter, incorrect adjustment will prevent the pinion from turning after it has been meshed with the ring gear. Don't bridge the terminals on these solenoids to test them. Test for a faulty starter switch by connecting a jumper cable from the battery live terminal to the solenoid coil terminal (usually connected to a brown cable). If the starter works, the switch or cable between the switch and solenoid is faulty

8
Engine will not rotate on the starter.
*Mechanical.

Starter pinion jammed in ring gear, engine seized.

Fortunately the most common cause is the jammed starter pinion – usually because the starter has become loose and the pinion has climbed up the teeth of the ring gear and jammed between the flywheel and the bell-housing. The remedy is to remove the starter and check the shaft. If this is still straight (it usually is) refit the motor and all will be well. If the shaft is bent, you need a reconditioned starter. A seized engine is something you will know about because the car will be on the move when it happens. The engine must be dismantled and given a complete rebuild.

9
Starter turns but will not engage with engine.
*Electrical.
*Mechanical.

Very weak battery; starter pinion sticking; teeth missing from ring gear.

Check the battery as in (7). A pinion that doesn't engage may be being blocked by dirt on the starter shaft – remove the starter and clean the pinion assembly in petrol but do not oil it. Old engines may have excessively worn ring gear teeth. Push the car with top gear engaged a yard or two to move the ring gear a little and try again. If the car starts, you will need a new ring gear sooner or later.

10
Starter turns engine very slowly – too slowly for it to start.

Battery almost fully discharged; corroded terminals, loose, dirty or corroded connections in feed to starter; short-circuit.

See section 7.

11
Engine starts but will not keep running.
*Ignition.

Loose low tension leads; distributor clamp loose; faulty ignition switch contact. Open circuit on ballast resistor or resistor cable on cold start coil.

Tighten any loose connections, by-pass a faulty ignition switch, damaged resistor or cable as detailed in section 1. If the distributor is loose, check the ignition timing (see section 3) before tightening the clamp.

12
Engine starts but will not keep running.
*Fuel.

Sticking choke; blocked fuel line; blocked air cleaner or fuel pump filter; sticking float valve; water in carburettor; idling jet or idling passages blocked; petrol tank air vent blocked; low fuel level.

Check the filters in the air cleaner and fuel pump. Pump filters can be cleaned and re-fitted, but paper-type air cleaner elements that are soaked in oil should be discarded and replaced with a new one as soon as possible. There are two main causes of fuel line blockage – either the pipe is flattened by driving over rough ground or by a stone thrown up by a wheel, or a small piece of debris in the tank drifts over the mouth of the fuel pipe. A flattened pipe is easily spotted from underneath. The debris problem can be temporarily solved by disconnecting the pipe at the fuel pump inlet and blowing down it. The tank will have to be drained to remove the cause of the blockage. See also sections 4, 5 and 13.

13
Engine will not idle or run slowly.
*Fuel.

Mixture too weak or too rich; slow-running improperly set; idling jet blocked; worn throttle plate; throttle plate loose on its spindle; worn spindle; air leaks into intake manifold; carburettor flooding; faulty fuel pump.

Rich running is most often caused by

a blocked air cleaner element – see section 12. If the element is not to blame, look for signs of leakage at the float chamber – maybe a speck of dirt has lodged under the float valve, jamming it open and causing flooding – this often happens after a fuel pipe has been renewed. Excessively weak running is indicated by engine over-heating and almost white deposits on the inside of the tail-pipe. Such an engine will usually perform a little better if the choke is pulled out slightly. Adjust the carburettor and unblock the idling jet by probing it with a bristle – do not use wire as this will enlarge the metering hole. If the manifold has not any obvious pipes disconnected, try the old trick of squirting a little oil from a can on the manifold joint. A leaking joint will draw in the oil and there will be a puff of blue smoke from the exhaust. Fit a new gasket to cure the leak. Carburettor spindles and throttle plates tend to wear together – check by gripping the linkage close to the carburettor body and attempt to move the spindle up and down. Just perceptible wear is allowable, but if there is a lot of slop, the carburettor draws in too much air and the engine will not idle – fit a recon. carburettor.

14
Engine starts but will not keep running.
*Mechanical.

Leaking valves; valves sticking or with incorrect clearances; broken or weak valve springs; worn guides; leaking cylinder head gasket; leakage past piston rings, scored cylinder bores.

As a cross-check, worn valve guides and leaking piston rings and scored bores will give a heavy oil consumption. Test compressions as detailed in Chapter 3 to sort out where the trouble lies. Worn or broken rings involve dismantling the pistons from the bores to fit new rings while scored bores will need re-boring. See section 6.

15
Engine starts but will not keep running.
*Ignition.

Incorrect plug gaps; plugs damaged, sooted or oiled-up; moisture on plugs,

loose or faulty HT leads; loose connections in LT circuit; flat battery; defective contact breaker; burnt contacts; ignition over-advanced.

Remove the plugs and check the gaps with a feeler gauge. Look for signs of cracking or burning of the ceramic round the centre electrode and renew any damaged plugs. Wipe soot or oil from the electrodes before re-fitting. A defective contact-breaker most likely has a short-circuit or poor connection in the 'pigtail' the small wire which runs from the side terminal on some Lucas distributors to the contact-breaker spring post. Connect a test lamp between the spring and a good earth, switch on the ignition and with the points open, the lamp should light. Waggle the 'pigtail' and see if the lamp flickers. If it does, renew the pigtail wire. See sections 1 and 3.

16
Engine runs erratically.
*Ignition.

Faulty plugs or leads; loose plug connections, defective, mal-adjusted or dirty contact-breaker points; incorrect ignition timing; faulty condenser; cracked distributor cap; sticking auto-advance mechanism; defective coil.

Intermittent mis-firing at high speeds is usually caused by a spark plug fault. Very old plugs or plugs of the wrong grade should be renewed with the correct item. See chapter 3 for further details. Check the centrifugal advance mechanism by removing the distributor cap (check it for cracks) and turn the rotor arm in the direction of normal rotation – it should return against spring pressure to its original position. If it does not the cam may have seized on the shaft or the advance weight springs have lost their tension. Before changing the springs check the advance with a stroboscope as in chapter 3. Test the action of the contact-breaker base plate by pressing it with a screwdriver – it should rotate a little. See sections 1, 3 and 11.

17
Engine runs erratically.
*Fuel.

Air leaks at intake manifold; blocked jets; mixture over-rich or over-weak; poor fuel supply; water in float chamber; petrol tank vent blocked.

A limited supply of fuel is the likeliest cause. Check for blockages at the fuel pump or in the line as detailed in section 12. See also sections 4, 5 and 13.

18
Engine runs erratically.
*Mechanical.

Valve trouble; leaking cylinder head gasket; exhaust system blocked.

The rough-and-ready way to check an exhaust pipe is to have a helper rev-up the engine while you feel the force of the exhaust gas at the tail-pipe. Blocked pipes have usually been flattened by driving over rough ground – a look underneath will confirm this. See also sections 4, 5, 12 and 13.

19
Engine does not give full power.
*Mechanical.

Wear in bores, broken or worn piston rings or ring grooves; incorrect valve timing; worn or leaking valves or guides; broken or weak valve springs; incorrect valve clearances; damaged head gasket; loose head nuts or bolts.

Check the valves first as detailed in sections 6 and 14. Now check the tightness of the head fixings. If all seems satisfactory, the head should come off to examine the state of the gasket and to look for ring and bore wear. New rings can be fitted without reboring (assuming the bores are not scored) if bore wear is less than .004 in per inch of bore diameter.

20
Engine does not give full power.
*Cooling.

On water-cooled engines, over-heating due to radiator or engine water jacket blocked by deposits; thermostat jammed shut; loose fanbelt. On air-cooled engines, look for blockages on the air intake, check

the drive-belt to the fan.

Flush-out a furred-up cooling system and use an inhibitor to break down the blockages. A jammed thermostat will allow a water-cooled engine to boil reasonably quickly although the water in the radiator will be cool – drain the radiator, lift the thermostat housing and fit a replacement. If air cannot flow past the radiator fins and tubes it will not dissipate heat. If the dirt blocking them is oily, brush it with an engine cleaner before flushing the fins clean with a jet of water. Loose fan belts may be worn beyond redemption in which case they should be renewed, or they may just need tightening. Some air-cooled engines draw their fresh air through a large bore flexible hose. If this collapses internally (sometimes they do when they get old) the engine is starved of air. Renew the hose if it looks a little frail.

21
Engine does not give full power.
*Fuel.

Blocked jets, faulty fuel pump, incorrect mixture strength; air leaks in intake manifold.

See sections 4 and 5.

22
Engine does not give full power.
*Ignition.

Ignition too far retarded; auto-advance sticking, wear in distributor drive or drive shaft bush; ignition wiring defect; faulty spark plugs.

Remove the distributor cap, grip the rotor arm and try to move the distributor cam sideways. If there is more than perceptible movement the distributor may need overhauling as detailed in Chapter 10. See sections 1, 2, 3 and 16.

23
Engine misfires on hard acceleration.
*Mechanical.

Overheating; valve/valve spring defects; burnt head gasket.

A gasket that is burned between two cylinders will allow combustion gases to burn a gutter across the exposed metal. If this is allowed to continue,

the cylinder block and head may need resurfacing to remove the damage. Check for gasket failure as detailed in Chapter 4. See also sections 6 and 20.

24
Engine misfires on hard acceleration.
*Ignition.

Plugs.

See sections 3 and 16.

25
Engine misfires on hard acceleration.
*Fuel.

Partial petrol blockage; damaged fuel pump; air leaks in intake manifold.

See sections 4 and 5.

26
Engine backfires.
*Ignition.

HT leads incorrectly connected; dampness or bad insulation allowing a short-circuit; bad connections; ignition switch or contact-breaker points dirty; CB points pitted or wrongly gapped; wrong ignition timing; auto-advance not working; distributor cap cracked or tracking; defective centre contact in cap; worn cap and electrodes; defective condenser/coil; unsuitable/worn plugs.

Most of these have been covered already except for worn electrodes in the distributor cap. It is tempting to clean off the deposits that accumulate on these at regular intervals. If this is done too often the gap between each electrode and the rotor arm gets too big and the supply to the plug suffers. It is best to leave these electrodes alone – although they get dirty, they still work. See sections 1, 2, 3 16.

27
Engine backfires.
*Fuel.

Weak mixture caused by blocked jets; incorrect carburettor setting; accelerator pump inoperative; poor fuel supply. Choked filters; air leaks in manifold; water in fuel; throttle not closing fully.

Accelerator pumps are used on fixed choke carburettors and squirt a syringe-like jet of fuel into the choke when the accelerator is pressed. Take off the air cleaner and watch for this while a helper presses the accelerator pedal. If there is no reaction, check the pump for lack of movement or a blockage. See sections 4 and 5.

28
Engine backfires.
*Mechanical/Ignition.

Incorrect grade of spark plug, valve trouble, wrong ignition timing; excess carbon.

Spark plugs are graded into heat ranges; using a plug which runs too hot in your engine means that the electrodes may glow red-hot and ignite the incoming mixture before a spark jumps across them, causing pre-ignition, which makes a knocking sound, and back-firing. Change to the correct grade of spark plug. Excessive carbon in the combustion chamber can give a similar effect when it glows red hot. See also sections 6 and 20.

29
Sudden engine failure.
*Fuel.

Lack of fuel. See sections 4, 5, 12, 13.

30
Sudden engine failure.
*Mechanical.

Excluding calamities such as a broken crankshaft, snapped con-rods, holed pistons and complete seizure, all of which are self-evident, the main mystery causes are a sheared distributor drive or a break in the drive to the camshaft.
Remove the distributor cap and check the rotor arm movement. If it rotates, do not fear the worst until you have checked the distributor clamp, as the body of the distributor may simply have jumped out, disengaging the distributor shaft from the driving shaft. To check the camshaft drive, remove the rocker or cam cover. On overhead camshaft engines the damage will be self-evident. On pushrod engines, take out the plugs and pull the engine over gently on the fanbelt, watching for movement at the rockers.

31
Sudden engine failure.
*Ignition.

Broken connections; contact-breaker rocker arm seized; HT lead between coil and distributor disconnected.

An ignition fault will make the engine cut dead without warning. Look for broken or disconnected cables on the LT side first, then check the HT cables – where these are shrouded by rubber covers, peel these back so you can inspect the connection. See sections 1, 2, 3.

32
Engine knocks or pinks.
*Ignition.
*Mechanical.
*Fuel.
*Cooling.

Ignition over-advanced; excess carbon; valve timing or clearances incorrect; petrol of too low an octane rating; overheating; incorrect spark plugs.

Try using petrol one grade higher. See sections 3, 6, 16, 20 and 28.

Clutch

33
Clutch drags or spins causing noisy or difficult gear selection and stalling at tick-over when a gear is engaged.

Poor pedal adjustment preventing full movement of the release bearing; friction faces coated with oil, or grease; dirt in clutch assembly; facings broken; distorted pressure plate or clutch cover; driven plate distorted and binding on splines.

On cars with provision for clutch pedal adjustment, re-set the pedal free play; where a self-adjusting clutch is fitted, lack of adjustment is caused by wear on the linings of the clutch plate and/ or the thrust bearing – renew both. If the plate is contaminated with lubricant it must be renewed, but first find the source of the grease or oil – it may be coming from the rear main bearing on the engine or grease may have come from a worn-out 'sealed; for life' ball-bearing thrust race. Distortion of the clutch plate is often caused by allowing the gearbox to hang unsupported on it during

assembly. Binding on the splines will be due to dirt or rust in the splines; clean them and apply just a trace of high melting point grease.

34
Clutch has a fierce action.

Oil or grease on linings; binding on clutch linkage or cable; misaligned clutch plate; worn-out friction linings.

In theory it shouldn't happen, but some cars with cables to operate the clutch suffer from the cable spearing a hole in the bulkhead after a few years. The average garage will weld up a new abutment plate, but if this is not accurately aligned, the cable can bind and cause the driver to blame the clutch disc for being unusually fierce. Fitting a new cable liberally greased at each end usually cures this problem – it also solves the snatching caused when two or three strands of the inner cable break and begin digging into the outer casing. Cars with rod-operated clutch linkages sometimes have a grease nipple for lubricating the pedal cross-shaft – lubricate this if the clutch action deteriorates. A worn out clutch plate must be renewed before the rivets holding the linings cut grooves in the pressure plate and flywheel – renew the release bearing at the same time. See section 33.

35
Clutch slips.

Oil or grease on linings; binding pedal mechanism; incorrect adjustment.

It is essential to have some free play at the clutch pedal before it begins to disengage the clutch, otherwise the slightest amount of wear will allow the clutch to slip. Check the adjustment in the handbook – usually most pedals have around 1 in of free play before they begin to release the clutch. See sections 33 and 34.

36
Clutch judders.

Oil or grease on linings; mis-alignment; pressure plate not parallel with flywheel; linings making uneven contact; clutch plate distorted; soft engine mounts; engine tie bar wrongly adjusted.

Split, soft or perished engine mountings permit the power unit too much movement and give the impression of clutch judder when the pedal is released; similarly a badly adjusted tie bar (when fitted) will give the same effect. Renew suspect mountings and re-set or re-bush the tie bar at the first sign of clutch judder. An out-of-line pressure plate must be renewed. See sections 33 and 34.

37
Clutch rattles.

Worn parts in release mechanism; clutch plate damaged; excessive transmission back-lash; gearbox bearings worn; first-motion shaft worn or bent.

Wear in the release mechanism tends to afflict cars with rod-operated clutch operating mechanisms. Wear in these is reasonably easy to track down and correct by fitting new parts. A damaged clutch plate usually adds up to a broken or loose spring near the hub – a new plate is the answer. Backlash in the transmission can occur in the gearbox, propshaft universal joints, differential, drive-shaft joints and splines or the hub splines. Some backlash is allowable and the noises only begin when it is excessive when the offending parts should be renewed or overhauled.

38
Clutch makes ticking or tapping noises.

Splines on clutch plate hub badly worn; pilot bearing worn.

All you can do is renew worn parts. If the hub splines are badly worn, look for the reason – maybe the clutch plate is mis-aligned or the first motion shaft is bent.

39
Clutch stops working – impossible to change gear.

Broken operating cable; linkage disconnected; loss of fluid from hydraulic clutch operating system; clutch plate broken away from hub.

Failure of the operating system between the pedal and the clutch will result in the pedal going down to the floorboards with very little resistance and complete non-functioning of the clutch. Usually a repair is easily carried out, renewing a broken cable or damaged linkage is fairly easy. A hydraulic system may need a new slave cylinder or master cylinder to get things working again. The broken clutch plate is rarer and is usually caused by allowing the gearbox to hang on it and distort it during fitting.

40
Linings wear abnormally quickly.

Vehicle continually heavily laden; driver "riding" the clutch pedal.

Cars which carry heavy loads or tow trailers or caravans on long journeys require more slipping of the clutch to get them off a standing start compared with a normally-laden vehicle. An accelerated rate of clutch wear is therefore to be expected. Driving with the left foot resting on the clutch pedal often causes small degrees of clutch slip and speeds up lining wear.

Gearbox

41
Gears difficult to engage.

Weak synchromesh; gear selector forks worn; wear on sliding hubs; gear lever pivot worn; clutch not disengaging fully.

Weak synchromesh is caused by wear on the synchromesh rings on the synchro. hubs. Assuming nothing else is worn, renewal of these rings will restore the synchromesh action. This is something of an optimistic view because by the time the synchromesh action has disappeared, most of the other parts mentioned immediately above will be worn too and normally the only long term solution is a complete gearbox overhaul or a reconditioned unit. If the gear lever pivot has worn either renew the lever or the housing that it pivots in. See section 33 for clutch.

42
Gears jump out of mesh.

Detent plunger spring weak or broken; plunger worn, faulty or broken. Selector forks badly worn.

Replacement will cure all these ills. A plunger spring will cost pennies but depending on where it is you may have to dismantle the gearbox to fit it. If you are lucky it may be accessible after taking off the gearbox top cover or unscrewing a plug. The gearbox must be partially dismantled to renew the selector forks.

43
Gears locked.

Detent out of action allowing two gears to be selected at once; selector shaft interlocking device seized; obstruction in gears.

It is almost certain you will have to strip down the gearbox to renew the offending parts. An obstruction usually turns out to be a broken tooth or part of a synchrohub. Trouble can often be diagnosed by draining the oil and looking for pieces of metal in it.

44
Excessive noise.

Lack of oil; worn or damaged bearings; bent or worn selector forks; worn selector linkage; spigot bearing worn; clutch thrust bearing worn.

First check the oil level. If it is low, topping-up will remove most of the noise. Worn bearings emit a low rumble which changes pitch as the engine goes from power to over-run. A grating noise suggests a badly worn bearing that is about to break up. Bent or worn forks will rattle while a worn spigot bearing which is in the centre of the engine flywheel and carries the front end of the first motion shaft, will emit a loud moan when the clutch pedal is depressed. Wear in the selector linkage often causes the gear lever to make a sizzling sound at certain road speeds. Removing the lever and replacing the bush immediately under it, or coating the lever pivot in thick grease generally cures it. A clutch release bearing that is failing can usually be felt as a vibration through the pedal when the clutch is used.

Rear axle

45
Noisy crownwheel and pinion.

Lack of oil; crownwheel and pinion incorrectly meshed; teeth damaged; differential bearings worn or damaged.

Top up the oil if the level is low. If the noise is still present ask yourself how many miles the car has covered, for some noise from the differential is almost inevitable with age – the pinion turns faster than the crown-wheel and wears out more quickly and this gives rise to a slight hum which you need not worry about. A consistently noisy hum on the over-run means the pinion is not meshing deeply enough with the crownwheel. A grinding noise on acceleration indicates they are too deeply in mesh. A constant noise from the differential when the car is in motion suggests damaged or excessively worn teeth. Worn bearings emit a rumbling sound. It is not normally possible for a home mechanic to set up a hypoid differential since the meshing of the teeth is critical and requires use of a dial gauge. In fact few garages overhaul them, preferring to supply a reconditioned unit.

46
Oil leaks from the differential pinion seal or past the half-shaft oil seals into the rear brakes.

Axle casing overfilled with oil; breather plug or ventilator blocked; defective oil seals.

Axle casings heat up in use and have a breather to allow the warm air to escape. If the breather is blocked, the air builds up pressure in the axle and forces oil past the oil seals. Unblock the breather to cure this – although in serious cases you will need to reline the rear brakes as well. Overfilling is often due to the car being supported at the rear on axle stands while the differential is topped up. It should only be filled with the car level. Damaged oil seals must be renewed.

Suspension and Steering

47
Heavy steering.

Tyres under-inflated; steering gear mal-adjusted; insufficient or incorrect lubricant in steering gear; excessive castor, front springs sagged, suspension misaligned; chassis twisted; steering swivels lacking lubricant.

Soft tyres are the most likely cause and the easiest to remedy. Check for over-adjusted steering gear by raising the front wheels clear of the ground and turning the wheel – tightness is often caused by over-enthusiastic tightening of adjusters. Oil level in the average steering box is checked by undoing a filler plug. Steering racks may have a grease nipple for lubrication, although nowadays most run in oil. To drain it, disconnect one rubber bellows and jack the car up on one side so the oil pours out. To refill, refit the bellows to the rack but loosen it where it clamps on to the track-rod. Raise the car on the side being worked on and inject the measured quantity of oil into the bellows using an oil can. Any misalignment of the front suspension can only be checked by a specialist with the right equipment. If anything is seriously bent, uneven tyre wear will give it away.

48
Excess play in the steering.

Steering gear loosely adjusted; worn track-rod ends; worn suspension parts; front wheel bearings worn or incorrectly adjusted.

Play or backlash in a steering box can be adjusted out. On a steering rack there should be virtually no play. If there is, the clearances between the rack and pinion have increased (possibly due to lack of oil) and the rack must be renewed. The ball-joints at the end of the track-rods tend to be 'sealed for life' so they require no lubrication. Unfortunately they seem

to have a relatively short life. When they wear, fit a new one. Worn suspension joints can be renewed and wheelbearings renewed or adjusted – see chapters 7 and 8.

49
Car weaves or pulls to one side when braking.

Uneven or low tyre pressures; brakes mal-adjusted; brake linings soaked in hydraulic fluid or oil; front springs soft; castor angles uneven or insufficient; steering gear loose or mis-aligned.

Check the tyre pressures first and adjust if necessary. Contaminated brake linings must be changed – the new linings must be fitted as sets on both wheels on the same axle. At the same time, cure the source of the leak – see chapter 9 and section 46. Change weak suspension springs, check tightness of steering gear fixings; have front wheel alignment garage-checked.

50
Car consistently pulls to one side.

Uneven tyre pressures; rear wheels not tracking with front wheels; brakes binding on one side, shock absorbers inoperative; front wheel alignment incorrect; weak front springs; misaligned suspension.

An out-of-line chassis or worn rear suspension pivots can cause the rear wheels to steer the car a little. Check suspension as in Chapter 8, have a suspect chassis checked professionally. Sometimes a rigid back axle shifts on its leaf spring mountings due to loose U-bolts – check underneath. Shock absorbers cause trouble if one is seized-up – a rare occurrence. Free off binding brakes, see sections 47, 48 and 49.

51
Tyres heavily and irregularly worn at the edges.

Pressures too low; wheel alignment incorrect; wheels or tyres out of true; uneven castor, toe-out on turns incorrect; suspension mis-aligned or badly worn.

Under-inflated tyres wear at the outside edges first, leaving the centre of the tread hardly worn. A badly buckled wheel or a tyre incorrectly centred on the rim will cause irregular wear – check the tyre fitting line close to the bead, it should be concentric with the edge of the rim. A buckled wheel can be spotted if the wheel is jacked up and spun. If the steering arms are bent it is possible for the wheel alignment to be correct in the straight-ahead position but hopelessly wrong when the wheels are turned – a garage with comprehensive wheel alignment equipment can check this. The remedy is new parts.

52
Tyres heavily worn in the centre.

Pressures too high; incorrect wheel alignment, wheels, tyres, brake-drums and hubs out of balance; suspension worn.

High tyre pressures push out the centre of the tread so it wears more quickly than the outside edges. An out-of-balance wheel assembly causes shake at the steering at certain speeds and because the heavy section of the tyre is being thrown against the road surface with a little more force than the rest, this patch will wear more quickly than the rest. For maximum life, tyres should be balanced when they are fitted and re-checked at regular intervals. See sections 48 and 49.

53
Front wheels wobble or 'shimmy'.

Low or unequal tyre pressures; worn or badly adjusted suspension; steering gear worn or badly adjusted; wheel bearings worn/adjusted too loosely; wheel, tyres, brake drums, hubs out of balance; wheels or tyres out of true; ineffective shock absorbers; steering idler worn.

Tyre pressures, wrongly adjusted or worn steering and suspension, out-of-balance wheels and worn wheel bearings have been covered in previous sections. Soft shock absorbers can give rise to shimmy – particularly on cars where lever-type shock absorbers form part of the suspension. Out-of-true new tyres are

uncommon, but well-worn ones sometimes develop bulges which can cause a lot of mysterious suspension movement – tyres in this condition must be scrapped. A worn steering idler can be repaired.

54
Front or rear wheels bounce or tramp when the car is travelling on a level surface.

Wheels, tyres, brake drums, hubs out of balance; soft springs, defective shock absorbers.

It is common for a wheel and tyre to be balanced off the car, but in a few cases this does not get rid of wheel vibration. When this happens, the brake drum or hub is contributing to the out-of-balance forces and the only remedy is to balance the wheel on the car. Once this has been done the wheel must always be fitted on its studs in the same way. If the springs are soft there will be a shiny mark where the bump stop has hit the chassis. On cars without discernible bump-stops, look at the attitude of the ; car – a pronounced nose-down inclination suggests weak front springs. For shock absorbers see 53.

55
Car wanders.

Low or uneven tyre pressures; steering incorrectly adjusted or worn; suspension misaligned or worn; loose hub bearings; loose steering gear; worn track-rod ends; road wheels loose.

On older cars wandering is likely to be caused by a combination of the causes shown. On newer models and cars that are maintained regularly, check for a loose track rod end. It's always worth checking the wheel nuts – they shouldn't work loose on their own, but sometimes someone forgets to tighten them fully. See sections 48 to 53.

56
Heavy road shocks felt through steering.

Low tyre pressures; steering gear mal-adjusted; excessive castor; tyres of wrong size or type.

In addition to giving an uncomfortable

ride and heavy steering, tyres that are seriously under-inflated cause severe flexing of the side-walls which can cause the tyre to overheat and fail. Some steering systems intentionally allow quite a lot of feed-back to the wheel, but if things get violent have the alignment checked.

Brakes

57
Brake pedal travel excessive.

Brake shoes need adjustment.

Brake shoes should be adjusted so they just clear the drums – it's allowable for them to brush the drums lightly as long as the wheel turns reasonably freely. Some drum brakes are self-adjusting – check the handbook to make sure.

58
Pedal feels spongy and slowly sinks to the floor.

Master cylinder or wheel cylinder seals worn; air in hydraulic system.

Worn master or wheel-cylinder seals allow air to be drawn in and pumped into the system – sometimes without any fluid leaking out. The method of isolating the trouble, using hose clamps is detailed in chapter 9. Once the leak has been cured, the air should be bled from the system.

59
Brakes inefficient.

Shoes incorrectly adjusted; air in hydraulic system; low fluid level; fluid leak; linings not bedded-in, worn or of the wrong material or contaminated with brake fluid oil or grease; drums or discs badly scored; servo inoperative.

If the fluid level gets too low air is drawn into the pipe-work and there is a poor reaction – or none at all – when you press the pedal. Bleed all the air out and keep the system topped up. Linings of the wrong material are unlikely if you purchased them from a dealer for the make of car. Badly scored brake drums should be renewed. Discs collect fine scoring on the surface as a matter of course, but they should be renewed if the surface is roughened up unevenly – this happens if a disc pad is allowed to wear down to the backing plate. Check servo connections to the engine intake manifold. As a quick test of a servo, run the engine for a moment, switch off, then push the brake pedal – the servo should be heard working.

60
Brakes drag or bind.

Shoes adjusted too tight; pull-off springs weak or broken; pedal return spring weak or broken; lack of free play at pedal; handbrake linkage seized on, wheel cylinder/disc caliper piston rusted on; master cylinder by-pass port blocked; filler cap air vent closed.

Shoe pull-off springs become 'tired' with age and should be renewed when the linings are changed. On some cars the brake pedal free play can be adjusted at the master cylinder pushrod – check the clearance with the handbook or the maker's manual as incorrect adjustment can cause the seal to block the port and hold the brakes on. Free off a sticking hand-brake linkage with plenty of penetrating oil and keep all pivots well greased. Wheel cylinder or disc caliper pistons only seize if their rubber dust excluders are damaged. Renew seized wheel cylinders. It is worth trying to save a caliper – see chapter 9. If a by-pass port is blocked by sludge, fit a new master cylinder and flush out the system with clean fluid. Use a pin to unblock a filler cap vent. See section 57.

61
Brakes remain on.

Shoes or the handbrake adjusted too tight; no pedal free travel at master cylinder; master cylinder and wheel cylinder seals swollen.

Seals in the hydraulic system swell if a spurious fluid is used. The answer is to pump out the fluid, flush it with cleaning fluid or methylated spirit, and fit new seals all round. For handbrake adjustments see chapter 9, see also section 60.

62
Car pulls to one side, brakes snatch.

Linings contaminated; drums distorted; suspension springs weak or broken; tyres unevenly inflated; brake backplate loose, worn steering or spring shackles; odd linings fitted.

Drums can become distorted if they have been 'skimmed' to remove scoring. The removal of metal from a cast-iron drum makes it lighter and less able to dissipate heat without distorting – fit new drums when this happens. You won't normally encounter odd linings unless you pick up a set second-hand. See sections 48, 49, 54, 59.

63
Pedal feels springy.

Linings not bedded-in, air in the hydraulic system; master cylinder loose; weak or cracked brake drum; weak hydraulic hose.

Ideally new brake linings should be used gently for around 200 miles until they conform exactly to the shape of the drum. If the brakes are used heavily during this period, high-spots develop on the lining and the pedal may have a springy feel to it until these high spots are worn off. Air in the system should be bled out after checking the cause. Watch flexible hoses for swelling while a helper pushes the brake pedal. Renew any doubtful ones.

Electrical

64
Battery flat.

Battery overloaded; fan belt slipping; faulty dynamo; voltage regulator faulty; electrolyte level low; battery disused for a long period; car parked with an auxiliary circuit in use.

The most common cause of a flat battery is leaving the car parked all day with the sidelights or a similar circuit in operation. To rectify, re-charge the battery – if you can get the car push-started, motoring ten miles or so will allow the generator to

re-charge it. A battery can be overloaded if a large number of electrical accessories are used at once. On cars with DC dynamos, for instance, it is possible to drain more from the battery than the dynamo can put in if, say, fog and spot lamps, headlamps, the heater blower, windscreen wipers and a heated rear window are all used at once. If you are keen on electrical accessories, and the car has a DC dynamo, fit an alternator. A loose fanbelt will slip and not drive the dynamo fast enough to keep pace with the demand from the battery. Often the dynamo will turn satisfactorily at tick-over speed, but when the engine speed rises and the effort to turn the dynamo pulley increases, slip takes place. Check drive belt tension and readjust if necessary. See sections 66 and 68 for dynamo faults. Regulators rarely go out of adjustment on their own although failure of the cut-out will allow the battery to leak its current through the dynamo. Regulators require special equipment for adjustment and should be checked by an auto electrician. The level of electrolyte in the battery should not be allowed to fall below the top of the plates. Batteries which are not in regular use should be charged up once very four weeks to discourage the formation of sulphate on the plates which acts as an insulator.

65
Battery continually needs topping-up.

One or more cells defective; charging rate too high.

Cells which are reaching the end of their useful life develop a heavy thirst for distilled water. Have the battery heavy discharge tested by a garage if one or two cells need very frequent topping-up. A battery with 'lazy' cells will not develop full power and is likely to let you down one cold morning. If all the cells need topping-up substantially each week, it is likely the charging rate, governed by the regulator is too high. This condition is also likely to cause corrosion of the battery terminals due to the over-charged electrolyte fizzing out the air holes. Remember that in hot weather, batteries lose a good deal of distilled water through evaporation – this does not cause terminal corrosion.

173

66

Ignition warning light comes on with engine above idling speed.

Dynamo drive belt slipping or broken; faulty regulator; dynamo failure.

It is tempting to drive on when the drive-belt breaks, but on many cars, besides turning the dynamo, this belt also turns the water pump, and a stationary water-pump will allow over-heating – see chapter 5. Complete dynamo failure without prior warning is unlikely, but can happen if a pulley breaks, a cable becomes disconnected, or one of the windings goes open circuit. Dynamo winding faults can only be cured by fitting an exchange unit or – if you can find one – fitting a replacement armature assembly. For regulators, see section 64.

67

Ignition warning light flickers at speeds above idle.

Slipping drive belt; dynamo brushes worn or oily; high resistance in armature; commutator dirty or glazed; faulty voltage regulator.

Oil on the commutator and brushes is caused by over-enthusiastic lubrication of the rear bearing – it should only be given two or three drops of oil at each service. Brushes wear in time and should be changed after about 20,000 miles – see chapter 10. If the dynamo armature has a high resistance, two or three commutator segments will be blackened – fit a new armature or reconditioned unit. A glazed commutator can be cleaned with a strip of glasspaper – see chapter 10. Worn commutators can be trued on a lathe providing the wear is not too serious, otherwise a reconditioned dynamo is needed. See section 64.

68

Light(s) fails to operate.

Break in circuit; short-circuit.

Vauxhall cars have a circuit breaker in their headlamp circuits and this switches them off in the event of a short-circuit. Check for the cause of the trouble – usually chafed insulation allowing a bare wire to earth on the chassis – before using the lights

again. A break in the circuit covers a multitude of possibilities from a blown fuse – some cars have their headlamps and sidelamps individually fuse-protected – to a bad earth connection. The way the lights fail will give a clue. If just one is dead, check for a blown bulb or light unit (light units will fail if the glass is cracked by a flying stone) then look for trouble at the various connections. If all the lights fail, the trouble is at a main feed – check first at the on–off switch then the dip switch.

69

Light(s) dim.

Low battery voltage; bulb envelope blackened; high resistance in circuit.

The state of charge of the battery is best checked using a hydrometer – see chapter 10. A bulb with a blackened envelope suggests that the lamp body is poorly earthed. If the surrounding bodywork is corroded, take an individual earth lead from the lamp body to a piece of sound bodywork; clean the bodywork down to the bare metal to make a sound earth connection. High resistance in the circuit may be due to poor connections in the feed cables or an almost-broken cable – check throughout the circuit.

70

Flashing indicator warning lamp operates at increased or reduced frequency, or is not working.

Failure of indicator bulb(s) or flasher canister; wiring fault.

If the indicator lamp does not operate, the flasher canister may or may not be at fault. To check, remove it and join together the three wires that connect to the base – if these are in the form of a socket, join the three holes using a paper-clip. When joined together, all the indicator lamps on one side should come on when the indicator switch selects them with the ignition on. Renew any damaged bulbs, or the canister as appropriate.

INDEX

Printed by Eyre & Spottiswoode Ltd at Grosvenor Press Portsmouth